C.-F. (Constantin-François) Volney

The Ruins, or, A survey of the Revolutions of Empires

C.-F. (Constantin-François) Volney

The Ruins, or, A survey of the Revolutions of Empires

ISBN/EAN: 9783743306370

Manufactured in Europe, USA, Canada, Australia, Japa

Cover: Foto ©ninafisch / pixelio.de

Manufactured and distributed by brebook publishing software (www.brebook.com)

C.-F. (Constantin-François) Volney

The Ruins, or, A survey of the Revolutions of Empires

CONTENTS.

Chap. I.
The Tour - - - - page 1

Chap. II.
Meditations - - - - - 6

Chap. III.
The Apparition - - - - 14

Chap. IV.
The Hemisphere - - - - 23

Chap. V.
Condition of man in the Universe - - 33

Chap. VI.
Original state of Man - - - 37

Chap. VII.
Principles of Society - - - 40

Chap. VIII.
Source of the evils of Society - - - 44

CONTENTS.

CHAP. IX.
Origin of Government and Laws - - page 48

CHAP. X.
General causes of the prosperity of Nations - 53

CHAP. XI.
General causes of the prosperity and ruin of ancient States - - - - - - - 61

CHAP. XII.
Lessons taught by ancient, repeated in modern Times 77

CHAP. XIII.
Will the Human Race be ever in a better condition than at present? - - - - - 103

CHAP. XIV.
Grand obstacle to Improvement - - - 117

CHAP. XV.
New Age - - - - - - 125

CHAP. XVI.
A free and legislative People - - - 132

CHAP. XVII.
Universal basis of all Right and all Law - - 136

CHAP. XVIII.
Consternation and conspiracy of Tyrants - - 141

CHAP. XIX.
General assembly of the people - - - 146

CONTENTS.

Chap. XX.
Investigation of Truth - - - - page 154

Chap. XXI.
Problem of religious contradictions - - 172

Chap. XXII.
Origin and genealogy of religious ideas - 218

Sect. I.
Origin of the idea of God: worship of the elements and the physical powers of Nature - - 226

Sect. II.
Second system: Worship of the stars, or Sabeism 231

Sect. III.
Third system: Worship of symbols, or Idolatry 237

Sect. IV.
Fourth system: Worship of two principles, or Dualism - - - - - - - 253

Sect. V.
Mystical or moral worship, or the system of a future state - - - - - 259

Sect. VI.
Sixth system: the animated World, or worship of the universe under different emblems - - 266

Sect. VII.
Seventh system: Worship of the Soul of the World, that is, the element of fire, the vital principle of the universe - - 271

Sect.

SECT. VIII.

Eighth system: The world a machine: worship of the Demi-ourgos, or supreme artificer — *page* 274

SECT. IX.

Religion of Moses, or worship of the soul of the world (You-piter) — 279

SECT. X.

Religion of Zoroaster — 281

SECT. XI.

Budoism, or religion of the Samaneans — 282

SECT. XII.

Braminism, or the Indian system — ibid.

SECT. XIII.

Christianity, or the allegorical worship of the sun under the cabalistical names of CHRIS-EN or CHRIST, and Yés-us or JESUS — 283

CHAP. XXIII.

End of all Religions the same — 297

CHAP. XXIV.

Solution of the problem of contradictions — 315

THE RUINS:

OR,

A SURVEY OF THE REVOLUTIONS OF EMPIRES.

CHAP. I.

THE TOUR.

In the eleventh year of the reign of Abd-ul Hamid, son of Ahmed, emperor of the Turks; when the Nogaian Tartars were driven from the Crimea, and a Muſſulman prince, of the blood of Gengis Khan, became the vaſſal and *guard* of a woman, a Chriſtian, and a queen *; I journeyed in the empire of the Ottomans, and traverſed the provinces which formerly were kingdoms of Egypt and of Syria.

* That is to ſay, in the year 1784. The reader is requeſted not to loſe ſight of this epocha. See the notes at the end of the volume.

Directing all my attention to what concerns the happiness of mankind in a state of society, I entered cities, and studied the manners of their inhabitants; I gained admission into palaces, and observed the conduct of those who govern; I wandered over the country, and examined the condition of the peasants: and no where perceiving aught but robbery and devastation, tyranny and wretchedness, my heart was oppressed with sorrow and indignation.

Every day I found in my route fields abandoned by the plough, villages deserted, and cities in ruins. Frequently I met with antique monuments; wrecks of temples, palaces, and fortifications; pillars, aqueducts, sepulchres. By these objects my thoughts were directed to past ages, and my mind absorbed in serious and profound meditation.

Arrived at **Hamsa** on the borders of the Orontes, and being at no great distance from the city of Palmyra, situated in the desert, I resolved to examine for myself its boasted monuments. After three days travel in barren solitude, and having passed through a valley filled with grottoes and tombs, my eyes

eyes were suddenly struck, on leaving this valley and entering a plain, with a most astonishing scene of ruins. It consisted of a countless multitude of superb columns standing erect, and which, like the avenues of our parks, extended in regular files farther than the eye could reach. Among these columns magnificent edifices were observable, some entire, others in a state half demolished. The ground was covered on all sides with fragments of similar buildings, cornices, capitals, shafts, entablatures, and pilasters, all constructed of a marble of admirable whiteness and exquisite workmanship. After a walk of three quarters of an hour along these ruins, I entered the inclosure of a vast edifice which had formerly been a temple dedicated to the sun; and I accepted the hospitality of some poor Arabian peasants, who had established their huts in the very area of the temple. Here I resolved for some days to remain, that I might contemplate, at leisure, the beauty of so many stupendous works.

Every day I visited some of the monuments which covered the plain; and one evening that, my mind lost in reflection, I had advanced

advanced as far as the *Valley of Sepulchres*, I ascended the heights that bound it, and from which the eye commands at once the whole of the ruins and the immensity of the desert. . . . The sun had just sunk below the horizon; a streak of red still marked the place of his descent, behind the distant mountains of Syria: the full moon, appearing with brightness upon a ground of deep blue, rose in the east from the smooth bank of the Euphrates: the sky was unclouded; the air calm and serene; the expiring light of day served to soften the horror of approaching darkness; the refreshing breeze of the night gratefully relieved the intolerable sultriness of the day that had preceded it; the shepherds had led the camels to their stalls; the grey firmament bounded the silent landscape; through the whole desert every thing was marked with stillness, undisturbed but by the mournful cries of the bird of night, and of some *chacals* *. . . . The dusk increased, and already I could distinguish nothing more than the

---

* An animal considerably like the fox, but less cunning, and of a frightful aspect. It lives upon dead bodies, and rocks and ruins are the places of its habitation.

pale

pale phantoms of walls and columns. ... The solitariness of the situation, the serenity of evening, and the grandeur of the scene, impressed my mind with religious thoughtfulness. The view of an illustrious city deserted, the remembrance of past times, their comparison with the present state of things, all combined to raise my heart to a strain of sublime meditations. I sat down on the base of a column; and there, my elbow on my knee, and my head resting on my hand, sometimes turning my eyes towards the desert, and sometimes fixing them on the ruins, I fell into a profound reverie.

CHAP. II.

MEDITATIONS.

Here, said I to myself, an opulent city once flourished; this was the seat of a powerful empire. Yes, these places, now so desert, a living multitude formerly animated, and an active crowd circulated in the streets which at present are so solitary. Within those walls, where a mournful silence reigns, the noise of the arts and the shouts of joy and festivity continually resounded. These heaps of marble formed regular palaces, these prostrate pillars were the majestic ornaments of temples, these ruinous galleries present the outlines of public places. There a numerous people assembled for the respectable duties of its worship, or the anxious cares of its subsistence: there industry, the fruitful inventor of sources of enjoyment, collected together the riches of every climate, and the purple of Tyre was exchanged for the precious thread of Serica; the soft tissues of Caffimere for the fumptuous carpets of Lydia; the amber of the Baltic for the pearls and perfumes of Arabia; the gold of Ophir for the pewter of Thule (*a*). . . .

And now a mournful fkeleton is all that fubfifts of this opulent city, and nothing remains of its powerful government but a vain and obfcure remembrance! To the tumultuous throng which crowded under thefe porticos, the folitude of death has fucceeded. The filence of the tomb is fubftituted for the hum of public places. The opulence of a commercial city is changed into hideous poverty. The palaces of kings are become the receptacle of deer, and unclean reptiles inhabit the fanctuary of the Gods. . . . What glory is here eclipfed, and how many labours are annihilated! . . . Thus perifh the works of men, and thus do nations and empires vanifh away!

The hiftory of paft times ftrongly prefented itfelf to my thoughts. I called to mind thofe diftant ages when twenty celebrated nations inhabited the country around me. I pictured to myfelf the Affyrian on the banks of the Tygris, the Chaldean on those of the Euphrates, the Persian whose power extended from the Indus to the Mediterranean. I enumerated the kingdoms of Damascus and Idumea; of Jerusalem and Samaria; and the warlike states of the Philistines; and the commercial republics of Phenicia. This Syria, said I to myself, now almost depopulated, then contained a hundred flourishing cities, and abounded with towns, villages, and hamlets (*b*). Every where one might have seen cultivated fields, frequented roads, and crowded habitations. Ah! what are become of those ages of abundance and of life? What are become of so many productions of the hand of man? Where are those ramparts of Nineveh, those walls of Babylon, those palaces of Persepolis, those temples of Balbec and of Jerusalem? Where are those fleets of Tyre, those dock-yards of Arad, those work-shops of Sidon, and that multitude of mariners, pilots, merchants, and soldiers? Where those husbandmen, those harvests, that picture of animated nature of which the earth seemed proud? Alas! I have traversed this desolate country, I have visited the places that were the

theatre

theatre of so much splendour, and I have nothing beheld but solitude and desertion! I looked for those ancient people and their works, and all I could find was a faint trace, like to what the foot of a passenger leaves on the sand. The temples are thrown down, the palaces demolished, the ports filled up, the towns destroyed, and the earth, stript of inhabitants, seems a dreary burying-place. ....Great God! from whence proceed such melancholy revolutions? For what cause is the fortune of these countries so strikingly changed? Why are so many cities destroyed? Why is not that ancient population re-produced and perpetuated?

Thus absorbed in contemplation, new ideas continually presented themselves to my thoughts. Every thing, continued I, misleads my judgment, and fills my heart with trouble and uncertainty. When these countries enjoyed what constitutes the glory and felicity of mankind, they were an *unbelieving* people who inhabited them: it was the Phenician, offering human sacrifices to Moloch, who brought together within his walls the riches of every climate; it was the Chaldean,

prostrating

prostrating himself before a serpent *, who subjugated opulent cities, and laid waste the palaces of kings and the temples of the Gods; it was the Persian, the worshipper of fire, who collected the tributes of a hundred nations; they were the inhabitants of this very city, adorers of the sun and stars, who erected so many monuments of affluence and luxury. Numerous flocks, fertile fields, abundant harvests, every thing that should have been the reward of *piety*, was in the hands of *idolaters:* and now that a *believing* and *holy* people occupy the countries, nothing is to be seen but solitude and sterility. The earth under these *blessed* hands produces only briars and wormwood. Man sows in anguish, and reaps vexation and cares; war, famine, and pestilence, assault him in turn. Yet, are not these the children of the prophets? This Christian, this Mussulman, this Jew, are they not the elect of Heaven, loaded with gifts and miracles? Why then is this race, beloved of the Divinity, deprived of the favours which were formerly showered upon the

* The dragon Bel.

Heathen?

Heathen? Why do these lands, consecrated by the blood of the martyrs, no longer boast their former temperature and fertility? Why have those favours been banished as it were, and transferred for so many ages to other nations and different climes?

And here, pursuing the course of vicissitudes which have in turn transmitted the sceptre of the world to people so various in manners and religion, from those of ancient Asia down to the more recent ones of Europe, my native country, designated by this name, was awakened in my mind, and turning my eyes towards it, all my thoughts fixed upon the situation in which I had left it *.

I recollected its fields so richly cultivated, its roads so admirably executed, its towns inhabited by an immense multitude, its ships scattered over every ocean, its ports filled with the produce of either India; and comparing the activity of its commerce, the extent of its navigation, the magnificence of its buildings, the arts and industry of its inhabitants, with all that Egypt and Syria

* In the year 1782, at the close of the American war.

could formerly boast of a similar nature, I pleased myself with the idea that I had found in modern Europe the past splendour of Asia: But the charm of my reverie was presently dissolved by the last step in the comparison. Reflecting that if the places before me had once exhibited this animated picture: who, said I to myself, can assure me that their present desolation will not one day be the lot of our own country? who knows but that hereafter some traveller like myself will sit down upon the banks of the Seine, the Thames, or the Zuyder sea, where now, in the tumult of enjoyment, the heart and the eyes are too slow to take in the multitude of sensations; who knows but he will sit down solitary amid silent ruins, and weep a people inurned, and their greatness changed into an empty name?

The idea brought tears into my eyes; and covering my head with the flap of my garment, I gave myself up to the most gloomy meditations on human affairs. Unhappy man! said I in my grief, a blind fatality plays with thy destiny (c)! a fatal necessity rules by chance the lot of mortals! But, no: they

are

are the decrees of celestial justice that are accomplishing! A mysterious God exercises his incomprehensible judgments! he has doubtless pronounced a secret malediction against the earth; he has struck with a curse the present race of men, in revenge of past generations. Oh! who shall dare to fathom the depths of the Divinity?

And I remained immoveable, plunged in profound melancholy.

CHAP.

CHAP. III.

THE APPARITION.

In the mean time a noise struck my ear, like to the agitation of a flowing robe, and the flow steps of a foot, upon the dry and rustling grass. Alarmed, I drew my mantle from my head; and casting round me a timid glance, suddenly, by the obscure light of the moon, through the pillars and ruins of a temple, I thought I saw, at my left, a pale apparition, enveloped in an immense drapery, similar to what spectres are painted when issuing out of the tombs. I shuddered; and while in this troubled state, I was hesitating whether to fly, or ascertain the reality of the vision, a hollow voice, in grave and solemn accents, thus addressed me:

How long will man importune the heavens with unjust complaint? How long, with vain clamours, will he accuse Fate as the author of his calamities? Will he then never open his
eyes

eyes to the light, and his heart to the infinuations of truth and reason! This truth every where presents itself in radiant brightness; and he does not see it! The voice of reason strikes his ear; and he does not hear it! Unjust man! if you can for a moment suspend the delusion which fascinates your senses; if your heart be capable of comprehending the language of argumentation, interrogate these ruins! read the lessons which they present to you!....And you, sacred temples! venerable tombs! walls once glorious! the witnesses of twenty different ages, appear in the cause of nature herself! come to the tribunal of sound understanding, to bear testimony against an unjust accusation, to confound the declamations of false wisdom or hypocritical piety, and avenge the heavens and the earth of man who calumniates them!

What is this blind fatality, that, without order or laws, sports with the lot of mortals? What this unjust necessity, which confounds the issue of actions, be they those of prudence or those of folly? In what consists the maledictions of Heaven denounced against these countries? Where is the divine curse that

perpetuates

perpetuates this scene of desolation? Monuments of past ages! say, have the heavens changed their laws, and the earth its course? Has the sun extinguished his fires in the region of space? Do the seas no longer send forth clouds? Are the rain and the dew fixed in the air? Do the mountains retain their springs? Are the streams dried up? and do the plants no more bear fruit and seed? Answer, race of falsehood and iniquity, has God troubled the primitive and invariable order which he himself assigned to nature? Has heaven denied to the earth, and the earth to its inhabitants, the blessings that were formerly dispensed? If the creation has remained the same, if its sources and its instruments are exactly what they once were, wherefore should not the present race have every thing within their reach that their ancestors enjoyed? Falsely do you accuse Fate and the Divinity: injuriously do you refer to God the cause of your evils. Tell me, perverse and hypocritical race, if these places are desolate, if powerful cities are reduced to solitude, is it he that has occasioned the ruin? Is it his hand that has thrown down

these

these walls, sapped these temples, mutilated these pillars ? or is it the hand of man ? Is it the arm of God that has introduced the sword into the city and set fire to the country, murdered the people, burned the harvests, rooted up the trees, and ravaged the pastures? or is it the arm of man ? And when, after this devastation, famine has started up, is it the vengeance of God that has sent it, or the mad fury of mortals ? When, during the famine, the people are fed with unwholesome provision, and pestilence ensues, is it inflicted by the anger of Heaven, or brought about by human imprudence ! When war, famine, and pestilence united have swept away the inhabitants, and the land is become a desert, is it God who has depopulated it? Is it his rapacity that plunders the labourer, ravages the productive fields, and lays waste the country; or the rapacity of those who govern? Is it his pride that creates murderous wars, or the pride of kings and their ministers ? Is it the venality of his decisions that overthrows the fortune of families, or the venality of the organs of the laws? Are they his passions that, under a thousand forms, torment individuals and nations; or the passions of human beings? And if in the anguish of their misfortunes they perceive not the remedies, is it the ignorance of God that is in fault, or their own ignorance? Cease, then, to accuse the decrees of Fate or the judgments of Heaven! If God is good, will he be the author of your punishment? If he is just, will he be the accomplice of your crimes? No, no; the caprice of which man complains, is not the caprice of destiny: the darkness that misleads his reason, is not the darkness of God; the source of his calamities, is not in the distant heavens, but near to him upon the earth; it is not concealed in the bosom of the divinity; it resides in himself, man bears it in his heart.

You murmur, and say: Why have an unbelieving people enjoyed the blessings of heaven and of the earth? Why is a holy and chosen race less fortunate than impious generations? Deluded man! where is the contradiction at which you take offence? Where the inconsistency in which you suppose the justice of God to be involved? Take the balance of blessings and calamities, of causes and effects,

and

and tell me—When those infidels observed the laws of the earth and the heavens, when they regulated their intelligent labours by the order of the seasons and the course of the stars, ought God to have troubled the equilibrium of the world to defeat their prudence? When they cultivated with care and toil the face of the country around you, ought he to have turned aside the rain, to have withheld the fertilizing dews, and caused thorns to spring up? When, to render this parched and barren soil productive, their industry constructed aqueducts, dug canals, and brought the distant waters across the deserts, ought he to have blighted the harvests which art had created; to have desolated a country that had been peopled in peace; to have demolished the towns which labour had caused to flourish; in fine, to have deranged and confounded the order established by the wisdom of man? And what is this *infidelity* which founded empires by prudence, defended them by courage, and strengthened them by justice; which raised magnificent cities, formed vast ports, drained pestilential marshes, covered the sea with ships, the earth with inhabitants, and, like the creative spirit, diffused life and motion through the world. If such is impiety, what is true belief? Does holiness consist in destruction? Is then the God that peoples the air with birds, the earth with animals, and the waters with reptiles; the God that animates universal nature, a God that delights in ruins and sepulchres? Does he ask devastation for homage, and conflagration for sacrifice? Would he have groans for hymns, murderers to worship him, and a desert and ravaged world for his temple? Yet such, *holy* and *faithful* generation, are your works! These are the fruits of your *piety!* You have massacred the people, reduced cities to ashes, destroyed all traces of cultivation, made the earth a solitude; and you demand the reward of your labours! Miracles are not too much for your advantage! For you the peasants that you have murdered should be revived; the walls you have thrown down should rise again; the harvests you have ravaged should flourish; the conduits that you have broken down should be renewed; the laws of heaven and earth, those laws which God has established for the

display

display of his greatness and his magnificence, those laws anterior to all revelations and to all prophets, those laws which passion cannot alter, and ignorance cannot pervert, should be superseded. Passion knows them not; ignorance, which observes no cause and predicts no effect, has said in the foolishness of her heart: " Every thing comes from " chance; a blind fatality distributes good " and evil upon the earth; success is not to " the prudent, nor felicity to the wise." Or else, assuming the language of hypocrisy, she has said: " Every thing comes from " God; and it is his sovereign pleasure to " deceive the sage, and to confound the " judicious." And she has contemplated the imaginary scene with complacency. " Good!" she has exclaimed. " I then am " as well endowed as the science that de- " spises me! The cold prudence which " evermore haunts and torments me, I will " render useless by a lucky intervention of " Providence." Cupidity has joined the chorus. " I too will oppress the weak; I " will wring from him the fruits of his " labour: for such is the decree of Heaven,

" such

"such the omnipotent will of fate."—For myself, I swear by all laws human and divine, by the laws of the human heart, that the hypocrite and the deceiver shall be themselves deceived; the unjust man shall perish in his rapacity, and the tyrant in his usurpation: the sun shall change its course, before folly shall prevail over wisdom and science, before stupidity shall surpass prudence in the delicate art of procuring to man his true enjoyments, and of building his happiness upon a solid foundation.

CHAP.

CHAP. IV.

THE HEMISPHERE.

Thus spoke the Apparition. Astonished at his discourse, and my heart agitated by a diversity of reflections, I was for some time silent. At length, assuming the courage to speak, I thus addressed him: O Genius of tombs and ruins! your sudden appearance and your severity have thrown my senses into disorder, but the justness of your reasoning restores confidence to my soul. Pardon my ignorance. Alas! if man is blind, can that which constitutes his torment be also his crime? I was unable to distinguish the voice of reason; but the moment it was known to me, I gave it welcome. Oh! if you can read my heart, you know how desirous it is of truth, and with what ardour it seeks it; you know that it is in this pursuit I am now found in these remote places. Alas! I have wandered over the earth, I have visited cities and countries;

countries; and perceiving every where misery and desolation, the sentiment of the evils by which my fellow creatures are tormented has deeply afflicted my mind! I have said to myself with a sigh: Is man, then, created to be the victim of pain and anguish? And I have meditated upon human evils, that I might find out their remedy. I have said, I will separate myself from corrupt societies; I will remove far from palaces where the soul is depraved by satiety, and from cottages where it is humbled by misery. I will dwell in solitude amidst the ruins of cities: I will enquire of the monuments of antiquity what was the wisdom of former ages: in the very bosom of sepulchres I will invoke the spirit that formerly in Asia gave splendour to states and glory to their people: I will enquire of the ashes of legislators what causes have erected and overthrown empires; what are the principles of national prosperity and misfortune; what the maxims upon which the peace of society and the happiness of man ought to be founded.

I stopped; and casting down my eyes, I waited the reply of the Genius. Peace and happiness,

happiness, said he, descend upon him who practises justice! Young man, since your heart searches after truth with sincerity; since you can distinguish her form through the mist of prejudices which blind the eyes, your enquiry shall not be vain: I will display to your view this truth of which you are in pursuit; I will show to your reason the knowledge which you desire; I will reveal to you the wisdom of the tombs, and the science of ages—Then approaching me, and placing his hand upon my head, Rise, mortal, said he, and disengage yourself from that corporeal frame with which you are incumbered—Instantly, penetrated as with a celestial flame, the ties that fix us to the earth seemed to be loosened; and lifted by the wing of the Genius, I felt myself like a light vapour conveyed in the uppermost region. There, from above the atmosphere, looking down towards the earth I had quitted, I beheld a scene entirely new. Under my feet, floating in empty space, a globe similar to that of the moon, but smaller, and less luminous, presented to me one of its faces*; and this

---

* See Plate I. representing half the terrestrial globe.

face had the appearance of a difk variegated with fpots, fome of them white and nebulous, others brown, green and grey; and while I exerted my powers in difcerning and difcriminating thefe fpots—Difciple of truth, faid the Genius to me, have you any recollection of this fpectacle? O Genius, I replied, if I did not perceive the moon in a different part of the heavens, I fhould fuppofe the orb below me to be that planet; for its appearance refembles perfectly the moon viewed through a telefcope at the time of an eclipfe; one might be apt to think the variegated fpots to be feas and continents.

Yes, faid he to me, they are the feas and continents of the very hemifphere you inhabit.

What, exclaimed I, is that the Earth that is inhabited by human beings?

It is, replied he. That brown fpace which occupies irregularly a confiderable portion of the difk, and nearly furrounds it on all fides, is what you call the main ocean, which, from the fouth pole advancing towards the equator, firft forms the great gulf of Africa and India, then ftretches to the eaft acrofs the Malay Iflands, as far as the confines of Tartary,

Tartary, while at the west it incloses the continents of Africa and of Europe, reaching to the north of Asia.

Under our feet, that peninsula of a square figure is the desert country of Arabia, and on the left you perceive that great continent, scarcely less barren in its interior parts, and only verdant as it approaches the sea, the inhabitants of which are distinguished by a sable complexion *. To the north, and on the other side of an irregular and narrow sea †, are the tracts of Europe, rich in fertile meadows and in all the luxuriance of cultivation. To the right from the Caspian, extend the rugged surface and snow-topt hills of Tartary. In bringing back the eye again to the spot over which we are elevated, you see a large white space, the melancholy and uniform desert of Cobi, cutting off the empire of China from the rest of the world. China itself is that furrowed surface which seems by a sudden obliquity to escape from the view. Farther on, those vast tongues of land and scattered points, are the peninsula,

* Africa. † The Mediterranean.

and

and islands of the Malayans, the unfortunate proprietors of aromatics and perfumes. Still nearer you observe a triangle which projects strongly into the sea, and is the too famous peninsula of India (*d*). You see the crooked windings of the Ganges, the ambitious mountains of Thibet, the fortunate valley of Cassimere (12), the discouraging deserts of Persia, the banks of the Euphrates, and the Tigris, the rough bed of the Jordan (4), and the mouths of the solitary Nile. (See the Plate.)

O Genius, said I, interrupting him, the organ of a mortal would in vain attempt to distinguish objects at so great a distance. Immediately he touched my eyes, and they became more piercing than those of the eagle; notwithstanding which rivers appeared to me no more than meandering ribbons, ridges of mountains irregular furrows, and great cities a nest of boxes varied among themselves like the squares in a chess-board.

The Genius proceeded to point out the different objects to me with his finger, and to develope them as he proceeded. These heaps of ruins, said he, that you observe in this

this narrow valley, laved by the Nile, are all that remain of the opulent cities that gave lustre to the ancient kingdom of Ethiopia (*e*). Here is the monument of its splendid metropolis, Thebes with its hundred palaces (*f*), the progenitor of cities, the memento of human frailty. It was there that a people, since forgotten, discovered the elements of science and art, at a time when all other men were barbarous, and that a race, now regarded as the refuse of society, because their hair is woolly, and their skin is dark, explored among the phenomena of nature, those civil and religious systems which have since held mankind in awe. A little lower the dark spots that you observe are the pyramids (1) whose masses have overwhelmed your imagination. Farther on, the coast (3) that you behold limited by the sea on one side, and by a ridge of mountains on the other, was the abode of the Phenician nations; there stood the powerful cities of Tyre, Sidon, Ascalon, Gaza, and Berytus. This stream of water, which seems to disembogue itself into no sea (4), is the Jordan; and these barren rocks were formerly the scene of events,

whose

whose tale may not be forgotten. Here you
find the desert of Horeb, and the hill of Si-
nai (5), where, by artifice which the vulgar
were unable to penetrate, a subtle and daring leader gave birth to institutions of memorable influence upon the history of mankind. Upon the barren strip of land which
borders upon this desert, you see no longer
any trace of splendour; and yet here was
formerly the magazine of the world. Here
were the ports of the Idumeans (g), from
whence the fleets of the Phenicians and the
Jews, coasting the peninsula of Arabia, bent
their voyages to the Persian gulf, and imported from thence the pearls of Havila, the
gold of Saba and Ophir. It was here, on
the side of Oman and Bahrain, that existed
that site of magnificent and luxurious commerce, which, as it was transplanted from
country to country, decided upon the fate of
ancient nations. Hither were brought the
vegetable aromatics, and the precious stones
of Ceylon, the shawls of Cassimere, the diamonds of Golconda, the amber of the Mal-
dives, the musk of Thibet, the aloes of Co-
chin, the apes and the peacocks of the continent

tinent of India, the incense of Hadramut, the myrrh, the silver, the gold dust, and the ivory of Africa. From hence were exported, sometimes by the Black Sea, in ships of Egypt and Syria, these commodities, which constituted the opulence of Thebes, Sidon, Memphis, and Jerusalem; sometimes ascending the course of the Tygris and the Euphrates, they awakened the activity of the Assyrians, the Medes, the Chaldeans, and the Persians, and according as they were used or abused, cherished or overturned their wealth and prosperity. Hence grew up the magnificence of Persepolis, of which you may observe the mouldering columns (8); of Ecbatana (9), whose seven-fold walls are levelled with the earth; of Babylon (10), the ruins of which are trodden under foot of men (b); of Nineveh (11), whose name seems to be threatened with the same oblivion, that has overtaken its greatness; of Thapsacus, of Anatho, of Gerra, and of the melancholy and memorable Palmyra. O names, for ever glorious! celebrated fields! famous countries! how replete is your aspect with sublime instruction! How many

profound

profound truths are written on the surface of this earth! Ye places that here witnessed the life of man, in so many different ages, aid my recollection while I endeavour to trace the revolutions of his fortune! Say, what were the motives of his conduct, and what his powers! Unveil the causes of his misfortunes, teach him true wisdom, and let the experience of past ages become a mirror of instruction, and a germ of happiness to present and future generations!

CHAP. V.

CONDITION OF MAN IN THE UNIVERSE.

After a short silence, the Genius thus resumed his instructions:

I have already observed to you, O friend of truth, that man vainly attributes his misfortunes to obscure and imaginary agents, and seeks out remote and mysterious causes, from which to deduce his evils. In the general order of the universe, his condition is doubtless subjected to inconveniencies, and his existence over-ruled by superior powers; but these powers are neither the decrees of a blind destiny, nor the caprices of fantastic beings. Man is governed, like the world of which he forms a part, by natural laws, regular in their operation, consequent in their effects, immutable in their essence; and these laws, the common source of good and evil, are neither written in the distant stars, nor concealed in mysterious codes: inherent in the nature of all terrestrial beings, identified with

with their existence, they are at all times and in all places present to the human mind; they act upon the senses, inform the intellect, and annex to every action its punishment and its reward. Let man study these laws, let him understand his own nature, and the nature of the beings that surround him, and he will know the springs of his destiny, the causes of his evils, and the remedies to be applied.

When the secret power that animates the universe, formed the globe of the earth, he stamped on the beings which compose it essential properties, that became the rule of their individual action, the tie of their reciprocal connections, and the cause of the harmony of the whole. He hereby established a regular order of causes and effects, of principles and consequences, which, under an appearance of chance, governs the universe, and maintains the equilibrium of the world. Thus he gave to fire motion and activity, to air elasticity, to matter weight and density; he made air lighter than water, metals heavier than earth, wood less cohesive than steel; he ordered the flame to ascend, the stone to fall, the plant to vegetate; to man,
whom

whom he decreed to expose to the encounter of so many substances, and yet wished to preserve his frail existence, he gave the faculty of perception. By this faculty, every action injurious to his life gives him a sensation of pain and evil, and every favourable action a sensation of pleasure and good. By these impressions, sometimes led to avoid what is offensive to his senses, and sometimes attracted towards the objects that soothe and gratify them, man has been necessitated to love and preserve his existence. Self-love, the desire of happiness, and an aversion to pain, are the essential and primary laws that nature herself imposed on man, that the ruling power, whatever it be, has established to govern him: and these laws, like those of motion in the physical world, are the simple and prolific principle of every thing that takes place in the moral world.

Such then is the condition of man: on one side, subjected to the action of the elements around him, he is exposed to a variety of inevitable evils; and if in this decree Nature appears too severe, on the other hand, just and even indulgent, she has not only tempered those evils with an equal portion of benefits, she has moreover given him the power of augmenting the one, and diminishing the other. She has seemingly said to him, "Feeble work of my hands, I owe you "nothing, and I give you life. The world "in which I place you was not made on "your account, and yet I grant you the use "of it. You will find in it a mixture of "good and evil. It is for you to distinguish "them; you must direct your own steps in "the paths of flowers and of thorns. Be the "arbitrator of your lot; I place your destiny "in your hands."——Yes, man is become the artificer of his fate; it is himself who has created in turn the vicissitudes of his fortune, his successes and his disappointments; and if, when he reflects on the sorrows which he has associated to human life, he has reason to lament his weakness and his folly, he has perhaps still more right to presume upon his force, and be confident in his energies, when he recollects from what point he has set out, and to what heights he has been capable of elevating himself.

CHAP.

CHAP. VI.

ORIGINAL STATE OF MAN.

In the origin of things, man, formed equally naked both as to body and mind, found himself thrown by chance upon a land confused and savage. An orphan, deserted by the unknown power that had produced him, he saw no supernatural beings at hand to advertise him of wants that he owed merely to his senses, and inform him of duties springing solely from those wants. Like other animals, without experience of the past, without knowledge of the future, he wandered in forests, guided and governed purely by the affections of his nature. By the pain of hunger he was directed to seek food, and he provided for his subsistence; by the inclemencies of the weather, the desire was excited of covering his body, and he made himself cloathing: by the attraction of a powerful pleasure, he approached a fellow-being, and perpetuated his species.

Thus the impressions he received from external objects, awakening his faculties, developed by degrees his understanding, and began to instruct his profound ignorance: his wants called forth his industry; his dangers formed his mind to courage; he learned to distinguish useful from pernicious plants, to resist the elements, to seize upon his prey, to defend his life; and his misery was alleviated.

Thus *self-love, aversion to pain, and desire of happiness*, were the simple and powerful motives which drew man from the savage and barbarous state in which Nature had placed him: and now that his life is sown with enjoyment, that he can every day count upon some pleasure, he may applaud himself and say: " It is I who have produced the
" blessings that encompass me; I am the
" fabricator of my own felicity; a secure
" habitation, commodious raiment, an abun-
" dance of wholesome provision in rich va-
" riety, smiling valleys, fertile hills, popu-
" lous empires, these are the works of my
" hand; but for me, the earth, given up to
" disorder, would have been nothing more
" than

"than a poisonous swamp, a savage forest, and a hideous desert!" True, mortal creator! I pay thee homage! Thou hast measured the extent of the heavens, and counted the stars, thou hast drawn the lightning from the clouds; conquered the fury of the sea and the tempest, and subjected all the elements to thy will! But, oh! how many errors are mixed with these sublime energies!

CHAP. VII.

PRINCIPLES OF SOCIETY.

In the mean time, wandering in woods and upon the borders of rivers, in pursuit of deer and of fish, the first human beings, hunters and fishermen, beset with dangers, assailed by enemies, tormented by hunger, by reptiles, and by the animals they chased, felt their individual weakness; and, impelled by a common want of safety, and a common sentiment of the same evils, they united their powers and their strength. When one man was exposed to danger, numbers succoured and defended him; when one failed in provision, another shared with him his prey. Men thus associated for the security of their existence, for the augmentation of their faculties, for the protection of their enjoyment; and the principle of society was that of *self-love*.

Afterwards, instructed by the repeated experience of diverse accidents, by the fatigues

of a wandering life, by the anxiety refulting from frequent fcarcity, men reafoned with themfelves, and faid: "Why fhould we con-
"fume our days in fearch of the fcattered
"fruits which a parfimonious foil affords?
"Why weary ourfelves in the purfuit of
"prey that efcape us in the woods or the
"waters? Let us affemble under our hand
"the animals that nourifh us; let us apply
"our cares to the increafe and defence of
"them. Their produce will afford us a fup-
"ply of food, with their fpoils we may
"clothe ourfelves, and we fhall live exempt
"from the fatigues of the day, and folicitude
"for the morrow." And aiding each other, they feized the nimble kid and the timid fheep; they tamed the patient camel, the ferocious bull, and the impetuous horfe; and applauding themfelves on the fuccefs of their induftry, they fat down in the joy of their hearts, and began to tafte repofe and tranquillity: and thus *self-love*, the principle of all their reafoning, was the inftigator to every art and every enjoyment.

Now that men could pafs their days in leifure, and the communication of their ideas,
they

they turned upon the earth, upon the heavens, and upon themselves an eye of curiosity and reflection. They observed the course of the seasons, the action of the elements, the properties of fruits and plants; and they applied their minds to the multiplication of their enjoyments. Remarking in certain countries the nature of seeds, which contain within themselves the faculty of re-producing the parent plant, they employed to their own advantage this property of Nature: they committed to the earth barley, wheat, and rice, and reaped a produce equal to their most sanguine hopes. Thus they found the means of obtaining within a small compass, and without the necessity of perpetual wanderings, a plentiful and durable stock of provision; and encouraged by this discovery, they prepared for themselves fixed habitations, they constructed houses, villages, and towns; they assumed the form of tribes and of nations: and thus was *self-love* rendered the parent of every thing that genius has effected, or human power performed.

By the sole aid then of his faculties, has man been able to raise himself to the astonishing

ing height of his present fortune. Too happy would have been his lot, had he, scrupulously observing the law imprinted on his nature, constantly fulfilled the object of it! But, by a fatal imprudence, sometimes overlooking and sometimes transgressing its limits, he plunged in an abyss of errors and misfortunes; and *self-love*, now disordered, and now blind, was converted into a prolific source of calamities.

CHAP. VIII.

SOURCE OF THE EVILS OF SOCIETY.

In reality, scarcely were the faculties of men expanded, than, seized by the attraction of objects which flatter the senses, they gave themselves up to unbridled desires. The sweet sensations which nature had annexed to their true wants, to attach them to life, no longer sufficed. Not satisfied with the fruits which the earth offered them, or their industry produced, they were desirous of heaping up enjoyments, and they coveted those which their fellow-creatures possessed. A strong man rose up against a weak one to tear from him the profit of his labour: the weak man solicited the succour of a neighbour, weak like himself, to repel the violence. The strong man in his turn associated himself with another strong man, and they said: " Why should we fatigue our arms in pro-
" ducing enjoyments which we find in the
" hands of the feeble, who are unable to de-
" fend

"fend themselves? Let us unite, and plun-
"der them. They shall toil for us, and we
"shall enjoy in indolence the fruit of their
"exertions." The strong thus associating
for the purpose of oppression, and the weak
for resistance, men reciprocally tormented
each other, and a fatal and general discord
was established upon the earth, in which the
passions, assuming a thousand new forms,
have never ceased to generate a regular train
of calamities.

Thus that very principle of self-love,
which, when restrained within the limits of
prudence, was a source of improvement and
felicity, became transformed, in its blind and
disordered state, into a contagious poison.
Cupidity, the daughter and companion of
ignorance, has produced all the mischiefs
that have desolated the globe.

Yes, ignorance and the love of accumulation, these are the two sources of all the
plagues that infest the life of man! They
have inspired him with false ideas of his
happiness, and prompted him to misconstrue
and infringe the laws of nature, as they related to the connection between him and
exterior

exterior objects. Through them his conduct
has been injurious to his own existence, and
he has thus violated the duty he owes to
himself; they have fortified his heart against
compassion, and his mind against the dictates
of justice, and he has thus violated the duty
he owes to others. By ignorance and inordinate desire, man has armed himself against
man, family against family, tribe against
tribe, and the earth is converted into a
bloody theatre of discord and robbery.
They have sown the seeds of secret war
in the bosom of every state, divided the
citizens from each other, and the same society is constituted of oppressors and oppressed, of masters and slaves. They have
taught the heads of nations, with audacious
insolence, to turn the arms of the society
against itself, and to build upon mercenary
avidity the fabric of political despotism:
or they have taught a more hypocritical
and deep-laid project, that imposed, as the
dictate of heaven, lying sanctions and a
sacrilegious yoke: thus rendering avarice
the source of credulity. In fine, they have
corrupted every idea of good and evil, just and

unjust,

unjust, virtue and vice: they have misled nations in a never-ending labyrinth of calamity and mistake. Ignorance and the love of accumulation!....These are the malevolent beings that have laid waste the earth; these are the decrees of fate that have overturned empires; these are the celestial maledictions that have struck those walls once so glorious, and converted the splendour of a populous city into a sad spectacle of ruins!... Since then it was from his own bosom all the evils proceeded that have vexed the life of man, it was there also he ought to have sought the remedies, where only they are to be found.

CHAP.

CHAP. IX.

THE ORIGIN OF GOVERNMENT AND LAWS.

In truth, the period soon arrived when men, tired of the ills they occasioned each other, sighed after peace; and reflecting on the nature and causes of those ills, they said: "We mutually injure one another by our "passions, and from a desire to grasp every "thing we in reality possess nothing. What "one ravishes to-day, another tears from "him to-morrow, and our cupidity rebounds "upon our own heads. Let us establish "arbitrators, who shall decide our claims "and appease our variances. When the "strong rises up against the weak, the arbi- "trator shall repel him; and the life and "property of each being under a common "guarantee and protection, we shall enjoy "all the blessings of nature."

Conventions, tacit or expressed, were thus introduced into society, and became the rule of the actions of individuals, the measure of
their

their claims, and the law of their reciprocal relations. Chiefs were appointed to enforce the obfervance of the compact, and to thefe the people entrufted the balance of rights, and the fword to punifh violations.

Then a happy equilibrium of powers and of action was eftablifhed, which conftituted the public fafety. The names of equity and juftice were acknowledged and revered. Every man, able to enjoy in peace the fruits of his labour, gave himfelf up to all the energies of his foul; and activity, awakened and kept alive by the reality or the hope of enjoyment, forced art and nature to difplay all their treafures. The fields were covered with harvefts, the valleys with flocks, the hills with vines, the fea with fhips, and man was happy and powerful upon the earth.

The diforder his imprudence had caufed, his wifdom thus remedied. But this wifdom was ftill the effect of the laws of nature in the organization of his being. It was to fecure his own enjoyments, that he was led to refpect thofe of another, and the defire of

accumulation

accumulation found its corrective in enlightened self-love.

Self-love, the eternal spring of action in every individual, was thus the necessary basis of all associations; and upon the observance of this natural law has the fate of every nation depended. Have the factitious and conventional laws of any society accorded with this law, and corresponded to its demands? In that case every man, prompted by an overpowering instinct, has exerted all the faculties of his nature, and the public felicity has been the result of the various portions of individual felicity. Have these laws, on the contrary, restrained the effort of man in his pursuit of happiness? In that case his heart, deprived of all its natural motives, has languished in inaction, and the oppression of individuals has engendered general weakness.

Self-love, impetuous and rash, renders man the enemy of man, and of consequence perpetually tends to the dissolution of society. It is for the art of legislation, and for the virtue of ministers, to temper the grasping

selfishness

selfishness of individuals, to keep each man's desire to possess every thing in a nice equipoise, and thus to render the subjects happy, in order that, in the struggle of this with any other society, all the members should have an equal interest in the preservation and defence of the commonwealth.

From hence it follows, that the internal splendour and prosperity of empires, have been in proportion to the equity of their governments; and their external power respectively, in proportion to the number of persons interested in the maintenance of the political constitution, and their degree of interest in that maintenance.

On the other hand, the multiplication of men by complicating their ties, having rendered the demarcation of their rights a point of difficult decision; the perpetual play of the passions having given rise to unexpected incidents; the conventions that were formed having proved vicious, inadequate, or null; the authors of the laws having either misunderstood the object of them, or dissembled it, and the persons appointed to execute them, instead of restraining the inordinate desires

desires of others, having abandoned themselves to the sway of their own avidity—society has, by these causes united, been thrown into trouble and disorder; and defective laws and unjust governments, the result of cupidity and ignorance, have been the foundation of the misfortunes of the people, and the subversion of states.

CHAP.

CHAP. X.

GENERAL CAUSES OF THE PROSPERITY OF ANCIENT STATES.

Such, O man, who enquirest after wisdom, have been the causes of the revolutions of those ancient states of which you contemplate the ruins! Upon whatever spot I fix my view, or to whatever period my thoughts recur, the same principles of elevation and decline, of prosperity and destruction, present themselves to the mind. If a people were powerful, if an empire flourished, it was because the laws of convention were conformable to those of nature; because the government procured to every man respectively the free use of his faculties, the equal security of his person and property. On the contrary, if an empire has fallen to ruin or disappeared, it is because the laws were vicious or imperfect, or a corrupt government has checked their operation. If laws and government, at first rational and just, have afterwards become depraved,

depraved, it is because the alternative of good and evil derives from the nature of the heart of man, from the succession of his inclinations, the progress of his knowledge, the combination of events and circumstances; as the history of the human species proves.

In the infancy of nations, when men still lived in forests, all subject to the same wants, and endowed with the same faculties, they were nearly equal in strength; and this equality was a circumstance highly advantageous to the formation of society. Each individual finding himself independent of every other, no one was the slave, and no one had the idea of being master of another. Untaught man knew neither servitude nor tyranny. Supplied with the means of providing sufficiency for his subsistence, he thought not of borrowing from strangers. Owing nothing, and exacting nothing, he judged of the rights of others by his own. Ignorant also of the art of multiplying enjoyments, he provided only what was necessary; and superfluity being unknown to him, the desire to engross of consequence remained unexcited; or if excited, as it attacked others

in

in those possessions that were wholly indispensible, it was resisted with energy, and the very foresight of this resistance maintained a salutary and immoveable equilibrium.

Thus original equality, without the aid of convention, maintained personal liberty, secured individual property, and produced order and good manners. Each man laboured separately and for himself: and his heart being occupied, he wandered not in pursuit of unlawful desires. His enjoyments were few, but his wants were satisfied: and as nature had made these wants less extensive than his ability, the labour of his hands soon produced abundance; abundance population; the arts developed themselves, cultivation extended, and the earth, covered with numerous inhabitants, was divided into different domains.

The relations of men becoming complicated, the interior order of society was more difficult to maintain. Time and industry having created affluence, cupidity awoke from its slumber; and as equality, easy between individuals, could not subsist between families, the national balance was destroyed.

It was necessary to supply the loss by means of an artificial balance; it was necessary to appoint chiefs, and establish laws; but as these were occasioned by cupidity, in the experience of primitive times they could not but partake of the origin from which they sprung. Various circumstances however concurred to temper the disorder, and make it indispensible for governments to be just.

States being at first weak, and having external enemies to fear, it was in reality of importance to the chiefs not to oppress the subject. By diminishing the interest of the citizens in their government, they would have diminished their means of resistance; they would have facilitated foreign invasion, and thus endangered their own existence for superfluous enjoyments.

Internally, the character of the people was repellent to tyranny. Men had too long contracted habits of independence; their wants were too limited, and the consciousness of their own strength too inseparable from their minds.

States being closely knit together, it was difficult to divide the citizens, in order to oppress

oppress some by means of others. Their communication with each other was too easy, and their interests too simple and evident. Beside, every man being at once proprietor and cultivator, he had no inducement to sell himself, and the despot would have been unable to find mercenaries.

If dissensions arose, it was between family and family, one faction with another; and a considerable number had still one common interest. Disputes, it is true, were in this case more warm, but the fear of foreign invasion appeased the discord. If the oppression of a party was effected, the earth being open before it, and men, still simple in their manners, finding every where the same advantages, the party migrated and carried their independence to another quarter.

Ancient states then enjoyed in themselves numerous means of prosperity and power.

As every man found his well-being in the constitution of his country, he felt a lively interest in its preservation; and if a foreign power invaded it, having his habitation and his field to defend, he carried to the combat the ardour of a personal cause, and his patriotic

triotic exertions were prompted by self-defence.

As every action useful to the public excited its esteem and gratitude, each was eager to be useful, and talents and civil virtues were multiplied by self-love.

As every citizen was called upon indiscriminately to contribute his proportion of property and personal effort, the armies and the treasuries of the state were inexhaustible.

As the earth was free, and its possession easy and secure, every man was a proprietor, and the division of property, by rendering luxury impossible, preserved the purity of manners.

As every man ploughed his own field, cultivation was more active, provisions more abundant, and individual opulence constituted the public wealth.

As abundance of provision rendered subsistence easy, population rapidly increased, and states quickly arrived at their plenitude.

As the produce was greater than the consumption, the desire of commerce started up, and exchanges were made between different nations, which were an additional stimulus to their

their activity, and increased their reciprocal enjoyments.

In fine, as certain places in certain epochas combined the advantage of good government with that of being placed in the road of circulation and commerce, they became rich magazines of trade, and powerful seats of dominion. It was in this manner that the riches of India and Europe, accumulated upon the banks of the Nile, the Tigris, and the Euphrates, gave succeffive exiftence to the fplendour of a thoufand metropoliffes.

The people, become rich, applied their fuperfluity of means to labours of public utility; and this was, in every ftate, the æra of thofe works, the magnificence of which aftonifhes the mind; thofe wells of Tyre (*i*), thofe artificial banks of the Euphrates, thofe conduits of Medea (*k*), thofe fortreffes of the Defert, thofe aqueducts of Palmyra, thofe temples, thofe porticos.... And thefe immenfe labours were little oppreffive to the nations that completed them, becaufe they were the fruit of the equal and united effort of individuals free to act and ardent to defire.

Thus

Thus ancient states prospered, because social institutions were conformable to the true laws of nature, and because the subjects of those states, enjoying liberty and the security of their persons and their property, could display all the extent of their faculties, and all the energy of self-love.

CHAP. XI.

GENERAL CAUSES OF THE REVOLUTIONS AND RUIN OF ANCIENT STATES.

In the mean time the inordinate desire of accumulation had excited a constant and universal struggle among men, and this struggle, prompting individuals and societies to reciprocal invasions, occasioned perpetual commotions and successive revolutions.

At first, in the savage and barbarous state of the first human beings, this inordinate desire, daring and ferocious in its nature, taught rapine, violence, and murder; and the progress of civilization was for a long time at a stand.

Afterwards, when societies began to be formed, the effect of bad habits communicating itself to laws and government, civil institutions became corrupt, and arbitrary and factitious rights were established, which gave the people depraved ideas of justice and morality.

Because

Because one man, for example, was stronger than another, this inequality, the result of accident, was taken for the law of nature (*l*); and because the life of the weak was in his power, and he did not take it from him, he arrogated over his person the absurd right of property, and individual slavery prepared the way for the slavery of nations.

Because the chief of a family could exercise an absolute authority in his own house, he made his inclinations and affections the sole rule of his conduct; he conferred and withheld the conveniences and enjoyments of life without respect to the law of equality or justice, and paternal tyranny laid the foundation of political despotism (*m*).

In societies formed upon such bases, time and industry having developed riches, inordinate desire, restricted by the laws, became artificial without being less active. Under the mask of union and civil peace, it engendered in the bosom of every state an intestine war, in which the citizens divided into opposite corps of orders, classes, and families, aimed to appropriate to themselves, under the name of *supreme power*, the ability of

grasping

grasping and controlling every thing at the will of their passions. It is this spirit of rapacity, the disguises of which are innumerable, but its operation and end uniformly the same, that has been the perpetual scourge of nations.

Sometimes opposing social compact, or destroying that which already existed, it has abandoned the inhabitants of a country to the tumultuous shock of all their jarring principles; and the dissolved states, under the name of *anarchy*, have been tormented by the passions of every individual member.

Sometimes a people jealous of its liberty, having appointed agents to administer, these agents have assumed to themselves the powers of which they were only the guardians; have employed the public funds in corrupting elections, gaining partizans, and dividing the people against itself. By these means, from temporary, they have become perpetual, from elective, hereditary magistrates; and the state, agitated by the intrigues of the ambitious, by the bribes of the wealthy leaders of factions, by the venality of the indolent poor, by the empiricism of declaimers,

ers, has been troubled with all the inconveniences of *democracy*.

In one country, the chiefs, equal in strength, mutually afraid of each other, have formed vile compacts and coalitions, and portioning out power, rank, honours, have arrogated to themselves privileges and immunities; have erected themselves into separate bodies and distinct classes; have tyrannised in common over the people, and, under the name of *aristocracy*, the state has been tormented by the passions of the wealthy and the great.

In another country, tending to the same end by different means, *sacred impostors* have taken advantage of the credulity of the ignorant. In the secrecy of temples, and behind the veil of altars, they have made the Gods speak and act; have delivered oracles, worked pretended miracles, ordered sacrifices, imposed offerings, prescribed endowments; and, under the name of *theocracy* and *religion*, the state has been tormented by the passions of priests.

Sometimes, weary of its disorders or of its tyrants, a nation, to diminish the sources of its evils, gave itself a single master. In that case, if the powers of the prince were limited,

his

his only defire was to extend them; if indefinite, he abufed the truft that was confided to him; and, under the name of *monarchy*, the ftate was tormented by the paffions of kings and princes.

Then the factious, taking advantage of the general difcontent, flattered the people with the hope of a better mafter; they fcattered gifts and promifes, dethroned the defpot to fubftitute themfelves in his ftead; and difputes for the fucceffion or the divifion of power, have tormented the ftate with the diforders and devaftations of *civil war*.

In fine, among thefe rivals, one individual more artful or more fortunate than the reft, gaining the afcendancy, concentred the whole power in himfelf. By a fingular phenomenon, one man obtained the maftery over millions of his fellow-creatures, againft their will, and without their confent; and thus the art of *tyranny* appears alfo to have been the offspring of inordinate defire. Obferving the fpirit of egotifm that divided mankind, the ambitious adroitly fomented this fpirit: he flattered the vanity of one, excited the jealoufy of another, favoured the avarice of a

third,

third, enflamed the resentment of a fourth, irritated the passions of all. By opposing interests or prejudices, he sowed the seeds of divisions and hatred. He promised to the poor the spoil of the rich, to the rich the subjugation of the poor; threatened this man by that, one class by another; and isolating the citizens by distrust, he formed his own strength out of their weakness, and imposed on them the yoke of *opinion*, the knots of which they tied with their own hands. By means of the army he extorted contributions; by the contributions he disposed of the army; by the corresponding play of money and places, he bound all the people with a chain that was not to be broken, and the states which they composed fell into the slow decay of *despotism*.

Thus did one and the same spring, varying its action under all the forms that have been enumerated, incessantly attack the continuity of states, and an eternal circle of vicissitudes have sprung from an eternal circle of passions.

This constant spirit of egotism operated two principal effects equally destructive: the one,

one, that by dividing focieties into all their fractions, a ftate of debility was produced, which facilitated their diffolution; the other, that always tending to concentre the power in a fingle hand, it occafioned a fucceffive abforption of focieties and ftates, fatal to their peace and to their common exiftence (*n*).

Juft as in a fingle ftate, the nation had been abforbed in a party, that party in a family, and that family in an individual, there alfo exifted an abforption of a fimilar kind between ftate and ftate, attended with all the mifchiefs in the relative fituation of nations, that the other produced in the civil relation of individuals. One city fubjected its neighbour city, and the refult of the conqueft was a province; province fwallowed up province, and thus produced a kingdom; between two kingdoms a conqueft took place, and thus furnifhed an empire of unweildy bulk. Did the internal force of thefe ftates increafe in proportion to their mafs? On the contrary, it was diminifhed; and far from the condition of the people being happier, it became every day more oppreffive and wretched,

F 2

wretched, by causes inevitably flowing from the nature of things.

Because, as the boundaries of states became extended, their administration became more complicated and difficult; and to give motion to the mass it was necessary to increase the prerogatives of the sovereign, and all proportion was thus annihilated between the duty of governors and their power.

Because despots, feeling their weakness, dreaded all those circumstances that developed the force of nations, and made it their study to attenuate it.

Because nations, estranged from each other by the prejudices of ignorance and the ferocity of hatred, seconded the perversity of governments, and employing a standing force for reciprocal offence, aggravated their slavery.

Because, in proportion as the balance between states was broken, it became easy for the strong to overwhelm the weak.

Because, in proportion as state became blended with state, the people were stripped of their laws, their customs, every thing by which they were distinguished from each other,

other, and thus loft the great mover *selfishness*, which gave them energy.

And despots, considering empires in the light of domains, and the people as their property, abandoned themselves to depredations, and the licentiousness of the most arbitrary authority.

And all the force and wealth of nations were converted into a supply for individual expence and personal caprice; and kings, in the wearisomeness of satiety, followed the dictates of every factitious and depraved taste (*o*). They must have gardens constructed upon arches, and rivers carried to the summit of mountains; for them fertile fields must be changed into parks for deer, lakes formed where there was no water, and rocks elevated in those lakes; they must have palaces constructed of marble and porphyry, and the furniture ornamented with gold and diamonds. Millions of hands were thus employed in sterile labours; and the luxury of princes being imitated by their parasites, and descending step by step to the lowest ranks, became a general source of corruption and empoverishment.

And the ordinary tributes being no longer adequate to the infatiable thirst of enjoyment, they were augmented: the consequence of which was, that the cultivator, finding his toil increase without any indemnity, lost his courage; the merchant, seeing himself robbed, took a disgust to industry; the multitude, condemned to a state of poverty, exerted themselves no farther than the procurement of necessaries required, and every species of productive activity was at a stand.

And the surcharge of taxes rendering the possession of lands burthensome, the humble proprietor abandoned his field, or sold it to the man of opulence; and the mass of wealth centered in a few individuals. As the laws and institutions favoured this accumulation, nations were divided into a small body of indolent rich, and a multiude of mercenary poor. The people, reduced to indigence, debased themselves; the great, cloyed with superfluity, became depraved; and the number of citizens interested in the preservation of the state decreasing, its strength and existence were by so much the more precarious.

In

In another view, as there was nothing to excite emulation or encourage instruction, the minds of men sunk into profound ignorance.

The administration of affairs being secret and mysterious, there existed no means of reform or hope of better times; and as the chiefs ruled only by violence and fraud, the people considered them but as a faction of public enemies, and all harmony between the governed and the governors was at an end.

The states of opulent Asia become enervated by all these vices, it happened at length that the vagrant and poor inhabitants of the deserts and the mountains adjacent, coveted the enjoyments of the fertile plains, and instigated by a common cupidity, they attacked polished empires, and overturned the thrones of despots. Such revolutions were rapid and easy, because the policy of tyrants had enfeebled the citizens, razed the fortresses, destroyed the warlike spirit of resistance, and because the oppressed subject was without personal interest, and the mercenary soldier without courage.

Hordes of barbarians having reduced whole

nations to a state of slavery, it followed that empires, formed of a conquering and a vanquished people, united in their bosom two classes of men essentially opposite and inimical to each other. All the principles of society were dissolved. There was no longer either a common interest, or public spirit: on the contrary, a distinction of casts and conditions was established, that reduced the maintenance of disorder to a regular system; and accordingly as a man was descended from this or that blood, he was born vassal or tyrant, live stock or proprietor.

The oppressors being in this case less numerous than the oppressed, it became necessary, in order to support this false equilibrium, to bring the science of tyranny to perfection. The art of governing was now nothing more than that of subjecting the many to the few. To obtain an obedience so contrary to instinct, it was necessary to establish the most severe penalties; and the cruelty of the laws rendered the manners atrocious. The distinction of persons also establishing in the state two codes of justice, two species of rights, the people, placed between

between the natural inclinations of their hearts, and the oath they were obliged to pronounce, had two contradictory consciences; and their ideas of just and unjust had no longer any foundation in the understanding.

Under such a system the people fell into a state of depression and despair; and the accidents of nature increasing the preponderance of evil, terrified at this groupe of calamities, they referred the causes of them to superior and invisible powers: because they had tyrants upon earth, they supposed there to be tyrants in heaven; and superstition came in aid to aggravate the disasters of nations.

Hence originated gloomy and misanthropic systems of religion, which painted the Gods malignant and envious like human despots. To appease them, man offered the sacrifice of all his enjoyments, punished himself with privations, and overturned the laws of nature. Considering his pleasures as crimes, his sufferings as expiations, he endeavoured to cherish a passion for pain, and to renounce self-love; he persecuted his senses;

senses, detested his life, and by a self-denying and unsocial system of morals, nations were plunged in the sluggishness of death.

But as provident nature had endowed the heart of man with inexhaustible hope, perceiving his desires disappointed of happiness here, he pursued it elsewhere; by a sweet illusion, he formed to himself another country, an asylum, where, out of the reach of tyrants, he should regain all his rights. Hence a new disorder arose. Smitten with his imaginary world, man despised the world of nature: for chimerical hopes he neglected the reality. He no longer considered his life but as a fatiguing journey, a painful dream; his body as a prison that withheld him from his felicity; the earth as a place of exile and pilgrimage, which he disdained to cultivate. A sacred sloth then established itself in the world; the fields were deserted, waste lands increased, empires were dispeopled, monuments neglected, and every where ignorance, superstition and fanaticism uniting their baleful effects, multiplied devastations and ruins.

Thus,

Thus, agitated by their own paſſions, men, whether in their individual capacity, or as collective bodies, always rapacious and improvident, paſſing from tyranny to ſlavery, from pride to abjectneſs, from preſumption to deſpair, have been themſelves the eternal inſtruments of their misfortunes.

Such was the ſimplicity of the principles that regulated the fate of ancient ſtates; ſuch was the ſeries of cauſes and effects, conſecutive and connected with each other, according to which they roſe or fell in the ſcale of human welfare, juſt as the phyſical cauſes of the human heart were therein obſerved or infringed. A hundred divers nations, a hundred powerful empires, in their inceſſant viciſſitudes, have read again and again theſe inſtructive leſſons to mankind... And theſe leſſons are mute and forgotten! The diſeaſes of paſt times have appeared again in the preſent! The heads of the different governments have practiſed again, without reſtraint, exploded projects of deception and deſpotiſm! The people have wandered as before in the labyrinths of ſuperſtition and ignorance!

And

And what, added the Genius, calling up his energies afresh, is the consequence of all this? Since experience is useless, since salutary examples are forgotten, the scenes which were acted before are now about to be renewed; revolutions will again agitate people and empires; powerful thrones will, as before, be overturned; and terrible catastrophes remind the human species, that the laws of nature, and the precepts of wisdom and truth, cannot be trampled upon in vain.

CHAP.

CHAP. XII.

LESSONS TAUGHT BY ANCIENT, REPEATED IN MODERN TIMES.

In this manner did the Genius addrefs me. Struck with the reafonablenefs and coherence of his difcourfe, and a multiplicity of ideas crowding upon my mind, which, while they thwarted my habits, led my judgment at the fame time captive, I remained abforbed in profound filence. Meanwhile, as in this fombre and thoughtful difpofition I kept my eyes fixed upon Afia, clouds of fmoke and of flames at the north, on the fhores of the Black Sea, and in the fields of the Crimea, fuddenly attracted my attention. They appeared to afcend at once from every part of the peninfula, and pafling by the ifthmus to the continent, they purfued their courfe, as if driven by an eafterly wind, along the miry lake of Afoph, and were loft in the verdant plains of the Coban. Obferving more attentively the courfe of thefe clouds, I perceived

ceived that they were preceded or followed by swarms of living beings, which, like ants disturbed by the foot of a passenger, were in lively action. Sometimes they seemed to move towards and rush against each other, and numbers after the concussion remained motionless. Disquieted at this spectacle, I was endeavouring to distinguish the objects, when the Genius said to me: Do you see those fires which spread over the earth, and are you acquainted with their causes and effects?—O Genius, I replied, I see columns of flame and smoke, and as it were insects that accompany them; but discerning with difficulty, as I do, the masses of towns and monuments, how can I distinguish such petty creatures? I can see nothing more than that these insects seem to carry on a sort of mock battles; they advance, they approach towards each other, they attack, they pursue.—It is no mockery, said the Genius, it is the thing itself.—And what name, replied I, shall we give to these foolish animalculæ that destroy each other? Do they live only for a day, and is this short life further abridged by violence and murder?—The Genius then once more

touched

touched my eyes and my ears. Listen, said
he to me, and observe.—Immediately, turning my eyes in the same direction, alas! said
I, transpierced with anguish, these columns
of flame, these insects, O Genius! they are
men, and the ravages of war! These torrents of flame ascend from towns and villages set on fire! I see the horsemen that
light them. I see them sword in hand overrun the country. Old men, women, and
children, in confused multitudes, fly before
them. I see other horsemen, who, with their
pikes upon their shoulders, accompany and
direct them: I can even distinguish by their
led horses, by their *kalpacks*, and by their
tufts of hair (*p*), that they are Tartars; and
without doubt those who pursue them in triangular hats and green uniforms are Muscovites. I understand the whole: I perceive
that the war has just broken out afresh between the empire of the Czars and the Sultans.—Not yet, replied the Genius; this is
only the prelude. These Tartars have been,
and would still be troublesome neighbours;
the Muscovites are ridding themselves of
them. Their country is an object of conve-

nience

nience to their less uncivilized enemies; it rounds and makes complete their dominions; and as the first step in the project that has been conceived, the throne of the Guerais is overturned.

In reality I saw the Russian flag hoisted over the Crimea, and their vessels scattered upon the Euxine.

Meanwhile, at the cries of the fugitive Tartars, the Mussulman empire was in commotion. " Our brethren," exclaimed the children of Mahomet, " are driven from their " habitations; the people of the prophet are " outraged; infidels are in possession of a con- " secrated land (*q*), and profane the temples " of Islamism! Let us arm ourselves to avenge " the glory of God and our own cause."

A general preparation for war then took place in the two empires. Armed men, provisions, ammunition, and all the murderous accoutrements of battle, were every where assembled. My attention was particularly attracted by the immense crowds that in either nation thronged to the temples. On one side the Mussulmans, assembled before their mosques, washed their hands and feet,

pared

pared their nails, and combed their beard: then spreading carpets upon the ground, and turning themselves towards the south, with their arms sometimes crossed and sometimes extended, they performed their genuflections and prostrations. Recollecting the disasters they had experienced during the last war, they cried: " God of clemency and pity, hast " thou then abandoned thy faithful people? " Why dost thou, who has promised to thy " prophet the dominion of nations, and sig- " nalized religion by so many triumphs, de- " liver up true believers to the sword of in- fidels?" And the Imans and the Santons said to the people: " It is the chastisement of " your sins. You eat pork, you drink wine, " you touch things that are unclean: God " has punished you. Do penance; purify " yourselves; say your creed*; fast from the " rising of the sun to its setting; give the " tenth of your goods to the mosques; go " to Mecca; and God will make your arms " victorious." Then, assuming courage, the people gave a general shout. " There is but

* There is but one God, and Mahomet is his prophet.

G one

" one God," said they in a transport of rage,
" and Mahomet is his prophet! accursed be
" every one that believeth not! .... Indul-
" gent God! grant us the favour to exter-
" minate these Christians: it is for thy glory
" we fight, and by our death we are mar-
" tyrs to thy name."—And having offered sacrifices, they prepared themselves for
battle.

On the other hand, the Russians on their
knees exclaimed: " Let us give thanks to
" God, and celebrate his power: he has
" strengthened our arm to humble his ene-
" mies. Beneficent God! incline thine ear
" to our prayers. To please thee we will
" for three days eat neither meat nor eggs.
" Permit us to exterminate these impious
" Mahometans, and overthrow their empire,
" and we will give thee the tenth of the spoil,
" and erect new temples to thy honour."
The priests then filled the churches with
smoke, and said to the people: " We pray
" for you, and God accepts our incense, and
" blesses your arms. Continue to fast and
" to fight; tell us the faults you have secret-
" ly committed; bestow your goods on the
" church;

"church; we will absolve you of your sins, "and you shall die in a state of grace." And they sprinkled water on the people, distributed among them little bones of departed saints to serve as amulets and talismans; and the people breathed nothing but war and destruction.

Struck with this contrasting picture of the same passions, and lamenting to myself their pernicious consequences, I was reflecting on the difficulty the common Judge would find in complying with such opposite demands, when the Genius, from an impulse of anger, vehemently exclaimed:

What madness is this which strikes my ear? What blind and fatal insanity possesses the human mind? Sacrilegious prayers, return to the earth from whence you came! Ye concave heavens, repel these murderous vows, these impious thanksgivings! Is it thus, O man, you worship the Divinity? And do you think that he, whom you call Father of all, can receive with complacence the homage of free-booters and murderers? Ye conquerors, with what sentiments does he behold your arms reeking with blood that he has created? Ye conquered, what hope can you place in useless moans? Is he a man that he should change, or the son of man that he should repent? Is he governed like you by vengeance and compassion, by rage and by weariness! Base idea, how much unworthy of the Being of Beings! Hear these men, and you would imagine that God is a Being capricious and mutable; that now he loves, and now he hates; that he chastises one, and indulges another; that hatred is engendered and nourished in his bosom; that he spreads snares for men, and delights in the fatal effects of imprudence; that he permits ill, and punishes it; that he foresees guilt, and acquiesces; that he is to be bought with gifts like a partial judge; that he reverses his edicts like an undiscerning despot; that he gives and revokes his favours because it is his will, and is to be appeased only by servility like a savage tyrant. I now completely understand what is the deceit of mankind, who have pretended that God made man in his own image, and who have really made God in theirs; who have ascribed to him their weakness, their errors, and their vices; and in the conclusion,

conclusion, surprised at the contradictory nature of their own assertions, have attempted to cloke it with hypocritical humility, and the pretended impotence of human reason, calling the delirium of their own understandings the sacred mysteries of heaven.

They have said, God is without variableness, and they pray to him to change. They have said that he is incomprehensible, and they have undertaken to be interpreters of his will.

A race of impostors has made its appearance upon the earth, who, pretending to be in the confidence of God, and taking upon themselves the office of instructing the people, have opened the flood-gates of falsehood and iniquity. They have affixed merit to actions which either are indifferent or absurd. They have dignified with the appellation of virtue the observance of certain postures, and the repetition of certain words and names. They have taught the impiety of eating certain meats on certain days rather than on others. It is thus the Jew would sooner die than work on the sabbath. It is thus the Persian would endure suffocation

before he would blow the fire with his breath. It is thus the Indian places supreme perfection in smearing himself with cow-dung, and mysteriously pronouncing the word *Aûm* (r). It is thus the Mussulman believes himself purified from all his sins by the ablution of his head and his arms; and disputes, sabre in hand, whether he ought to begin the ceremony at the elbow (s) or the points of his fingers. It is thus the Christian would believe himself damned, were he to eat the juice of animal food instead of milk or butter. What sublime and truly celestial doctrines! What purity of morals, and how worthy of apostleship and martyrdom! I will cross the seas to teach these admirable laws to savage people and distant nations. I will say to them: " Chil-
" dren of nature, how long will you wander
" in the paths of ignorance? How long will
" you be blind to the true principles of mo-
" rality and religion? Visit civilized na-
" tions, and take lessons of pious and learn-
" ed people. They will teach you, that, to
" please God, you must in certain months
" of the year faint all day with hunger and
" thirst,

"thirst. They will teach you how you
"may shed the blood of your neighbour,
"and purify yourselves from the stain, by
"repeating a profession of faith, and mak-
"ing a methodical ablution: how you may
"rob him of his goods, and be absolved
"from the guilt, by sharing them with cer-
"tain persons whose profession it is to live
"in idleness upon the labour of others."

Sovereign and mysterious Power of the Universe! secret Mover of Nature! universal Soul of every thing that lives! infinite and incomprehensible Being, whom, under so many forms, mortals have ignorantly worshipped! God, who in the immensity of the heavens dost guide revolving worlds, and people the abyss of space with millions of suns: say, what appearance do those human insects, which I can with difficulty distinguish upon the earth, make in thy eyes? When thou directest the stars in their orbits, what to thee are the worms that crawl in the dust? Of what importance to thy infinite greatness are their distinctions of sects and parties? And how art thou concerned with the subtleties engendered by their folly?

And you, credulous men, shew me the efficacy of your practices! During the many ages that you have observed or altered them, what change have your *prescriptions* wrought in the laws of nature? Has the sun shone with greater brilliance? Has the course of the seasons at all varied? Is the earth more fruitful, are the people more happy? If God be good, how can he be pleased with your penances? If he be infinite, what can your homage add to his glory? Inconsistent men, answer these questions!

Ye conquerors, who pretend by your arms to serve God, what need has he of your aid? If he wishes to punish, are not earthquakes, volcanoes, and the thunderbolt in his hand? And does a God of clemency know no other way of correcting but by extermination?

Ye Mussulmans, if your misfortunes were the chastisements of heaven for the violation of the *five precepts*, would prosperity be showered on the Franks who laugh at these things? If it is by the laws of the Koran that God judges the earth, what were the principles

principles by which he governed the nations that existed before the prophet, the numerous people who drank wine, ate pork, and travelled not to Mecca, yet to whom it was given to raise powerful empires? By what laws did he judge the Sabeans of Nineveh and of Babylon; the Persian, who worshipped fire; the Greek and Roman idolaters; the ancient kingdoms of the Nile, and your own progenitors the Arabs and Tartars? How does he at present judge the various nations that are ignorant of your worship, the numerous casts of Indians, the vast empire of the Chinese, the swarthy tribes of Africa, the islanders of the Atlantic Ocean, the colonies of America!

Presumptuous and ignorant men, who arrogate to yourselves the whole earth, were God to summon at once all past and present generations, what proportion would those Christian and Mussulman sects, calling themselves *universal*, bear in the vast assemblage? What would be the judgment of his fair and impartial justice respecting the actual mass of mankind? It is in estimating the general system of his government that you wander among

among multiplied abfurdities; and it is there that, in reality, truth prefents itfelf in all its evidence. It is there that we trace the fimple but powerful laws of nature and reafon; the laws of the common mover, the general caufe; of a God impartial and juft, who, that he might fend his rain upon a country, afks not who is its prophet; who caufes his fun equally to fhine on all tribes of men, whether diftinguifhed by a fair or a fable complexion, on the Jew as on the Muffulman, on the Chriftian as on the Heathen; who multiplies the inhabitants of every country with whom order and induftry reign; who gives profperity to every empire where juftice is obferved, where the powerful is reftrained, and the poor man protected by the laws; where the weak lives in fafety, and where all enjoy the rights which they derive from nature and an equitable compact.

Such are the principles by which nations are judged! This is the true religion by which the fate of empires is regulated, and which, O Ottomans, has ever decided that of your own empire! Interrogate your anceftors; afk them by what means they rofe to greatness, when, idolators, few in number and poor, they came from the deserts of Tartary to encamp in these fertile countries? Ask them if it was by islamism, at that period unknown to them, that they conquered the Greeks and Arabs; or by their courage, prudence, moderation, and unanimity, the true powers of the social state? Then the Sultan himself administered justice and maintained order: then the prevaricating judge and the rapacious governor were punished, and the multitude lived in ease: the cultivator was secure from the rapine of the janizary, and the fields were productive: the public roads were safe, and commerce flourished. It is true you were a league of robbers, but among yourselves you were just. You subjugated nations, but you did not oppress them. Vexed by their own princes they preferred being your tributaries. "Of what importance is it to me, said the "Christian, whether my master be pleased "with images or breaks them in pieces, "provided he is just towards me? God will "judge his doctrine in heaven." You were temperate and hardy; your enemies soft and effeminate;

effeminate: you were skilled in the art of battle; they had forgotten its principles: you had experienced chiefs, warlike and disciplined troops; the hope of booty excited ardour; bravery was recompensed; disobedience and cowardice punished, and all the springs of the human heart were in action. You thus conquered a hundred nations, and out of the mass founded an immense empire.

But other manners succeeded. The laws of nature, however, did not less operate in your misfortunes than in your prosperity. You destroyed your enemies, and your grasping ambition, still in force, preyed upon yourselves. Having become rich, you commenced an internal contest respecting the division and the enjoyment of your riches, and disorder was generated through every class of your society. The Sultan, intoxicated with his greatness, misunderstood the object of his functions, and all the vices of arbitrary power presently unfolded themselves. Meeting with no obstacle to his desires, he became a depraved character. Weak, and arrogant at the same time, he spurned the people, and would no longer be influenced and directed by their voice.

voice. Ignorant, and yet flattered, he neglected all instruction, all study, and sunk into total incapacity. Become himself unqualified for the conduct of affairs, he committed the trust to hirelings, and these hirelings deceived him. To satisfy their own passions, they stimulated and increased his; they multiplied his wants, and his enormous luxury devoured every thing. He was no longer content with the frugal table, the modest attire, and the simple habitation of his ancestors: the earth and sea must be exhausted to satisfy his pride; scarce furs must be fetched from the pole, and costly tissues from the equator; he consumed at a meal the tribute of a city, and in a day the revenue of a province. He became infested with an army of women, eunuchs, and courtiers. He was told that the virtue of kings consisted in liberality; and the munificence and treasures of the people were delivered into the hands of parasites. In imitation of the master, the slaves were also desirous of having magnificent houses, furniture of exquisite workmanship, carpets richly embroidered, vases of gold and silver for the vilest uses; and all

the

the wealth of the empire was swallowed up in the *Seraï*.

To supply this inordinate luxury the slaves and the women sold their influence; and venality introduced a general depravation. They sold the favour of the prince to the Visier, and the Visier sold the empire. They sold the law to the Cadi, and the Cadi sold justice. They sold the altar to the priest, and the priest sold heaven. And gold obtaining every thing, nothing was left unpractised to obtain gold. For gold, friend betrayed friend; the child his father; the servant his master; the wife her honour; the merchant his conscience; and there no longer existed in the state either good faith, manners, concord, or stability.

The Pacha, who purchased his office, presently had recourse to the system of farming it for a revenue, and exercising upon it every species of extortion. He sold the collection of the taxes, the command of the troops, the administration of the districts; and in proportion as every employment was temporary, rapine, diffusing itself from rank to rank, was rapid and precipitate. The exciseman oppressed

pressed the merchant by his exactions, and trade was annihilated. The Aga stript the husbandman, and cultivation was degraded. The labourer, robbed of his little capital, had not wherewith to sow his field: taxes nevertheless became due, and he was unable to pay them; he was threatened with corporal punishment, and driven to the expedient of a loan: specie, for want of security, was withdrawn from circulation; the interest of money became enormous, and usury aggravated the misery of the poor.

Inclement seasons, periods of dearth, had rendered the harvests abortive, but government would neither forgive nor postpone its demands. Distress began its career: a part of the inhabitants of the villages took refuge in the cities; the burthen upon those that remained became greater, their ruin was consummated, and the country depopulated.

Driven to the last extremity by tyranny and insult, certain villages broke out into rebellion. The Pacha considered the event as a subject of rejoicing; he made war upon them, took their houses by storm, ransacked their goods, and carried off their cattle. The
soil

foil became a defert, and he exclaimed!
" What care I; I fhall be removed from it
to-morrow."

Yet again, the want of cultivation led one
ftep farther. Periodical rains or fwelling
tides overflowed the banks and covered the
country with fwamps: thefe fwamps exhaled
a putrid air, which fpread chronical difeafes,
peftilence, and ficknefs of a thoufand forms,
and was followed by a ftill farther decreafe
of population, by penury and ruin.

Oh! who can enumerate all the evils of
this tyrannical fyftem of government!

Sometimes the Pachas make war of themfelves, and to avenge their perfonal quarrels,
provinces are laid wafte. Sometimes, dread-
ing their mafters, they aim at independence,
and draw upon their fubjects the chaftife-
ment of their revolt. Sometimes, fear-
ing thefe very fubjects, they call to their
aid and keep in pay foreign troops, and to
be fure of them, they indulge them in every
kind of robbery. In one place, they commence an action againft a rich man, and
plunder him upon falfe pretences. In another, they fuborn witneffes, and impofe a

fine

fine for an imaginary offence. On all occasions they excite the hatred of sects against each other, and encourage informations for the sake of increasing their own corrupt advantages. They extort from men their property; they attack their persons; and when their imprudent avarice has heaped into one mass the riches of a province, the supreme government, with execrable perfidy, pretending to avenge the oppressed inhabitants, draws to itself their spoil in the spoil of the culprit, and wantonly and vainly expiate in blood the crime of which it was itself the accomplice.

O iniquitous beings, sovereigns or ministers, who sport with the life and property of the people! was it you who gave breath to man, that you take it from him? Is it you who fertilize the earth, that you dissipate its fruits? Do you fatigue your arms with ploughing the field? Do you expose yourselves to the heat of the sun, and endure the torment of thirst in cutting down the harvest and binding it into sheaves? Do you watch like the shepherd in the nocturnal dew?

dew? Do you traverse deserts like the indefatigable merchant? Alas! when I have reflected on the cruelty and insolence of the powerful, my indignation has been roused, and I have said in my anger: What! will there never appear upon the earth a race of men who shall avenge the people and punish tyrants! A small number of robbers devour the multitude, and the multitude suffer themselves to be devoured! O degraded people, awake to the recognition of your rights! authority proceeds from you, yours is all the power. Vainly do kings command you *in the name of God* and *by their lance:* soldiers, obey not the summons. Since God supports the Sultan, your succour is useless; since the sword of heaven suffices him, he has no need of yours; let us see what he can do of himself.... The soldiers have laid down their arms; and lo, the masters of the world are as feeble as the meanest of their subjects! Ye people, know then that those who govern you are your chiefs and not your masters; your guardians appointed by yourselves, and not your proprietors; that your wealth is

your

your own, and to you they are accountable for the adminiſtration of it; that kings or ſubjects, God has made all men equal, and no human being has a right to oppreſs his fellow-creature.

But this nation and its chiefs acknowledge not theſe ſacred truths.... Be it ſo; they will ſuffer the conſequences of their error. The decree is gone forth; the day approaches when this coloſſus of power ſhall be daſhed to pieces, and fall cruſhed by its own weight. Yes, I ſwear by the ruins of ſo many demoliſhed empires, that the creſcent ſhall undergo the ſame fate as the ſtates whoſe mode of government it has imitated! A foreign people ſhall drive the Sultans from their metropolis; the throne of Orkhan ſhall be ſubverted; the laſt ſhoot of his race ſhall be cut off; and the horde of the Oguzians (*t*), deprived of their chief, ſhall be diſperſed like that of the Nogaians. In this diſſolution the ſubjects of the empire, freed from the yoke that held them together, will reſume their ancient diſtinctions, and a general anarchy will take place, as happened in the empire of the Sophis (*u*), till there shall arise among the Arabs, the Armenians, or the Greeks, legislators who shall form new states. Oh! were a sagacious and hardy race of men to be found, what materials of greatness and glory are here!.... But the hour of destiny is arrived. The cry of war strikes my ear, and the catastrophe is about to commence. In vain the Sultan draws out his armies; his ignorant soldiers are beaten and scattered. In vain he calls upon his subjects: their hearts are callous; his subjects reply: " It " is decreed; and what is it to us who is " to be our master? we cannot lose by the " change." In vain these true believers invoke heaven and the prophet, the prophet is dead, and heaven without pity answers: " Cease to call upon me. You are the au- " thors of your calamities, find yourselves " their remedy. Nature has established " laws, it becomes you to practise them. " Examine and reflect upon the events that " take place, and profit by experience. It " is the folly of man that works his destruc- " tion; it is his wisdom that must save him.

" The

"The people are ignorant; let them get un-
"derstanding: their chiefs are depraved; let
"them correct their vices and amend their
"lives, for such is the decree of nature:
"*Since the evils of society flow from* IGNO-
"RANCE *and* INORDINATE DESIRE, *men
"will never cease to be tormented till they
"shall become intelligent and wise; till they
"shall practise the art of justice, founded on
"a knowledge of the various relations in
"which they stand, and the laws of their own
"organization* *."

CHAP.

---

* A singular moral phenomenon made its appearance in Europe in the year 1788. A great nation, jealous of its liberty, contracted a fondness for a nation the enemy of liberty; a nation friendly to the arts for a nation that detests them; a mild and tolerant nation for a persecuting and fanatic one; a social and gay nation for a nation whose characteristic are gloom and misanthropy; in a word, the French were smitten with a passion for the Turks: they were desirous of engaging in a war for them, and that at a time when a revolution in their own country was just at its commencement. A man who perceived the true nature of the situation, wrote a book to dissuade them from the war: it was immediately pretended that he was paid by the government, which in reality wished the war, and which was upon the point of shutting him up in a state prison. Another man wrote

CHAP. XIII.

WILL THE HUMAN RACE BE EVER IN A BETTER CONDITION THAN AT PRESENT.

OPPRESSED with sorrow at the predictions of the Genius, and the severity of his reasoning: Unhappy nations, cried I, bursting

to recommend the war; he was applauded, and his word was taken in payment for the science, the politeness and importance of the Turks. It is true that he believed in his own thesis, for he had found among them people who cast a nativity, and alchemists who ruined his fortune; as he found Martinists at Paris, who enabled him to sup with Sesostris, and Magnetisers who concluded with destroying his existence. Notwithstanding this, the Turks were beaten by the Russians, and the man who then predicted the fall of their empire, persists in the prediction. The result of this fall will be a complete change of the political system, as far as it relates to the coast of the Mediterranean. If, however, the French become important in proportion as they become free, and if they make use of the advantage they will obtain, their progress may easily prove of the most honourable sort, inasmuch as, by the wise decrees of fate, the true interest of mankind evermore accords with their true morality.

ing into tears! Unhappy my own lot! I now despair of the felicity of man! since his evils flow from his own heart, since he must himself apply the remedy, woe for ever to his existence! For what can restrain the inordinate desire of the powerful? Who shall enlighten the ignorance of the weak? Who instruct the multitude in the knowledge of its rights, and force the chiefs to discharge the duties of their station? Individual will not cease to oppress individual, one nation to attack another nation, and never will the day of prosperity and glory again dawn upon these countries. Alas! conquerors will come; they will drive away the oppressors, and will establish themselves in their place; but, succeeding to their power, they will succeed also to their rapacity, and the earth will have changed its tyrants, without lessening the tyranny.

Then turning towards the Genius: O Genius! said I, despair has taken hold of my heart. While you have instructed me in the nature of man, the depravity of governors, and the abjectness of those who are governed, have given me a difguft to life; and fince there is no alternative but to be the accomplice or the victim of oppreffion, what has the virtuous man to do but to join his afhes to thofe of the tombs!

The Genius, fixing upon me a look of feverity mixed with compaffion, was filent. After a few minutes he replied: Is it then in dying that virtue confifts? The wicked man is indefatigable in the confummation of vice, and the juft difheartened at the firft obftacle which ftands in the way of doing good!.... But fuch is the human heart: fuccefs intoxicates it to prefumption, difappointment dejects and terrifies it. Always the victim of the fenfation of the moment, it judges not of things by their nature but by the impulfe of paffion.... Mortal, who defpaireft of the human race, upon what profound calculation of reafonings and events is your judgment formed? Have you fcrutinized the organization of fenfible beings, to determine with precifion whether the fprings that incline them to happinefs are weaker than thofe which repel? or rather,

viewing

viewing at a glance the history of the species, and judging of the future by the example of the past, have you hence discovered with certainty, that all proficiency is impossible? Let me ask: Have societies, since their origin, made no step towards instruction and a better state of things? Are men still in the woods, destitute of every thing, ignorant, stupid, and ferocious? Are there no nations advanced beyond the period, when nothing was to be seen upon the face of the globe but savage freebooters or savage slaves? If individuals have at certain times, and in certain places, become better, why should not the mass improve? If particular societies have attained a considerable degree of perfection, why should not the progress of the general society advance? If first obstacles have been overcome, why should succeeding ones be insurmountable?

But you are of opinion that the human race is degenerating? Guard yourself against the illusion and paradoxes of misanthropy. Dissatisfied with the present, man supposes in the past a perfection which does not exist,

and

and which is merely the discoloration of his chagrin. He praises the dead from enmity to the living, and employs the bones of the fathers as an instrument of chastisement against the children.

To establish this principle of a retrograde perfection, it is necessary that we should contradict the testimony of facts and reason. Nor is this all; the facts of history might indeed be equivocal, but it is farther necessary that we should contradict the living fact of the nature of man; that we should assert that he is born with a perfect science in the use of his senses; that, previous to experience, he is able to distinguish poison from aliment; that the sagacity of the infant is greater than that of his bearded progenitor; that the blind man can walk with more assurance than the man endued with sight; that man, the creature of civilization, is less favoured by circumstances than the cannibal; in a word, that there is no truth in the existing gradation of instruction and experience.

Young man, believe the voice of tombs and

and the testimony of monuments. There are countries which have doubtless fallen off from what they were at certain epochas: but if the understanding were to analyse thoroughly the wisdom and felicity of their inhabitants at those periods, their glory would be found to have less of reality than of splendour; it would be seen, that even in the most celebrated states of antiquity, there existed enormous vices and cruel abuses, the precise cause of their instability; that in general the principles of government were atrocious; that, from people to people, audacious robbery, barbarous wars, and implacable animosities were prevalent (*x*); that natural right was unknown; that morality was perverted by senseless fanaticism and deplorable superstition; that a dream, a vision, an oracle, were the frequent occasion of the most terrible commotions. Nations are not perhaps yet free from the power of these evils; but their force is at least diminished, and the experience of past times has not been wholly lost. Within the three last centuries especially, the light of knowledge

has

has been increased and disseminated; civilization, aided by various happy circumstances, has perceptibly advanced, and even inconveniences and abuses have proved advantageous to it: for if conquests have extended kingdoms and states beyond due bounds, the people of different countries, uniting under the same yoke, have lost that spirit of estrangement and division which made them all enemies to one another. If the hands of power have been strengthened, an additional degree of system and harmony has at least been introduced in its exercise. If wars have become more general in the mass of their influence and operation, they have been less destructive in their details. If the people carry to the combat less personality and less exertion, their struggles are less sanguinary and ferocious. If they are less free, they are less turbulent; if they are more effeminate, they are more pacific. Despotism itself seems not to have been unproductive of advantages: for if the government has been absolute, it has been less perturbed and tempestuous; if thrones have been

been regarded as hereditary property, they have excited less dissention, and exposed the people to fewer convulsions; in fine, if despots, with timid and mysterious jealousy have interdicted all knowledge of their administration, all rivalship for the direction of affairs, the passions of mankind, excluded from the political career, have fixed upon the arts and the science of nature; the sphere of ideas has been enlarged on every side; man, devoted to abstract studies, has better understood his place in the system of nature, and his social relations; principles have been more fully discussed, objects more accurately discerned, knowledge more widely diffused, individuals made more capable, manners more sociable, life more benevolent and pleasing; the species at large, particularly in certain countries, have been evidently gainers: nor can this improvement fail to proceed, since its two principal obstacles, those which have hitherto rendered it so slow, and frequently retrograde, the difficulty of transmitting ideas from age to age, and communicating them rapidly from man to man, have been removed.

With the people of antiquity, every canton and every city, having a language peculiar to itself, stood aloof from the rest, and the result was favourable to ignorance and anarchy: they had no communication of ideas, no participation of discoveries, no harmony of interests or of will, no unity of action or conduct. Beside, the only means of diffusing and transmitting ideas being that of speech, fugitive and limited, and that of writing, slow of execution, expensive, and acquired by few, there resulted an extreme difficulty as to instruction in the first instance, the loss of advantages one generation might derive from the experience of another, instability, retrogradation of science, and one unvaried scene of chaos and childhood.

On the contrary, in the modern world, and particularly in Europe, great nations having allied themselves by a sort of universal language, the firm of opinion has been placed upon a broader basis; the minds of men have sympathised, their hearts have enlarged; we have seen agreement in thinking, and concord in acting: in fine, that sacred

sacred art, that memorable gift of celestial genius, the press, furnished a means of communicating, of diffusing at one instant any idea to millions of the species, and of giving it a permanence which all the power of tyrants has been able neither to suspend nor to suppress. Hence has the vast mass of instruction perpetually increased; hence has the atmosphere of truth continually grown brighter, and a strength of mind been produced that is in no fear of counteraction. And this improvement is the necessary effect of the laws of nature; for by the law of sensation, man as invincibly tends to make himself happy, as the flame to ascend, the stone to gravitate, the water to gain its level. His ignorance is the obstacle which misleads him as to the means, and deceives him respecting causes and effects. By force of experience he will become enlightened; by force of errors he will set himself right; he will become wise and good, because it is his interest to be so: and ideas communicating themselves through a nation, whole classes will be instructed, science will be universally

sally familiar, and all men will understand what are the principles of individual happiness and of public felicity; they will understand what are their respective relations, their rights, and their duties, in the social order; they will no longer be the dupes of inordinate desire; they will perceive that morality is a branch of the science of physics, composed it is true of elements complicated in their operation, but simple and invariable in their nature, as being no other than the elements of human organization itself. They will feel the necessity of being moderate and just, because therein consists the advantage and security of each; that to wish to enjoy at the expence of another is a false calculation of ignorance, because the result of such proceeding, are reprisals, enmity, and revenge; and that dishonesty is invariably the offspring of folly.

Individuals will feel that private happiness is allied to the happiness of society:

The weak, that instead of dividing their interests, they ought to unite, because equality constitutes their strength:

The

The rich, that the measure of enjoyment is limited by the constitution of the organs, and that lassitude follows satiety:

The poor, that the highest degree of human felicity consists in peace of mind and the due employment of time:

Public opinion, reaching kings on their thrones, will oblige them to keep themselves within the bounds of a regular authority:

Chance itself, serving the cause of nations, will give them sometimes incapable chiefs, who, through weakness, will suffer them to become free; and sometimes enlightened chiefs, who will virtuously emancipate them:

Individuality will be a term of greater comprehension, and nations, free and enlightened will hereafter become one complex individual, as single men are now: the consequences will be proportioned to the state of things. The communication of knowledge will extend from society to society, till it comprehends the whole earth. By the law of imitation the example of one people will be followed by others, who will adopt its spirit and its laws. Despots themselves, perceiving that they can no longer maintain their power without justice and beneficence, will be induced, both from necessity and rivalship, to soften the rigour of their government; and civilization will be universal.

Among nations there will be established an equilibrium of force, which, confining them within the limits of just respect for their reciprocal rights, will put an end to the barbarous practice of war, and induce them to submit to civil arbitration the decision of their disputes (*y*); and the whole species will become one grand society, one individual family governed by the same spirit, by common laws, and enjoying all the felicity of which human nature is capable.

This great work will doubtless be long accomplishing, because it is necessary that one and the same motion should be communicated to the various parts of an immense body; that the same leaven should assimilate an enormous mass of heterogeneous elements: but this motion will effectually operate. Already society at large, having passed through the same stages as particular societies have done, promises to lead to the same results. At first, disconnected in its parts, each individual

dividual stood alone; and this intellectual solitude constituted its age of anarchy and childhood. Divided afterwards into sections of irregular size, as chance directed, which have been called states and kingdoms, it has experienced the fatal effects which result from the inequality of wealth and conditions; and the aristocracy by which great empires have domineered over their dependencies, have formed its second age. In process of time, these paramount chiefs of the globe have disputed with each other for superiority, and then was seen the period of factions and civil broils. And now the parties, tired of their discords and feeling the want of laws, sigh for the epocha of order and tranquillity. Let but a virtuous chief arise, a powerful and just people appear, and the earth will arrive at supreme power. It waits a legislative people; this is the object of its wishes and its prayers, and my heart hears its voice..... Then turning to the quarter of the West: Yes, continued he, a hollow noise already strikes my ear; the cry of liberty, uttered upon the farther shore of the Atlantic, has reached to the old continent. At
this

this cry a secret murmur against oppression is excited in a powerful nation; a salutary alarm takes place respecting its situation; it enquires what it is and what it ought to be; it examines into its rights, its resources, and what has been the conduct of its chiefs.... One day, one reflection more.... and an immense agitation will arise, a new age will make its appearance, an age of astonishment to vulgar minds, of surprise and dread to tyrants, of emancipation to a great people, and of hope to the whole world.

CHAP.

CHAP. XIV.

GRAND OBSTACLE TO IMPROVEMENT.

THE Genius ſtopt. My mind however, preoccupied with gloomy forebodings, yielded not to perſuaſion; but fearful of offending him by oppoſition, I made no reply. After a ſhort interval; fixing on me a look that tranſpierced my ſoul: You are ſilent, ſaid he, and your heart is agitated with thoughts which it dares not utter!—Confuſed and terrified: O Genius, I made anſwer, pardon my weakneſs: truth alone has doubtleſs proceeded from your lips; but your celeſtial intelligence can diſtinguiſh its traits, where to my groſs faculties there appear nothing but clouds. I acknowledge it, conviction has not penetrated my ſoul, and I feared that my doubts might give you offence.

And what is doubt, replied he, that it ſhould be regarded as a crime? Has man the power of thinking contrary to the impreſſions that are made upon him? If a truth be palpable, and its observance important, let us pity the man who does not perceive it: his punishment will infallibly spring from his blindness. If it be uncertain and equivocal, how is he to find in it what does not exist? To believe without evidence and demonstration is an act of ignorance and folly. The credulous man involves himself in a labyrinth of contradictions; the man of sense examines and discusses every question, that he may be consistent in his opinions; he can endure contradiction, because from the collision evidence arises. Violence is the argument of falsehood; and to impose a creed authoritatively, is the index and proceeding of a tyrant.

Emboldened by these sentiments, I replied: O Genius, since my reason is free, I strive in vain to welcome the flattering hope with which you would console me. The sensible and virtuous soul is prone enough to be hurried away by dreams of fancied happiness; but a cruel reality incessantly recals its attention to suffering and wretchedness. The more I meditate on the nature of man, the more I examine the present state of society, the less possible does it appear to me that

that a world of wifdom and felicity fhould
ever be realized. I furvey the face of our
whole hemifphere, and no where can I perceive the germ of a happy revolution. All
Afia is buried in the moft profound darknefs. The Chinefe, fubjected to an infolent defpotifm (z), dependent for their fortune upon the decifion of lots, and held in
awe by ftrokes of the bamboo, enflaved by
the immutability of their code, and by the
irremediable vice of their language, offer to
my view an abortive civilization and a race
of automata. The Indian, fettered by prejudice, and manacled by the inviolable infti-
tution of his cafts, vegetates in an incurable
apathy. The Tartar, wandering or fixed,
at all times ignorant and ferocious, lives in
the barbarity of his anceftors. The Arab,
endowed with a happy genius, lofes its force
and the fruit of his labour in the anarchy of
his tribes, and the jealoufy of his families.
The African, degraded from the ftate of
man, feems irremediably devoted to fervi-
tude. In the North I fee nothing but ferfs,
reduced to the level of cattle, the live ftock
of the eftate upon which they live (1). Ignorance,

norance, tyranny, and wretchedness have every where struck the nations with stupor; and vicious habits, depraving the natural senses, have destroyed the very instinct of happiness and truth. In some countries of Europe, indeed, reason begins to expand its wings; but even there, is the knowledge of individual minds common to the nation? Has the superiority of the government been turned to the advantage of the people? And these people, who call themselves polished, are they not those who three centuries ago filled the earth with their injustice? Are they not those who, under the pretext of commerce, laid India waste, dispeopled a new continent, and who at present subject Africa to the most inhuman slavery? Can liberty spring up out of the bosom of despots, and justice be administered by the hands of rapacity and avarice? O Genius! I have beheld civilized countries, and the illusion of their wisdom has vanished from my sight. I saw riches accumulated in the hands of a few individuals, and the multitude poor and destitute. I saw all right and power concentered in certain classes, and the mass

of

of the people paſſive and dependent. I ſaw the palaces of princes, but no incorporation of individuals as ſuch, no common-hall of nations. I perceived the deep attention that was given to the intereſts of government; but no public intereſt, no ſympathetic ſpirit. I ſaw that the whole ſcience of thoſe who command conſiſted in prudently oppreſſing; and the refined ſervitude of poliſhed nations only appeared to me the more irremediable.

With one obſtacle in particular my mind was ſenſibly ſtruck. In ſurveying the globe, I perceived that it was divided into twenty different ſyſtems of religious worſhip. Each nation has received, or formed for itſelf, oppoſite opinions, and aſcribing to itſelf excluſively the truth, has imagined every other to be in error. But if, as is the fact, in this diſcordance the majority deceive themſelves, and deceive themſelves with ſincerity, it follows that the human mind as readily imbibes falſehood as truth; and in that caſe how is it to be enlightened? How are prejudices to be extirpated that firſt take root in the mind? How is the bandage to be removed from the eyes, when the firſt article

in

in every creed, the first dogma of all religions, is the proscription of doubt, of examination, and of the right of private judgment? How is truth to make itself known? If she resort to the demonstration of argument, pusillanimous man appeals against evidence to his conscience. If she call in the aid of divine authority, already prepossessed, he opposes an authority of a similar kind, and treats all innovation as blasphemy. Thus, in his blindness, riveting the chains upon himself, does he become the sport of his ignorance and passions. To dissolve these fatal shackles, a miraculous concurrence of happy circumstances would be necessary. It would be necessary that a whole nation, cured of the delirium of superstition, should no longer be liable to the impressions of fanaticism; that, freed from the yoke of a false doctrine, it should voluntarily embrace the genuine system of morality and reason; that it should become at once courageous and prudent, wise and docile; that every individual, acquainted with his rights, should scrupulously observe their limits; and the poor should know how to resist seduction, and the rich the allurements

ments of avarice; that there should be found upright and disinterested chiefs; that its tyrants should be seized with a spirit of madness and folly; that the people, recovering their powers, should perceive their inability to exercise them, and consent to appoint delegates; that having first created their magistrates, they should know both how to respect and how to judge them; that in the rapid renovation of a whole nation pervaded with abuse, each individual, removed from his former habits, should suffer patiently the pains and self-denials annexed; in fine, that the nation should have the courage to conquer its liberty, the wisdom to secure it, the power to defend it, and the generosity to communicate it. Can sober judgment expect this combination of circumstances? Should fortune in the infinite variety of her caprices produce them, is it likely that I should live to see that day? Will not this frame long before that have mouldered in the tomb?

Here, oppressed with sorrow, my heart deprived me of utterance. The Genius made no reply; but in a low tone of voice I heard him

him say to himself: "Let us revive the hope
"of this man; for if he who loves his fellow-
"creatures be suffered to despair, what is to
"become of nations? The past is perhaps
"but too much calculated to deject him.
"Let us then anticipate futurity; let us un-
"veil the astonishing age that is about to
"arise, that virtue, seeing the end of its
"wishes, animated with new vigour, may
"redouble its efforts to hasten the accom-
"plishment of it."

CHAP. XV.

NEW AGE.

SCARCELY had the Genius uttered to himself these words than an immense noise proceeded from the West, and turning my eyes to that quarter, I perceived at the extremity of the Mediterranean, in the country of one of the European nations, a prodigious movement, similar to what exists in the bosom of a large city when, pervaded with sedition, an innumerable people, like waves, fluctuate in the streets and public places. My ear, struck with their cries, which ascended to the very heavens, distinguished at intervals these phrases:

"What is this new prodigy? What this
"cruel and mysterious scourge? We are a
"numerous people, and we want strength!
"We have an excellent soil, and we are
"destitute of provision! We are active and
"laborious, and we live in indigence! We
"pay enormous tributes, and we are told
                                    "that

"that they are not sufficient! We are at
"peace without, and our persons and pro-
"perty are not safe within! What then is
"the secret enemy that devours us?"

From the midst of the concourse, some individual voices replied: "Erect a standard
"of distinction, and let all those who, by
"useful labours, contribute to the support
"and maintenance of society, gather round
"it, and you will discover the enemy that
"preys on your vitals."

The standard being erected, the nation found itself suddenly divided into two bodies of unequal magnitude and dissimilar appearance: the one innumerable and nearly integral, exhibited, in the general poverty of their dress, and in their meagre and sunburnt faces, the marks of toil and wretchedness; the other a pretty groupe, a valueless faction, presented, in their rich attire, embroidered with gold and silver, and in their sleek and ruddy complexions, the symptoms of leisure and abundance. Considering these men more attentively, I perceived that the large body was constituted of labourers, artisans, tradesmen, and every profession useful

to

to society; and that in the lesser groupe there were none but priests, courtiers, public accountants, commanders of troops, in short, the civil, military, or religious agents of government.

The two bodies being front to front assembled, and having looked with astonishment at each other, I saw the feelings of indignation and resentment spring up in the one, and a sort of panic in the other; and the large said to the small body:

Why stand you apart? Are you not of our number?

No, replied the groupe; you are the people; we are a privileged class; we have laws, customs, and rights peculiar to ourselves.

People.

And what labour do you perform in the society?

Privileged Class.

None: we are not made to labour.

People.

How then have you acquired your wealth?

Privileged Class.

By taking the pains to govern you.

People.

People.

To govern us! and is this what you call governing? We toil, and you enjoy; we produce, and you diffipate; wealth flows from us, and you abforb it.... Privileged men, clafs diftinct from the people, form a nation apart, and govern yourfelves (2).

Then, deliberating on their new fituation, fome among the groupe faid: Let us join the people, and partake their burthens and cares; for they are men like ourfelves. Others replied: To mix with the herd would be degrading and vile; they are born to ferve us, who are men of a fuperior race. The civil govenors faid: the people are mild and naturally fervile; let us fpeak to them in the name of the king and the law, and they will return to their duty.... People! the king decrees, the fovereign ordains.

People.

The king cannot decree any thing which the fafety of the people does not demand; the fovereign cannot ordain but according to law.

Civil Governors.

The law calls upon you for fubmiffion.

People,

People.

The law is the general will; and we will a new order.

Civil Governors.

You are in that cafe rebels.

People.

A nation cannot be a rebel; tyrants only are rebels.

Civil Governors.

The king is on our fide, and he enjoins you to fubmit.

People.

Kings cannot be feparated from the nation in which they reign. Our king cannot be on your fide; you have only the phantom of his countenance.

Then the military governors advanced, and they faid: The people are timorous; it is proper to threaten them; they will yield to the influence of force....Soldiers, chaftife this infolent multitude!

People.

Soldiers, our blood flows in your veins! will you ftrike your brothers? If the people be deftroyed, who will maintain the army?

And the foldiers, grounding their arms, faid

said to their chiefs: We are a part of the people; we whom you call upon to fight against them.

Then the ecclesiastical governors said: There is but one resource left. The people are superstitious; it is proper to overawe them with the names of God and religion.

Priests.

Our dear brethren, our children, God has commissioned us to govern you.

People.

Produce the patent of his commission.

Priests.

You must have faith; reason leads men into guilt.

People.

And would you govern us without reason?

Priests.

God is the God of peace; religion enjoins you to obey.

People.

No; justice goes before peace; obedience implies a law, and renders necessary the cognizance of it.

Priests.

This world was intended for trial and suffering.

People.

People.

Do you then shew us the example of suffering.

Priests.

Would you live without Gods or kings?

People.

We abjure tyranny of every kind.

Priests.

You must have mediators, persons who may act in your behalf.

People.

Mediators with God, and mediators with the king! Courtiers and priests, your services are too expensive; henceforth we take our affairs into our own hands.

Then the smaller groupe exclaimed: It is over with us; the multitude are enlightened. And the people replied: You shall not be hurt; we are enlightened, and we will commit no violence. We desire nothing but our rights: resentment we cannot but feel, but we consent to pass it by: we were slaves, we might now command; but we ask only to be free, and free we are.

CHAP. XVI.

A FREE AND LEGISLATIVE PEOPLE.

I Now reflected with myself that public power was at a stand, that the habitual government of this people was annihilated, and I shuddered at the idea of their falling into the dissolution of anarchy. But taking their affairs immediately into their consideration, they quickly dispelled my apprehensions.

"It is not enough, said they, that we
"have freed ourselves from parasites and
"tyrants, we must prevent for ever the re-
"vival of their power. We are human
"beings, and we know, by dear-bought ex-
"perience, that every human being inces-
"santly grasps at authority, and wishes to
"enjoy it at the expence of others. It is
"therefore necessary to guard ourselves be-
"forehand against this unfortunate propen-
"sity, the prolific parent of discord; it is
"necessary to establish rules by which our
"rights

"rights are to be determined and our con-
"duct governed. But in this investigation
"abstruse and difficult questions are in-
"volved, which demand all the attention
"and faculties of the wisest men. Occupied
"in our respective callings, we have neither
"leisure for these studies, nor are we com-
"petent of ourselves to the exercise of such
"functions. Let us select from our body
"certain individuals, to whom the employ-
"ment will be proper. To them let our
"common powers be delegated, to frame for
"us a system of government and laws: let us
"constitute them the representatives of our
"interests and our wills; and that this re-
"presentation may be as accurate as possible,
"and have comprehended in it the whole
"diversity of our wills and interests, let the
"individuals that comprize it be numerous,
"and citizens like ourselves."

The selection being made, the people thus addressed their delegates: " We have hither-
"to lived in a society formed by chance,
"without fixed clauses, without free con-
"ventions, without stipulation of rights,
"without reciprocal engagements; and a
"multitude

" multitude of disorders and evils have been
" the result of this confused state of things.
" We would now, with mature deliberation,
" frame a regular compact; and we have
" made choice of you to draw up the articles
" of it. Examine then with care what
" ought to be its basis and principles. In-
" vestigate the object and tendency of every
" association; observe what are the rights
" which every individual brings into it, the
" powers he cedes for the public good, and
" the powers which he reserves entire to
" himself. Communicate to us equitable
" laws and rules of conduct. Prepare for
" us a new system of government, for we
" feel that the principles, which to this day
" have guided us, are corrupt. Our fathers
" have wandered in the paths of ignorance,
" and we from habit have trod in their steps.
" Every thing is conducted by violence,
" fraud, or delusion; and the laws of mo-
" rality and reason are still buried in obscu-
" rity. Do you unfold the chaos; discover
" the time, order, and connexion of things;
" publish your code of laws and rights; and
" we will conform to it."

And this people raised an immense throne in the form of a pyramid, and seating upon it the men they had chosen, said to them: "We raise you this day above us, that you "may take a more comprehensive view of "our relations, and be exalted above the at-"mosphere of our passions.

"But remember that you are citizens like "ourselves; that the power which we con-"fer upon you belongs to us; that we give "it as a trust for which you are responsible, "not as exclusive property, or hereditary "right; that the laws which you make, you "will be the first to submit to; that to-"morrow you will descend from your sta-"tions, and rank again with us; that you "will have acquired no distinguishing right, "but the right to our gratitude and esteem. "And oh! with what glory will the uni-"verse, that reveres so many apostles of "error, honour the first assembly of en-"lightened and reasonable men, who shall "have declared the immutable principles of "justice to mankind, and consecrated in the "very face of tyrants the rights of na-"tions!"

CHAP. XVII.

UNIVERSAL BASIS OF ALL RIGHT AND ALL LAW.

THESE men, chosen by the people to investigate the true principles of morality and reason, then proceeded to the object of their mission: and after a long examination, having discovered a universal and fundamental principle, they said to their constituents: "We "have employed our faculties in the investi- "gation you demand of us, and we conceive "the following to be the primordial basis "and physical origin of all justice and all "right.

"Whatever be the active power, the mov- "ing cause that directs the universe, this "power having given to all men the same "organs, the same sensations, and the same "wants, has thereby sufficiently declared "that it has also given them the same rights "to the use of its benefits; and that in the "order of nature all men are equal.

"Secondly,

"Secondly, inasmuch as this power has
"given to every man the ability of preserv-
"ing and maintaining his own existence, it
"clearly follows, that all men are constitut-
"ed independent of each other, that they
"are created free, that no man can be sub-
"ject and no man sovereign, but that all
"men are the unlimited proprietors of their
"own persons.

"Equality, therefore, and liberty, are two
"essential attributes of man, two laws of
"the Divinity, not less essential and immu-
"table, than the physical properties of ina-
"nimate nature.

"Again, from the principle, that every
"man is the unlimited master of his own
"person, it follows, that one inseparable
"condition in every contract and engage-
"ment is the free and voluntary consent of
"all the persons therein bound.

"Farther, because every individual is
"equal to every other individual, it fol-
"lows, that the balance of receipts and
"payments in political society, ought to be
"rigorously in equilibrium with each other;
"so that from the idea of equality immedi-
"ately

"ately flows that other idea of equity and
"juſtice *.

"Finally, equality and liberty conſtitute
"the phyſical and unalterable baſis of every
"union of men in ſociety, and of conſe-
"quence the neceſſary and generating prin-
"ciple of every law and regular ſyſtem of
"government (3).

"It is becauſe this baſis has been invaded,
"that the diſorders have been introduced
"among you, as in every other nation, which
"have at length excited you to reſiſtance. It
"is by returning once more to a conformity
"with this rule, that you can reform abuſes
"and reconſtitute a happy order of ſociety.

"We are bound however to obſerve to
"you, that from this regeneration there will
"reſult an extreme ſhock to be endured in
"your habits, in your fortunes, and in your
"prejudices. Vicious contracts muſt be
"diſſolved, unjuſt prejudices aboliſhed, ima-
"ginary diſtinctions ſurrendered, and iniqui-

* The etymology of the words themſelves trace out to us this connexion: *equilibrium, equalitas, equitas,* are all of one family, and the phyſical idea of *equality* in the ſcales of a balance is the ſource and type of all the reſt.

"tous

"tous descriptions of property abrogated: "in fine, you must set out once more from "the state of nature. Consider whether you "are capable of these mighty sacrifices."

They concluded: and while I reflected upon the inherent cupidity of the human heart, I was induced to believe that the people would reject a melioration presented under such austere colours. I was mistaken. Instantly a vast crowd of men thronged towards the throne, and solemnly abjured all riches and all distinctions. "Unfold to us, "cried they, the laws of equality and liberty; "we disclaim all future possession that is not "held in the sacred name of justice. *Equality,* "*liberty, justice,* these are our inviolable code, "these names shall inscribe our standard."

Immediately the people raised a mighty standard, varied with three colours, and upon which those three words were written. They unfurled it over the throne of the legislators, and now for the first time the symbol of universal and equal justice appeared upon the earth. In front of the throne the people built an altar, on which they placed golden scales, a sword, and a book, with this legend:

legend: TO EQUAL LAW, THE PROTECTOR, AND THE JUDGE. They then drew round the throne a vast amphitheatre, and the nation seated itself to hear the publication of the law. Millions of men, in act of solemn appeal to heaven, lifted up their hands together, and swore, "that they would "live equal, free, and just; that they would "respect the rights and property of each "other; that they would yield obedience to "the law and its ministers regularly ap-"pointed."

A sight like this, so full of sublimity and energy, so interesting by the generous emotions it implied, melted me into tears; and addressing myself to the Genius, I said: "Now may I live, for after this there is "nothing which I am not daring enough to "hope."

CHAP. XVIII.

CONSTERNATION AND CONSPIRACY OF TYRANTS.

MEANWHILE, scarcely had the solemn cry of liberty and equality resounded through the earth, than astonishment and apprehension were excited in the different nations. In one place, the multitude, moved by desire, but wavering between hope and fear, between a sense of their rights and the habitual yoke of slavery, betrayed symptoms of agitation: in another kings, suddenly roused from the sleep of indolence and despotism, were alarmed for the safety of their thrones: every where those classes of civil and religious tyrants, who deceive princes and oppress the people, were seized with rage and consternation; and concerting plans of perfidy, they said to one another: "Woe be to us, should "this fatal cry of liberty reach the ear of the "multitude, and this destructive spirit of "justice

" juſtice be diſſeminated."..... And ſeeing the
ſtandard waving in the air: " What a ſwarm
" of evils, cried they, are included in theſe
" three words! If all men are equal, where
" is our excluſive right to honours and
" power? If all men are, or ought to be free,
" what becomes of our ſlaves, our vaſſals,
" our property? If all are equal in a civil
" capacity, where are our privileges of birth
" and ſucceſſion, and what becomes of no-
" bility? If all are equal before God, where
" will be the need of mediators, and what
" is to become of the prieſthood? Ah! let us
" accompliſh without a moment's delay the
" deſtruction of a germ ſo prolific and con-
" tagious! let us employ the whole force
" of our art againſt this calamity. Let us
" ſound the alarm to kings, that they may
" join in our cauſe. Let us divide the peo-
" ple; let us engage them in war, and turn
" aſide their attention by conqueſts and na-
" tional jealouſy. Let us excite their ap-
" prehenſions reſpecting the power of this
" free nation. Let us form a grand league
" againſt the common enemy. Let us pull
" down this ſacrilegious ſtandard, demoliſh
" this

"this throne of rebellion, and quench this
"fire of revolution in its outset."

And in reality, the civil and religious tyrants of the people entered into a general combination, and having gained, either by constraint or seduction, multitudes on their side, they advanced in an hostile manner against the free nation. Surrounding the altar and the throne of natural law, they demanded, with loud cries: " What is this new and he-
" retical doctrine? What this impious altar,
" this sacrilegious worship? ....True believ-
" ers and loyal subjects! Would you not sup-
" pose that to day truth has been first disco-
" vered, and that hitherto you have been in-
" volved in error? Would you not suppose
" that these men, more fortunate than your-
" selves, have alone the privilege of being
" wise? And you, rebel and guilty nation, do
" you not feel that your chiefs mislead you?
" That they adulterate the principles of your
" faith, and overturn the religion of your fa-
" thers? Tremble lest the wrath of heaven
" be lighted against you; and hasten by speedy
" repentance to expiate your error."

But inaccessible to seduction as to terror, the free nation kept silence; it maintained an an exact discipline in arms, and continued to exhibit an imposing attitude.

And the legislators said to the chiefs of nations: " If when we went on with our " eyes hood-winked, our steps did not fail " to be enlightened, why, now that the " bandage is removed, should we conceive " that we are involved in darkness? If we, " who prescribe to mankind to exert their " faculties, deceive and mislead them, what " can be expected from those who de- " sire only to maintain them in blind- " ness? Ye chiefs of nations, if you possess " truth communicate it: we shall receive it " with gratitude; for with ardour we pur- " sue it, and with interest shall engage in " the discovery. We are men, and may be " deceived; but you also are men and as " fallible as ourselves. Assist us in this la- " byrinth, in which the human species has " wandered for so many ages: assist us to " dissipate the illusion of evil habits and " prejudice. Enter the lists with us in " the shock of opinions which dispute for " our acceptance, and engage with us in " tracing the pure and proper character of " truth. Let us terminate to day the long
" combat

"combat of error: let us establish between
"it and truth a solemn contest: let us call
"in men of every nation to assist us in the
"judgment: let us convoke a general assem-
"bly of the world; let them be judges in
"their own cause; and in the successive trial
"of every system, let no champion and no
"argument be wanting to the side of preju-
"dice or of reason. In fine, let a fair exami-
"nation of the result of the whole, give birth
"to universal harmony of minds and opi-
"nions."

L   CHAP.

CHAP. XIX.

GENERAL ASSEMBLY OF THE PEOPLE.

Thus spoke the legiflators of this free people; and the multitude, feized with the fpirit of admiration, which every reafonable propofition never fails to infpire, fhouted their applaufe, and the tyrants remained alone, overwhelmed with confufion.

A fcene of a new and aftonifhing nature then prefented itfelf to my view. All the people and nations of the globe, every race of men from every different climate, advancing on all fides, feemed to affemble in one inclofure, and form in diftinct groupes an immenfe congrefs. The motley appearance of this innumerable crowd, occafioned by their diverfity of drefs, of features and of complexion, exhibited a moft extraordinary and moft attractive fpectacle.

On one fide I could diftinguifh the European with his fhort and clofe habit, his triangular hat, fmooth chin, and powdered hair;

hair; and on the opposite side the Asiatic with a flowing robe, a long beard, a shaved head and circular turban. Here I observed the inhabitants of Africa, their skin of the colour of ebony, their hair woolly, their body girt with white and blue fish-skin, and adorned with bracelets and collars of corals, shells and glass-beads; there the northern tribes inveloped in bags of skin; the Laplander with his piked bonnet and his snow shoes; the Samoiede with glowing limbs and with a strong odour; the Tongouse with his bonnet shaped like a horn, and carrying his idols pendent from his neck; the Yakoute with his freckled skin; the Calmuc with flattened nose and with little eyes, forced as it were to have no correspondence with each other. Farther in the distance were the Chinese, attired in silk, and with their hair hanging in tresses; the Japanese of mingled race; the Malayans with spreading ears, with a ring in their nose, and with a vast hat of the leaves of the palm-tree (4); and the *Tatoued* inhabitants of the islands of the ocean and of the continent of the Antipodes *. The

* The country of the *Papons*, or New Guinea.

contemplation

contemplation of one species thus infinitely varied, of one understanding thus modified with extravagance, of one organization assuming so contrary appearances, gave me a a very complicated sensation, and excited in me a thousand thoughts (5). I contemplated with astonishment this gradation of colour, from a bright carnation to a brown scarcely less bright, a dark brown, a muddy brown, bronze, olive, leaden, copper, as far as to the black of ebony and jet. I observed the Cassimerean, with his rose-coloured cheek, next in vicinity to the sun-burnt Hindoo; the Georgian standing by the Tartar; and I reflected upon the effect of climate hot or cold, of soil mountainous or deep, marshy or dry, wooded or open. I compared the dwarf of the pole with the giant of the temperate zone; the lank Arab with the pot-bellied Hollander; the squat figure of the Samoiede with the tall and slender form of the Sclavonian and the Greek; the greasy and woolly head of the Negro with the shining locks of the Dane; the flat-faced Calmuc, with his eyes anglewise to each other and his nose crushed, to the oval and

swelling

swelling visage, the large blue eyes, and the aquiline nose, of the Circassian and the Abassin. I contrasted the painted linens of India with the workmanlike cloths of Europe; the rich furs of Silesia; the various clothing of savage nations, skins of fishes, platting of reeds, interweaving of leaves and of feathers, together with the blue-stained figures of serpents, stars, and flowers, with which their skin is varied. Sometimes the general appearance of this multitude, reminded me of the enamelled meadows of the Nile and the Euphrates, when, after rains and inundations, millions of flowers unfold themselves on all sides; and sometimes it resembled, in murmuring sound and busy motion, the innumerable swarms of grasshoppers which alight in the spring like a cloud upon the plains of Hauran.

At sight of so many living and percipient animals, I recollected, on one side, the immense multitude of thoughts and sensations which were crowded into this space; and on the other, reflected on the contest of so many opinions and prejudices, and the struggle of so many capricious passions; and I was struck with

with astonishment, admiration, and apprehension.... When the legislators, having enjoined silence, presently fixed my attention on themselves.

"Inhabitants of the earth, said they, a
"free and powerful nation addresses you in
"the name of justice and of peace, and offers
"as the sure pledge of its sincerity, its convic-
"tion and experience. We were for a long
"time tormented with the same evils as you;
"we have enquired into their origin, and we
"have found them to be derived from vio-
"lence and injustice, which the inexperience
"of past ages established into laws, and the
"prejudices of the present generation have
"supported and cherished. Then, abolish-
"ing every factitious and arbitrary institution,
"and ascending to the source of reason and
"of right, we perceived that there existed in
"the order of the universe, and in the physi-
"cal constitution of man, eternal and immu-
"table laws, which waited only his obser-
"vance to render him happy. O men of dif-
"ferent climes, look to the heavens that give
"you light, to the earth that nourishes you!
"Since they present to you all the same gifts;
"since

"since the Power that directs their motions
"has bestowed on you the same life, the
"same organs, the same wants, has it not
"also given you the same right to the use of
"its benefits! Has it not hereby declared
"you to be all equal and free? What mortal
"then shall dare refuse to his fellow-crea-
"ture that which is granted him by nature?
"O nations! let us banish all tyranny and
"discord; let us form one society, one vast
"family; and since mankind are all consti-
"tuted alike, let there henceforth exist but
"one law, that of nature; one code, that of
"reason; one throne, that of justice; one
"altar, that of union."

They ceased: and the multitude rended the skies with applause and acclamation; and in their transports made the earth resound with the words *equality, justice, union*. But different feelings presently succeeded to this first emotion. The doctors and chiefs of the people exciting in them a spirit of disputation, there arose a kind of murmur, which, spreading from groupe to groupe, was converted into uproar, and from uproar into disorder of the first magnitude. Every nation

tion assumed exclusive pretensions, and claimed the preference for its own opinions and code.

"You are in error," said the parties pointing at each other; "we alone are in possession
"of reason and truth: ours is the true law,
"the genuine rule of justice and right, the
"sole means of happiness and perfection; all
"other men are either blind or rebellious."
And the agitation became extreme.

But the legislators having proclaimed silence: "People," said they, "by what im-
"pulse of passion are you agitated? Where
"will this quarrel conduct you? What ad-
"vantage do you expect from this dissension?
"For ages has the earth been a field of dis-
"putation, and torrents of blood have been
"shed to decide the controversy: what profit
"have you reaped from so many combats and
"tears? When the strong has subjected the
"weak to his opinion, has he thereby fur-
"thered the cause of evidence and truth? O
"nations, take council of your own wisdom!
"If disputes arise between families, or in-
"dividuals, by what mode do you reconcile
"them! Do you not appoint arbitrators?"

"*Yes*,"

"*Yes*," exclaimed the multitude unanimously. "Treat then the authors of your pre-
"sent diffensions in a similar manner. Com-
"mand those who call themselves your in-
"structors, and who impose on you their
"creed, to discuss in your presence the argu-
"ments on which it is founded. Since they
"appeal to your interests, understand in what
"manner your interests are treated by them.
"... And you, chiefs and doctors of the
"people, before you involve them in the
"discordance of your opinions, let the rea-
"sons for and against these opinions be
"fairly discussed. Let us establish a solemn
"controversy, a public investigation of truth,
"not before the tribunal of a frail indivi-
"dual, or a prejudiced party, but in presence
"of the united information and interests of
"mankind; and let the natural sense of the
"whole species be our arbitrator and judge."

CHAP.

CHAP. XX.

INVESTIGATION OF TRUTH.

The people having by shouts expressed their approbation, the legislators said: "That we may proceed in this grand work with order and regularity, let a spacious amphitheatre be formed in the sand before the altar of union and peace: let each system of religion and each particular sect, erect its proper and distinguishing standard in points of the circumference; let its chiefs and its doctors place themselves round it, and let their followers be ranged in a right line terminated by the standard."

The amphitheatre being traced out, and order proclaimed, a prodigious number of standards were instantly raised, similar to what is seen in a commercial port, when, on days of festivity, the flags of a hundred nations stream from a forest of masts. At sight of this astonishing diversity, I addressed myself to the Genius: I scarcely supposed the earth, said

said I, to be divided into more than eight or ten different systems of religion, and I then despaired of conciliation: how can I now hope for concord when I behold thousands of different parties!—These, however, replied the Genius, are but a part of what exist; and yet they would be intolerant!

As the groupes advanced to take their stations, the Genius, pointing out to me the symbols and attributes of each, thus explained to me their meaning.

That first groupe, said he, with a green standard, on which you see displayed a cross, a bandage, and a sabre, is formed of the followers of the Arabian prophet. To believe in a God (without knowing what he is); to have faith in the words of a man (without understanding the language in which he speaks); to travel into a desert in order to pray to the Deity (who is every where); to wash the hands with water (and not abstain from blood); to fast all day (and practise intemperance at night); to give alms of their own property (and to plunder the property of their neighbour): such are the means of perfection instituted by Mahomet, such the
signals

signals and characteristics of his true followers; and whoever professes not these tenets, is considered as a reprobate, has the sacred anathema denounced against him, and is devoted to the sword. A God of clemency, the author of life, has, according to them, instituted these laws of oppression and murder; has instituted them for the whole universe, though he has condescended to reveal them but to one man; has established them from all eternity, though they were made known by him but yesterday. These laws are sufficient for all the purposes of life, and yet a volume is added to them; this volume was to diffuse light, to exhibit evidence, to lead to perfection and happiness, and yet, in the very life-time of its prophet, its pages, every where abounding with obscure, ambiguous, and contradictory passages, needed explanation and commentaries; and the persons who undertook to interpret them, varying in opinion, became divided into sects and parties opposite and inimical to each other. One maintains that Ali is the true successor, and another takes the part of Omar and Aboubekre. This denies the eternity of the Koran,

Koran, that the neceſſity of ablutions and prayers. The Carmite proſcribes pilgrimage, and allows the uſe of wine; the Hakemite preaches the doctrine of tranſmigration, and thus are there ſects to the number of ſeventy-two, of which you may enumerate the different ſtandards (6). In this diſcordance, each aſcribing the evidence excluſively to itſelf, and ſtigmatizing the reſt with hereſy and rebellion, has turned againſt them its ſanguinary zeal. And this religion, which celebrates a beneficent and merciful God, the common parent of the whole human race, converted into a torch of diſcord and an incentive to war, has never ceaſed for twelve hundred years to whelm the earth in blood, and ſpread ravage and deſolation from one extremity of the ancient hemiſphere to the other (7).

The men you ſee diſtinguiſhed by their vaſt white turbans, their hanging ſleeves and long roſaries, are the Imans, the Mollas, and the Muftis; and not far from them are the Derviſes with a pointed bonnet, and the Santons with their ſacred tonſure. They utter with vehemence their ſeveral confeſſions

sions of faith; they dispute with eagerness respecting the more or less important sources of impurity; the mode of performing ablutions; the attributes and perfections of God; the Chaîtan and the good and evil Genii; death; the resurrection; the interrogatory which succeeds the tomb; the passage of the perilous bridge, and its hair-breadth escapes; the balance of good and bad works; the pains of hell, and the joys of paradise.

By the side of these, that still more numerous groupe, with standards of a white ground strewed with crosses, consists of the worshippers of Jesus. Acknowledging the same God as the Mussulmans, founding their belief on the same books, admitting like them a first man, who lost the whole human race by eating an apple, they yet feel towards them a holy horror; and from motives of *piety*, these two sects reciprocally treat each other as *impious* men and blasphemers. Their chief point of dissension is, that the Christian, after admitting the unity and indivisibility of God, proceeds to divide him into three persons, making of each an entire and complete God, and yet preserving an
identical

identical whole: he adds, that this Being, who fills the universe, reduced himself to the stature and form of a man, and assumed material, perishable, and limited organs, without ceasing to be immaterial, eternal, and infinite. The Mussulman, on the contrary, not able to comprehend these mysteries, though he readily conceives of the eternity of the Koran, and the mission of the prophet, treats them as absurdities, and rejects them as the visions of a disordered brain. Hence result the most implacable animosities.

Divided among themselves, the Christian sects are not less numerous than those of the Mussulman religion; and the quarrels that agitate them are by so much the more violent, since the objects for which they contend being inaccessible to the senses, and of consequence incapable of demonstration, the opinions of each sectary can have no other foundation than that of his will or caprice. Thus agreeing that God is an incomprehensible and unknown being, they nevertheless dispute respecting his essence, his mode of acting, and his attributes. Agreeing that his supposed transformation into man, is an
enigma

enigma above the human understanding, they still dispute respecting the confusion or the distinction of two wills and two natures, the change of substance, the real or fictitious presence, the mode of incarnation, &c. &c. Hence innumerable sects, of which two or three hundred have already perished, and three or four hundred others still exist, and are represented by that multitude of colours in which your sight is bewildered. The first in order, surrounded by a groupe absurd and discordant in their attire, red, purple, black, white, and speckled, with heads wholly or partially shaved, or with their hair short, with red caps, square caps, here with mitres, there with beards, is the standard of the Roman pontiff, who, applying to the priesthood the pre-eminence of his city in the civil order, has erected his supremacy into a point of religion, and made of his pride an article of faith.

At the right, you see the Greek Pontiff, who, proud of the rivalship set up by his metropolis, opposes equal pretensions, and supports them against the Western church, by the superior antiquity of that of the East.

At

At the left, are the standards of two recent
chiefs *, who, throwing off a yoke that was
become tyrannical, have, in their reform,
erected altars against altars, and gained half
Europe from the Pope. Behind them are
the inferior sects into which these grand
parties are again subdivided, the Nestorians,
the Eutycheans, the Jacobites, the Icono-
clasts, the Anabaptists, the Presbyterians, the
Wiclifites, the Osiandrins, the Manicheans,
the Pietists, the Adamites, the Enthusiasts,
the Quakers, the Weepers, together with a
hundred others (8); all of distinct parties,
of a persecuting spirit when strong, tolerant
when weak, hating each other in the name
of a God of peace, forming to themselves an
exclusive paradise in a religion of universal
charity, each dooming the rest, in another
world, to endless torments, and realizing
here the imaginary hell of futurity.

Next to this groupe, observing a single
standard of a hyacinth colour, round which
were gathered men in all the various dresses
of Europe and Asia: Here, said I to the
Genius, we shall at least find unanimity.—

* Luther and Calvin.

At first sight, replied he, and from an incidental and temporary circumstance this would seem to be the case: but do you not know what system of worship it is?—Then perceiving in Hebrew letters the monogram of God, and branches of the palm-tree in the hands of the Rabbins: Are not these, said I, the children of Moses, dispersed over the earth, and who, holding every nation in abhorrence, have been themselves universally despised and persecuted?—Yes, replied the Genius, and it is for this very reason that, having neither time nor liberty to dispute, they have preserved the appearance of unanimity. But in their re-union, no sooner shall they compare their principles, and reason upon their opinions, than they will be divided, as formerly, at least into two principal sects *, one of which, taking advantage of the silence of their legislator, and confining itself to the literal sense of his books, will deny every dogma not therein clearly understood, and of consequence will reject as inventions, the immortality of the soul, its transmigration into an abode of hap-

* The Sadducees and the Pharisees.

pines

pinefs or feat of pain, its refurrection, the last judgment, the existence of angels, the revolt of a fallen spirit, and the poetical system of a world to come: and this favoured people, whose perfection consists in the cutting off a morsel of their flesh, this atom of people that in the ocean of mankind is but as a small wave, and that pretends that the whole was made for them alone, will farther reduce by one half, in consequence of their schism, their already trivial weight in the balance of the universe.

The Genius then directed my attention to another groupe, the individuals of which were clothed in white robes, had a veil covering the mouth, and were ranged round a standard of the colour of the clouds gilded by the rising sun. On this standard was painted a globe, one hemisphere of which was black and the other white. The fate of these disciples of Zoroaster (9), continued he, this obscure remnant of a people once so powerful, will be similar to that of the Jews. Dispersed as they are at present among other nations, and persecuted by all, they receive without discussion the precepts that are taught them: but so soon as their Mobed and their Destours (10) shall be restored to their full prerogatives, the controversy will be revived respecting the good and the bad principle, the combats of Ormuz, God of light, and Ahrimanes, God of darkness; the literal or allegorical senses of these combats; the good and evil Genii; the worship of fire and the elements; pollution and purification; the resurrection of the body, or the soul, or both (11); the renovation of the present world, or the production of a new which is to succeed it. The Parses will ever divide themselves into sects, by so much the more numerous as their families shall have contracted different manners or opinions during their dispersion.

Next to these are standards which exhibit upon a blue ground monstrous figures of human bodies, double, triple, or quadruple, with the heads of lions, boars, and elephants, and tails of fishes, tortoises, &c. These are the standards of the Indian sects, who find their Gods amidst the animal creation, and the souls of their kindred in reptiles and insects. These men anxiously support hospitals

pitals for the reception of hawks, serpents, and rats, and look with horror upon their brethren of mankind! They purify themselves with the dung and urine of a cow, and consider themselves as polluted by the touch of a heretic! They wear a net over their mouths, lest by accident a fly should get down their throat, and they should thus interrupt the progress of a purified spirit in its purgatory; but with all this humanity in unintelligible cases, they think themselves obliged to let a Paria (12) perish with hunger rather than relieve him! They worship the same Gods, but inlist themselves under hostile standards.

This first standard, separated from the rest, and on which you see represented a figure with four heads, is the standard of Brama, who, though the Creator of the universe, has neither followers nor temples, and who, reduced to serve as a pedestal to the Lingam (13), receives no other mark of attention than a little water sprinkled every morning over his shoulder by the Bramin, and a barren song in his praise.

The second standard on which you see painted

painted a kite, his body scarlet and his head white, is that of the Vichenou, who, though preserver of the universe, has passed a part of his life in malevolent actions. Sometimes you see him under the hideous forms of a boar and a lion tearing the entrails of mankind; sometimes under that of a horse (14), soon to appear upon the face of the earth, with a sabre in his hand, to destroy the present inhabitants of the world, to darken the stars, to drive the planets from their spheres, to shake the whole earth, and to oblige the mighty serpent to vomit a flame which shall consume the globes.

The third standard is that of Chiven, the destroyer of all things, the God of desolation, and who nevertheless has for his emblem the instrument of production; he is the most detestable of the three, and he has the greatest number of followers. Proud of his attribute and character, his partizans in their devotions (15) express every sort of contempt for the other Gods, his equals and his brothers, and imitating the inconsistency that characterises him, they profess modesty and chastity, and at the same time publicly

publicly crown with flowers, and bathe with milk and honey, the obscene image of the Lingam.

Behind them came the less magnificent standards of a multitude of Gods, male, female, and hermaphrodite, related to and connected with the three principal, who pass their lives in intestine war, and are in this respect imitated by their worshippers. These Gods have need of nothing, and receive offerings without ceasing. Their attributes are omnipotence and ubiquity, and a Bramin with some petty charm imprisons them in an image, or in a pitcher, and retails their favours according to his will and pleasure.

At a still greater distance you will observe a multitude of other standards, which, upon a yellow ground, common to them all, have different emblems figured, and are the standards of one God, who, under various names, is acknowledged by the nations of the East. The Chinese worship him under the name of *Fôt* (16); the Japanese denominate him *Budso*; the inhabitants of Ceylon, *Beddhou*; the people of Laos, *Chekia*; the Peguan, *Phta*; the Siamese, *Sommona-Kodom*; the

people

people of Thibet, *Budd* and *La*; all of them
agree as to moſt points of his hiſtory; they
celebrate his penitence, his ſufferings, his
faſts, his functions of mediator and expiator,
the enmity of another God his adverſary,
the combats of that adverſary and his defeat: but they diſagree reſpecting the means
of recommending themſelves to his favour,
reſpecting rites and ceremonies, reſpecting
the dogmas of their interior and their public
doctrine. Thus the Japaneſe Bonze, in a
yellow robe, and with his head uncovered,
preaches the eternity of ſouls and their ſucceſſive tranſmigration into different bodies;
while his rival, the Sintoiſt, denies that the
ſoul can exiſt independently of the ſenſes
(17), and maintains that it is the mere reſult of the organization with which it is
connected, and with which it periſhes, as
the ſound of a flute is annihilated when you
break it in pieces. Near him the Siameſe,
with ſhaved eye-brows, and with the Talipat ſcreen in his hand (18), recommends
alms-giving, purifications and offerings, at
the very time that he believes in blind neceſſity and immutable fate. The Chineſe
Ho-Chang

Ho-Chang sacrifices to the souls of his ancestors, while his neighbour, the follower of Confucius, pretends to discover his future destiny by the tossing of counters and the conjunction of the stars (19). Observe this infant attended by a numerous crowd of priests with yellow garments and bonnets: he is the grand Lama, and the God of Thibet has just become incarnate in his person (20). He however has a rival on the banks of the Baikal; nor is the Calmuc Tartar in this respect any way behind the Tartar of La-sa. They are agreed in this important doctrine, that God can become incarnate only in a human body, and scorn the stupidity of the Indian, who looks down with reverence upon cow-dung, though they themselves preserve with no less awe the excrements of their pontiff (21).

As these standards passed, an innumerable crowd of others presented themselves to our eyes, and the Genius exclaimed: I should never come to a conclusion, were I to detail to you all the different systems of belief which divide these nations. Here the Tartar Hordes adore, under the figure of animals, insects,

insects, and birds, the good and the evil Genii, who, under a principal but indolent divinity, govern the universe, by their idolatry giving us an image of the ancient paganism of the western world. You see the strange dress of their Chamans, a robe of leather fringed with little bells and rattles, embroidered with idols of iron, claws of birds, skins of serpents, and heads of owls: they are agitated with artificial convulsions, and with magical cries evoke the dead to deceive the living. In this place you behold the footy inhabitants of Africa, who, while they worship their *Fetiches*, entertain the same opinions. The inhabitant of Juida adores God under the figure of an enormous serpent, which for their misfortune the swine regard as a delicious morsel (22). The Teleutean dresses the figure of his God in a variety of gaudy colours, like a Russian soldier; and the Kamchadale, finding that every thing goes on ill in this world and under his climate, represents God to himself under the figure of an ill-natured and arbitrary old man (23), smoking his pipe and sitting in his *traineau* employed in

the

the hunting of foxes and martins. In fine, there are a hundred other savage nations, who, entertaining none of these ideas of civilized countries respecting God, the soul, and a future state, exercise no species of worship, and yet are not less favoured with the gifts of nature, in the irreligion to which nature has destined them.

CHAP.

CHAP. XXI.

PROBLEM OF RELIGIOUS CONTRADICTIONS.

The different groupes having taken their stations, and profound silence succeeding to the confused uproar of the multitude, the legislators said: " Chiefs and doctors of the " people! you perceive how the various " nations of mankind, living apart, have hi- " therto pursued different paths, each be- " lieving its own to be that of truth. If " truth, however, is one, and your opinions " are opposite, it is manifest that some of " you must be in error; and since so many " men deceive themselves, what individual " shall dare say, I am not mistaken? Begin, " then, by being indulgent respecting your " disputes and dissentions. Let us all seek " truth, as if none of us had possession of it. " The opinions which to this day have go- " verned the earth, produced by chance, " disseminated in obscurity, admitted with- " out discussion, credited from a love of

" novelty

"novelty and imitation, have in a manner "clandestinely usurped their empire. It is "time, if they are founded in reality, to "give them the solemn stamp of certainty, "and to legitimate their existence. Let us "this day cite them to a common and ge-"neral examination; let each make known "his creed; let the united assembly be the "judge, and let us acknowledge that to be "the only true one, which is proper for the "whole human race."

Then, in order of position, the first standard at the left being desired to speak: "There can be no doubt," said they, "that "ours is the only true and infallible doc-"trine. In the first place, it is revealed "by God himself."

"So also is ours," exclaimed all the other standards, "and there can be no room for "doubt."

"But it is at least necessary to explain it," said the legislators, "for it is impossible for "us to believe any thing of which we are "ignorant."

"Our doctrine," resumed the first standard, "is proved by numerous facts, by a "crowd of miracles, by resurrections from
"the

" the dead, by torrents suddenly dried up,
" mountains removed from their situations,
" &c. &c."

" We also," cried the rest, " are in posses-
" sion of miracles without number;" and each
began to recite the most incredible things.

" Their miracles," replied the first standard, " are imaginary, or the prestiges of the
" evil spirit who has deluded them."

To this it was answered by the others:
" They are yours, on the contrary, that are
" imaginary;" and each speaking of himself
added: " Ours are the only true ones, all
" other miracles are false."

" Have you living witnesses of their
" truth?" the legislators asked.

" No," they universally answered: " they
" are ancient facts, of which the witnesses
" are dead, but these facts are recorded."

" Be it so," replied the legislators: " but
" as they contradict each other, who shall
" reconcile them?"

" Just arbiters!" cried one of the standards, " as a proof that our witnesses have
" seen the truth, they died in confirmation
" of it; and our creed is sealed with the
" blood of martyrs."

" So

"So also is ours," exclaimed the rest: "we have thousands of martyrs, who have "died in the most agonizing tortures, with- "out in a single instance abjuring the truth." And the Christians of every sect, the Musſulmans, the Indians, the Japanese, recounted endless legends of confessors, martyrs, penitents, &c.

One of these parties having denied the martyrology of the others: "We are ready," cried they, "to die ourselves to prove the "infallibility of our creed."

Instantly a crowd of men of every sect and of every religion, presented themselves to endure whatever torments might be inflicted on them; and numbers of them began to tear their arms, and to beat their head and their breast, without discovering any symptom of pain.

But the legislators putting a stop to this violence: "O men!" said they to them, "hear with composure the words we ad- "dress to you. If you die to prove that two "and two make four, will this truth gain "additional confirmation by your death?"

"No," was the general answer.

"If

"If you die to prove they are five, will
"this make them five?"

"No," they again replied.

"What, then, does your perſuaſion prove,
"ſince it makes no alteration in the exiſt-
"ence of things. Truth is one; your opi-
"nions are various; many of you muſt
"therefore be miſtaken. And ſince man, as
"is evident, can perſuade himſelf of error,
"how can his perſuaſion be regarded as the
"demonſtration of evidence? Since error
"has its martyrs, what is the ſignet of
"truth? Since the evil ſpirit works mira-
"cles, what is the diſtinguiſhing character-
"iſtic of the Divinity? Beſide, why this
"uniform reſort to incomplete and inſuffi-
"cient miracles? Why not rather, inſtead
"of theſe violations of nature, change the
"opinions of rational beings? Why mur-
"der and terrify men, inſtead of enlighten-
"ing and inſtructing them?

"O credulous mortals, and obſtinate in
"your credulity! as we are none of us cer-
"tain of what paſſed yeſterday, of what is
"paſſing this very day before our eyes, how
"can we ſwear to the truth of what hap-
"pened

"pened two thousand years ago? Weak, and
"at the same time proud beings! the laws
"of nature are immutable and profound, our
"understandings full of illusion and frivolity,
"and yet we would decide upon and com-
"prehend every thing. But in reality it is
"easier for the whole human race to fall into
"error, than an atom of the universe to
"change its nature."

"Well then," said one of the doctors,
"let us leave the evidence of facts, since such
"evidence is equivocal, and let us attend to
"the proofs of reason, and the intrinsic me-
"rit of the doctrine itself."

An Iman of the law of Mahomet, with a look of confidence, then advanced in the sand, and having turned himself towards Mecca, and uttered with emphasis his confession of faith: "Let God be praised!" said he, in a grave and authoritative voice; "the "light shines in all its splendour, and the "truth has no need of examination." Then exhibiting the Koran: "Behold the light "and the truth in their genuine colours! In "this book every doubt is removed; it will "conduct the blind man safely, who shall
                                        "receive

"receive without discussion the divine word, given to the prophet to save the simple and confound the wise. God hath appointed Mahomet to be his minister upon earth; he has delivered up the world to him, that he might subdue by his sword such as refuse to believe in his law. Infidels dispute his authority, and resist the truth: their obduracy proceeds from God, who has hardened their hearts that he might inflict upon them the most dreadful chastisements *."

Here a violent murmur from all sides interrupted the Iman. "What man is this," cried every groupe, " who thus gratuitously commits outrage? By what right does he pretend, as conqueror and tyrant, to impose his creed on mankind? Has not God created us as well as him with eyes, understanding, and reason? Have we not an equal right to make use of them in determining

* This passage contains the sense and nearly the very words of the first chapter of the Koran; and the reader will observe in general, that, in the pictures that follow, the writer has endeavoured to give as accurately as possible the letter and spirit of the opinions of each party.

"what

"what we ought to reject, and what to be-
"lieve? If he have the right to attack, have
"not we the right to defend ourselves? If he
"be content to believe without examination,
"are we therefore not to employ our reason
"in the choice of our creed?

"And what is this *splendid* doctrine which
"fears the *light?* What this apostle of a God
"of clemency who preaches only carnage
"and murder? What this God of justice who
"punishes a blindness which himself has
"caused? If violence and persecution are the
"arguments of truth, mildness and charity
"must they be the indices of falsehood?"

A man advancing from the next groupe
then said to the Iman: "Admitting that
"Mahomet is the apostle of the better doc-
"trine, the prophet of the true religion,
"condescend to tell us, in practising this
"doctrine whom we are to follow, his son-
"in-law Ali, or his vicars Omar and Abou-
"bekre (24)?"

At the mention of these names a terrible
schism arose among the Mussulmans. The
partisans of Omar and of Ali, treating each
other as heretics and blasphemers, were
equally

equally lavish of execrations. The dispute even became so violent, that it was necessary for the neighbouring groupes to interpose to prevent their coming to blows.

Some degree of tranquillity being at length restored, the legislators said to the Imans: " You see what are the consequences which " result from your principles! were they " carried into practice, you would by your " enmity destroy each other till not an in- " dividual would remain: and is it not the " first law of God, that man should live?" Then addressing themselves to the other groupes: " This spirit of intolerance and " exclusion," said they, " is doubtless shock- " ing to every idea of justice, and destroys " the whole basis of morals and society: shall " we not, however, before we entirely reject " this code, agree to hear some of its dogmas " recited, that we may not decide from " forms only, without having investigated " the religion itself?"

The groupes having consented to the proposal, the Iman began to explain to them how God, who before time had spoken to the nations sunk in idolatry by twenty-four

thousand

thousand prophets, had at length sent the last, the extract and perfection of all the rest, Mahomet, in whom was vested the salvation of peace: he informed them that to prevent the word of truth from being any more perverted by infidels, the divine clemency had written with its own fingers the chapters of the Koran; and that the Koran, by virtue of its character of the word of God, was, like its author, uncreated and eternal. He proceeded to explain to them the dogmas of Islamism; that this book had been transmitted from heaven leaf by leaf in twenty-four thousand miraculous visions of the angel Gabriel; that the angel announced his approach by a small still knocking, which threw the prophet into a cold sweat; that Mahomet had in one night traversed ninety heavens, mounted upon the animal called Borak, one half woman and one half horse; that being endowed with the gift of miracles, he walked in the sunshine unattended by a shadow, caused with a single word trees already withered to resume their verdure, filled the wells and the cisterns with water, and cut in two equal parts the body of the moon; that, authorized by a commission
from

from heaven, he had propagated, sword in hand, a religion the most worthy of God for its sublimity, the most suitable to man for the simplicity of its injunctions, consisting indeed only of eight or ten principal doctrines, such as the unity of God; the authority of Mahomet, the only prophet of God; our duty to pray five times in a day; to fast one month in the year; to repair to Mecca once at least in our lives; to pay the tenth of all that we possess; to drink no wine, to eat no pork, and to make war upon the infidels (25); upon which conditions every Mussulman, being himself an apostle and a martyr, should enjoy in this life a thousand blessings, and in the world to come, after a solemn trial, his soul being weighed in the balance of good works, his absolution pronounced by the two black angels, and his progress performed over the bridge that crosses the infernal pit, as narrow as a hair and as keen as a razor, should be received in the seat of delights, bathed in rivers of milk and honey, embalmed in the perfumes of India and Arabia, and live in uninterrupted commerce with those chaste females, the celestial Houris, who present a
perpetually

perpetually renewed virginity to the elect, who preserve a perpetual vigour.

An involuntary smile was visible in the countenance of every one at this relation; and the various groupes, reasoning upon these articles of belief, unanimously said: "Is it "possible for reasonable beings to have faith "in such reveries? Might one not suppose "that a chapter had been just read to us "from the *Thousand and One Nights?*"

A Samoiede advancing in the sand then said: "The paradise of Mahomet is in my "opinion excellent: but one of the means "of obtaining it puzzles me extremely. If, "as this prophet ordains, it is necessary to "abstain from meat and drink between the "rising and setting of the sun, how in our "country is such a fast practicable, where "the sun continues above the horizon for six "months together?"

To vindicate the honour of their prophet, the Mussulman doctors denied the possibility of this; but a hundred people bearing testimony to the fact, the infallibility of Mahomet sustained a violent shock.

"It is singular," said a European, "that God "should

"should continually have revealed what was going on in heaven, without ever having informed us of what passes upon earth."

"Their pilgrimage," said an American, "is to me an insuperable difficulty. For let us suppose a generation to be twenty-five years, and the number of males existing on the globe to be a hundred millions: in this case, each being obliged to travel to Mecca once during his life, there would be annually engaged in the pilgrimage four millions of men; and as it would be impracticable for them to return in the same year, the number would be doubled, or in other words would amount to eight millions. Where are provisions, accommodation, water, and vessels to be found for this universal procession? What numerous miracles would it not be necessary to work!"

"The proof," said a Catholic Divine, "that the religion of Mahomet is not a revealed religion, is, that the majority of ideas upon which it is founded existed for a long time before it, and that it is nothing more than a confused mixture formed out of the truths of our holy religion and that of the Jews,

"which

"which an ambitious man has made serve
"his projects of dominion, and his worldly
"views. Turn over the pages of his book:
"you will see little else than the histories of
"the Old and New Testament travestied
"into the most absurd tales, and the rest a
"tissue of vague and contradictory declama-
"tion, and ridiculous or dangerous precepts.
"Analyze the spirit of these precepts, and
"the conduct of their apostle: you will find
"a subtle and daring character, which, to ar-
"rive at its end, works, it is true, with ad-
"mirable skill upon the passions of those
"whom it wishes to govern. It addresses
"itself to simple and credulous men, and it
"tells them of prodigies: they are ignorant
"and jealous, and it flatters their vanity by
"despising science; they are poor and rapa-
"cious, and it excites their avidity by the hope
"of plunder; having nothing at first to give
"them on earth, it creates treasures in hea-
"ven; it makes them long for death, as the
"supreme blessing; the dastardly it threa-
"tens with hell; to the brave it promises
"paradise; the weak it strengthens by the
"principle of fatality: in short, it produces
"the

"the attachment it requires, by every al-
"lurement of the senses, and the fascination
"of all the passions.

"How different is the character of the
"Christian doctrine! and how much does its
"empire, established on the wreck of every
"natural inclination and the extinction of
"all the passions, prove its celestial origin!
"How forcibly does its mild and compas-
"sionate morality attest its emanation from
"the Divinity! Many of its dogmas, it is
"true, are beyond the reach of human un-
"derstanding, and impose on reason a re-
"spectful silence; but this very circum-
"stance the more fully confirms its revela-
"tion, since the faculties of men could never
"have invented such sublime mysteries."—
Then, with the Bible in one hand, and the
Four Evangelists in the other, the doctor
began to relate that in the beginning, God
(after having passed an eternity without doing any thing) conceived at length the design (without apparent motive) of forming
the world out of nothing: that having in six
days created the whole universe, he found
himself tired on the seventh: that having

placed

placed the first pair of human beings in a delightful garden to make them completely happy, he nevertheless forbad them to taste of the fruit of one tree which he planted within their reach : that these first parents having yielded to temptation, all their race (as yet unborn) were condemned to suffer the penalty of a fault which they had no share in committing: that after permitting the human species to damn themselves for four or five thousand years, this God of compassion ordered his well-beloved son, engendered without a mother and of the same age as himself, to descend upon the earth in order to be put to death, and this for the salvation of mankind, the majority of whom have nevertheless continued in the road to sin and damnation : that to remedy this inconvenience, this God, the son of a woman, who was at once a mother and a virgin, after having died and risen again, commences a new existence every day, and under the form of a morsel of dough is multiplied a thousand fold at the pleasure of the basest of mankind. Having explained these dogmas, he was going on to treat of the doctrine of the

the Sacraments, of abfolution and anathema, of the means of purifying men from crimes of every fort with a drop of water and the muttering half a dozen words; but he had no fooner pronounced the names of indulgence, papal prerogative, fufficient grace, and effectual grace, than he was interrupted by a thoufand voices at once. It is a horrid corruption, cried the Lutherans, to pretend to fell for money the pardon of fin; it is contrary to the fenfe of the gofpel, faid the Calvinifts, to talk of the real prefence in the Sacrament. The Pope, exclaimed the Janfenifts, has no power to decide upon any thing without a council. Thirty fects at once mutually accufed each other of herefy and blafphemy, and their voices were fo confufed that it was no longer poffible to diftinguifh a word they uttered.

After fome time, filence being at length reftored, the Muffulmans faid to the legiflators: " Since you have rejected our doctrine
" as containing things incredible, can you
" poffibly admit that of the Chriftians, which
" is ftill more contrary to juftice and com-
" mon fenfe? An immaterial and infinite
" God

"God to transform himself into a man!
"To have a son as old as himself! This
"God-man to become bread, which is eaten
"and undergoes digestion! What absurdi-
"ties have we equal to these? Is it to these
"men belong the exclusive right of exact-
"ing a blind obedience? And will you ac-
"cord to them privileges of faith, to our
"detriment?"

Some savage tribes then advanced: "What," said they, "because a man and a woman eat
"an apple six thousand years ago, is the
"whole human race to be involved in dam-
"nation? And do you call God just? What
"tyrant ever made the children responsible
"for the sins of their fathers? How can one
"man answer for the actions of another?
"Would not this be overthrowing every
"principle of equity and reason?"

"Where," exclaimed others, "are the
"witnesses and proofs of all these pretended
"facts? It is impossible to receive them
"without evidence. The most trivial ac-
"tion in a court of judicature requires two
"witnesses, and are we to believe all this
"upon mere tradition and hearsay?"

A Jewish

A Jewish Rabbin then, addressing the assembly, said: "For the general facts we are "indeed sureties; but as to the form and ap-"plication of those facts, the case is different, "and the Christians are here condemned out "of their own mouth. They cannot deny "that we are the stock from which they are "descended, the trunk upon which they "have been grafted: from whence it fol-"lows by an inevitable dilemma, that either "our law is from God, and then theirs is a "heresy, since it differs from ours; or our law "is not from God, and then whatever proves "its falsehood is destructive of theirs."

"But there is a proper line of distinction," said the Christian, "to which it is necessary "to attend. Your law is of God as typical "and preparative, not as final and absolute; "you are but the image, of which we are "the reality."

"We are not ignorant," replied the Rabbin, "that such are your pretensions; but "they are perfectly suppositious and false. "Your system rests entirely on mystical (26), "visionary, and allegorical interpretations. "You pervert the letter of our books, sub-
"stitute

" ftitute continually for the true senfe of a
" paffage the moft chimerical ideas, and find
" in them whatever is agreeable to your
" fancy, juft as a roving imagination difco-
" vers figures in the clouds. You have thus
" imagined a fpiritual Meffiah, where our
" prophets fpeak only of a political king.
" You have interpreted into a redemption of
" the human race, what refers folely to the
" re-eftablifhment of our nation. Your pre-
" tended conception of the virgin is derived
" from a phrafe which you have wrefted
" from its true meaning. You conftrue
" every thing as you pleafe. You even find
" in our books your doctrine of the Trinity,
" though they contain not the moft indirect
" allufion to it, and though the idea was an
" invention of profane nations, and admitted
" into your code, together with a multitude
" of other opinions of every worfhip and fect
" of which it is compofed, during the chaos
" and anarchy of the three firft ages."

At thefe words, tranfported with indignation, and crying out facrilege, blafphemy!
the Chriftian doctors were difpofed to lay
violent hands upon the Jew: and a motley

groupe

groupe of monks, some in black, some in white, advancing with a standard on which *pincers, a gridiron,* and *a funeral pile,* and the words *justice, charity,* and *mercy,* were painted*, exclaimed: " It is proper to make an " example of this impious heretic, and to " burn him alive for the glory of God." And already they had pictured to their imaginations the scene of torture, when the Mussulmans in a tone of irony said to them: " Such is the religion of peace, whose hum-
" ble and humane spirit you have so loudly
" vaunted! Such that evangelical charity
" which combats incredulity with no other
" weapon than mildness, and opposes only
" patience to injuries! Hypocrites, it is thus
" you deceive nations! It is in this manner
" you have propagated your destructive er-
" rors! When weak, you have preached li-
" berty, toleration, and peace; when power
" has been in your hands, you have prac-
" tised violence and persecution!"..... And they were beginning to recite the wars and murders of Christianity, when the legis-

* This description answers exactly to the colours of the Inquisition of Spanish Jacobins.

lators.

lators, demanding silence, assuaged for a while the discord.

"It is not," replied the monks in a tone of affected mildness and humility, "ourselves "that we would avenge, we are desirous "only of defending the cause and glory of "God."

"And what right have you," said the Imans, "to constitute yourselves his repre- "sentatives more than we? Have you pri- "vileges that we are not favoured with? "Are you beings of a different nature from "us?"

"To take upon ourselves to defend God, "is to insult his wisdom and power," said another groupe. "Does he not know bet- "ter than mortals what is becoming his "dignity!"

"Certainly," rejoined the monks; "but "his ways are secret."

"You, however," said the Rabbins, "will "always find the difficulty insuperable of "proving that you enjoy the exclusive pri- "vilege of comprehending them." And the Jews, proud of finding their cause supported, fondly pleased themselves with the idea that their books would be triumphant; when the Mobed * of the Parfes begged leave to speak.

"We have heard," said he to the legisla‑
"tors, the account of the Jews and Chriſtians
"reſpecting the origin of the world, and
"though they have introduced various cur‑
"ruptions, they have related a number of
"facts which our religion admits; but we
"deny that they are to be attributed to the
"Hebrew legiſlator. It was not he who
"made known to mankind theſe ſublime
"dogmas, theſe celeſtial events: it was not
"to him that God revealed them, but to our
"holy prophet Zoroaſter; and proofs of
"this are to be found in the very books in
"queſtion. If you examine with attention
"the detail of laws, of rights, and of pre‑
"cepts eſtabliſhed by Moſes, you will no
"where find the moſt tacit indication of
"what conſtitutes at preſent the baſis of the
"Jewiſh and Chriſtian theology. You will
"perceive no trace either of the immortality
"of the ſoul, or a life to come, or hell, or

* Highprieſt.

"paradiſe,

"paradise, or the revolt of the principal an-
"gel, author of all the evils which have af-
"flicted the human race, &c. These ideas
"were unknown to Moses, and this appears
"from indisputable evidence, since it was not
"till four hundred years after him that they
"were first promulgated by Zoroaster in
"Asia (27)."

The Mobed added, addressing himself to the Rabbins: "It was not till this epocha,
"till after the age of your first kings, that
"these ideas appeared in your writings; and
"then their appearance was furtive and
"gradual, according as there grew up a po-
"litical relation between your ancestors and
"ours. It was particularly at the period
"when, conquered and dispersed by the
"kings of Nineveh and Babylon, your pro-
"genitors resorted to the banks of the Ti-
"gris and the Euphrates, and resided in our
"country for three successive generations,
"that they imbibed our manners and opi-
"nions, which before they had regarded
"with aversion, as contrary to their law.
"When our king, Cyrus, had delivered them

"from slavery they felt attached to us from
"sentiments of gratitude; they became our
"disciples and imitators, and introduced
"our peculiar doctrines into the corrected
"publication of their sacred books (28);
"for your Genesis in particular was never
"the work of Moses, but a compilation di-
"gested after the return from the Babylo-
"nish captivity, and containing in it the
"Chaldean opinions respecting the origin
"of the world.

"At first the pure followers of the law,
"opposing to the emigrants the letter of the
"text and the absolute silence of the pro-
"phet, endeavoured to overpower these in-
"novations; but they ultimately prevailed,
"and our doctrines, modified according to
"your ideas, gave rise to a new sect. You
"expected a king, the restorer of your poli-
"tical independence; we announced a God,
"the regenerator of the world, and the sa-
"viour of mankind. These ideas blended
"together, constituted the tenets of the Es-
"senians, and through them became the
"basis of Christianity. Jews, Christians,
"Mahometans, however lofty may be your
"pretensions,

" pretensions, you are, in your spiritual and
" immaterial system, only the blundering
" followers of Zoroaster!"

Having thus commenced his discourse, the Mobed went on to the detail of his religion; and supporting his sentiments by quotations from the Zadder and the Zendavesta, he recounted in the same order as they are found in the book of Genesis, the creation of the world in six *gahans* (29); the formation of a first man and a first woman in a peculiar and celestial habitation, under the reign of perfect good; the introduction of evil into the world by the great lizard, the emblem of Ahrimanes; the revolt and combat of this magnificent genius of darkness, against Ormuz the benevolent God of light; the distribution of angels into white and black, good and ill; their hierarchy consisting of cherubim, seraphim, thrones, dominions, &c.; the end of the world at the close of six thousand years; the coming of the Lamb, the regenerator of nature; the new world; the life to come in an abode of felicity or anguish; the passage of souls over the bridge of the abyss; the celebration of the mysteries of Mithra; the

unleavened

unleavened bread that is set apart for the initiated: the baptism of new-born children; extreme unction and auricular confession (30); in a word, he repeated so many articles analogous to those of the three preceding religions, that his discourse seemed to be a commentary or a continuation of the Koran or the Apocalypse.

But the Jewish, Christian, and Mahometan doctors excepted to this detail, and treating the Parses as idolatrous worshippers of fire, charged them with falsehood, invention, and alteration of facts. A violent dispute then arose respecting the dates of events, their order and succession, respecting the origin of opinions, their transmission from one people to another, the authenticity of the books which establish them, the epocha when these books were composed, the character of their compilers, the value of their testimony; and the various parties proving, each against the rest, contradictions, improbabilities, and the counterfeit nature of their books, accused one another of having founded their creed upon popular rumours, upon vague traditions, upon absurd fables, invented by folly, and admitted

mitted without examination by unknown, ignorant, or partial writers, at doubtful periods, and different from those to which their partisans referred them.

A loud rumour was now excited under the standards of the various Indian sects, and the Bramins, entering their protest against the claims of the Jews and the Parses, said:
" What are these upstart and almost un-
" known people, who thus arrogantly con-
" sider themselves as the founders of nations,
" and the depositories of the sacred archives?
" To hear their calculations of five or six
" thousand years, one would suppose that
" the world was but of yesterday, whereas
" our monuments prove a duration of many
" thousands of centuries. And in what re-
" spect are their books preferable to ours?
" Are then the Vedes, the Chastres, the
" Pourans, inferior to the Bible, the Zenda-
" vesta, the Sadder (31)? Is not the testi-
" mony of our progenitors and our Gods, of
" equal value with that of the Gods and
" progenitors of the western world? Oh!
" were we permitted to reveal to profane
" men the mysteries of our religion! Did

" not

"not a sacred veil justly hide our doctrine
"from every eye!"....

The Bramins suddenly observing a profound silence: "How," said the legislators, "can we admit your doctrine, if you refuse "to make it known? How could its first "authors propagate it, when, having sole "possession of it, they regarded even their "own people as profane? Has heaven re- "vealed it that it might be kept a secret?"

The Bramins however persisted in their silence; and a European at this moment offering to speak, remarked, that their secrecy was at present an empty form, that their sacred books were divulged and their doctrine explained: he accordingly undertook to recapitulate its several articles.

Beginning with an abstract of the four Vedes, the twenty-eight Pourans, and the five or six Chastres, he recounted how an immaterial, infinite, eternal, and *round* Being, after having passed an unlimited portion of time in self-contemplation, desirous at length of manifesting himself, separated the faculties of male and female which were in him, and operated an act of generation of which the

Lingam

Lingam remains the emblem: how from this first act were born three divine powers, of the names of Brama, Bichen, or Vichenou, and Chib or Chiven (32), the first deputed to create, the second to preserve, the third to destroy or change the form of the universe. He then detailed the history of their exploits and adventures, and related how Brama, proud of having created the world and the eight Bobouns (or spheres) of probation, and of being preferred to his equal Chib, this pride occasioned between them a combat, in which the globes or celestial orbits were broken to pieces, as if they had been a basket of eggs: how Brama overcome in this contest, was reduced to serve as a pedestal to Chib, metamorphosed into the Lingam: how Vichenou, the preserver of the universe, had, in the discharge of his function, assumed nine animal and mortal forms; how under the first, that of a fish, he saved from the universal deluge a family by whom the earth was re-peopled; afterwards, in the shape of a tortoise (33), drew from the sea of milk the mountain *Mandreguiri* (the Pole); then, under that of a boar, tore the entrails of the giant

giant *Erenniacheffen*, by whom the earth had been sunk in the abyss of *Djole*, from which he delivered it; how he became incarnate under the form of the Black Shepherd, and bearing the name of *Chris-en* rescued the world from the venomous serpent Calengam, whose head he crushed, after having himself received a wound in his heel.

Passing to the history of the secondary Genii, unfolded to the assembly how the Eternal, for the display of his glory, had created divers orders of angels, whose office it was to sing his praises and direct the universe: that a part of these angels had revolted under the conduct of an ambitious chief, who wished to usurp the power of God, and take the reigns of government into his own hands: that God precipitated them into a world of darkness as a punishment for their misdeeds: that at last, touched with compassion, he consented to withdraw them from thence, and to receive them again into favour, after previously subjecting them to a long state of probation: that for this purpose, having created fifteen orbits or regions of planets, and bodies to inhabit them, he obliged these

rebellious

rebellious angels to undergo eighty-seven
tranfmigrations: that the fouls, thus purified,
returned to their primitive fource, to the
ocean of life from which they had emanated:
that as all living beings contained a portion
of this univerfal foul, it was an act of great
criminality to deprive them of it. He was
proceeding to develope the rites and ceremonies of this religion, when, fpeaking of
offerings and libations of milk and butter to
Gods of wood and of brafs, he was interrupted by a univerfal murmur mixed with loud
burfts of laughter.

Each of the different groupes reafoned in its
own particular manner refpecting this fyftem.
" They are idolaters," faid the Muffulmans,
" it is our duty to exterminate them"....
" They are mad," faid the followers of Confucius, " it is our duty to cure them"....
" What abfurd Gods," cried the reft, " a fet
" of fat monkeys begrimmed with fmoke,
" whom they wafh like children in clouts,
" and from whom they drive away the flies,
" lured by the tafte of honey, who would
" otherwife defile them with their excre-
" ments!"

At thefe words a Bramin, burfting with
indignation,

§

indignation, exclaimed: "These are in-
"scrutable mysteries, the profound em-
"blems of truth, which you are not wor-
"thy to know."

"And how comes it," replied a Lama of
Thibet, "that you are more worthy than we?
"Is it because you pretend to be sprung
"from the head of Brama, while the rest of
"mankind derive their origin from the less
"noble parts of his body? If you would
"support the fable of your origin, and the
"vain distinctions of your casts, prove that
"you are of a nature different from us; prove
"at least by historical testimony the allego-
"ries you maintain; nay, prove that you are
"really the authors of this system; for on our
"part we are able to prove, if that were
"necessary, that you have only stolen and
"disfigured it; that you have borrowed the
"ancient paganism of the western world,
"and blended it by an absurd conceit with
"the purely spiritual nature of our Gods
"(34), a nature which stoops not to address
"itself to the senses, and was wholly unknown
"to the world till the mission of Beddou."

Instantly innumerable voices demanded to
be informed of this nature, and to hear of
that

that God with whose very name the majority of them were unacquainted. In pursuance of this demand, the Lama resumed.

"In the beginning," said he, "there was "one God, self-existent, who passed through "a whole eternity, absorbed in the contem- "plation of his own reflections, ere he de- "termined to manifest those perfections to "created beings, when he produced the "matter of the world. The four elements, "at their production, lay in a state of mingled "confusion, till he breathed upon the face of "the waters, and they immediately became "an immense bubble, shaped like an egg, "which when complete became the vault or "globe of the heavens in which the world is "inclosed (35). No sooner was the earth "and the bodies of animals produced, than "God, the source of motion, bestowed upon "them as a living soul a portion of his sub- "stance. Thus the soul of every living "thing, being only a fraction or separate "part of the universal soul, no percipient "being is liable to perish, but merely changes "its form and mould as it passes successively "into different bodies. But of all the sub-
"stantial

"stantial forms that of man is most pleasing
"to the Divine Being, as most resembling
"his uncreated perfections; and man, when,
"by withdrawing himself from the com-
"merce of the senses, he becomes absorbed
"in the contemplation of his own nature,
"discovers the Divinity that resides in it, and
"himself becomes worthy of Divinity. Thus
"is God incessantly rendering himself incar-
"nate; but his greatest and most solemn in-
"carnation was three thousand years ago,
"in the province of Cassimere, under the
"name of Fôt or Beddou, for the purpose of
"teaching the doctrine of self-denial and self-
"annihilation." The Lama proceeded to detail the history of Fôt, observing, that he had
sprung from the right intercostal of a virgin of
the royal blood, who, when she became a mother, did not the less continue to be a virgin:
that the king of the country, uneasy at his
birth, was desirous to put him to death, and
caused all the males who were born at the
same period to be massacred: that being saved
by shepherds, Beddou lived in the desert to
the age of thirty years, at which time he
opened his commission, preaching the doctrine

trine of truth and casting out devils; that he performed a multitude of the most astonishing miracles, spent his life in fasting and the severest mortifications, and at his death bequeathed to his disciples the volume in which the principles of his religion are contained. The Lama then began to read—

"He that forsaketh his father and his "mother," says Fôt, "to follow me, shall "become a perfect Samanean (a heavenly "being).

"He that keepeth my precepts to the "fourth degree of perfection, shall acquire "the power of flying in the air, of moving "earth and heaven, of protracting or short- "ening his life, and of rising again.

"The Samanean looks with contempt on "riches, and makes use only of such things "as are strictly necessary. He mortifies the "flesh, subdues his passions, fixes his desires "and affections on nothing terrestrial, medi- "tates without ceasing upon my doctrine, "endures injuries with patience, and bears "no enmity against his neighbour.

"Heaven and earth," says Fôt, "shall pass "away; despise therefore your bodies which
"are

" are composed of the four perishable ele-
" ments, and think only of your immortal soul.

" Hearken not to the suggestions of the
" flesh: fear and sorrow are the produce of
" the passions: stifle the passions, and fear
" and sorrow will thus be destroyed.

" Whosoever dies," says Fôt, " without
" having received my doctrine, becomes
" again and again an inhabitant of the earth,
" till he shall have embraced it."

The Lama was going on with his extracts when the Christians interrupted him, observing, that this religion was an alteration of theirs; that Fôt was Jesus himself disfigured, and that the Lamas were nothing more than a degenerate sect of the Nestorians and Manicheans.

But the Lama (36), supported by all the Chamans, Bonzes, Gonnis, Talapoins of Siam, of Ceylon, of Japan, and of China, demonstrated to the Christians from their own Theologians, that the doctrine of the Samaneans was known through the East upwards of a thousand years before Christianity existed; that their name was cited previous to the reign

of Alexander, and that that of Boutta or
Beddou could be traced to a more remote
antiquity than that of Jesus—" And now,
said they, retorting upon the Christians,
" do you prove to us that you are not your-
" selves degenerated Samaneans; that the
" man whom you consider as the author of
" your sect is not Fôt himself in a different
" form. Demonstrate his existence by his-
" torical monuments of so remote a period
" as those which we have adduced (37);
" for as it appears to be founded on no au-
" thentic testimony, we absolutely deny its
" truth; and we maintain that your gospels
" are taken from the books of the Mythriacs
" of Persia, and the Essenians of Syria, who
" were themselves only reformed Sama-
" neans (38)."

These words excited a general outcry on
the part of the Christians, and a new dispute more violent than any preceding one
was on the point of taking place, when a
groupe of Chinese Chamans, and Talapoins
of Siam came forward, pretending that they
could easily adjust every difference, and produce in the assembly a uniformity of opinion,

nion, and one of them speaking for the rest, said: " It is time that we should put an end to all these frivolous disputes, by drawing aside the veil and exposing to your view the *interior* and *secret* doctrine which Fôt himself, on his death-bed, revealed to his disciples (39). These various theological opinions are mere chimeras; these accounts of the attributes, actions and life of the Gods are nothing more than allegories and mysterious symbols, under which moral ideas, and the knowledge of the operations of nature in the action of the elements and the revolutions of the planets, are ingeniously depicted.

" The truth is, that there is no reality in any thing; that all is illusion, appearance, a dream; that the moral metemsychosis is nothing more than a figurative sense of the physical metemsychosis, of that successive motion by which the elements of which a body is composed, and which never perish, pass, when the body itself is dissolved, into a thousand others, and form new combinations. The soul is
" merely

" merely the vital principle resulting from
" the properties of matter, and the action of
" the elements in bodies, in which they
" create a spontaneous movement. To sup-
" pose that this result of organization, which
" is born with it, developed with it, sleeps
" with it, continues to exist when organiza-
" tion is no more, is a romance that may be
" pleasing enough, but that is certainly chi-
" merical. God himself is nothing more
" than the principal mover, the occult power
" diffused through every thing that has be-
" ing, the sum of its laws and its properties,
" the animating principle, in a word, the
" soul of the universe; which, by reason of
" the infinite diversity of its connections and
" operations, considered sometimes as simple
" and sometimes as multiple, sometimes as
" active and sometimes as passive, has ever
" presented to the human mind an insolv-
" able enigma. What we can comprehend
" with greatest perspicuity is, that matter
" does not perish; that it possesses essential
" properties, by which the world is go-
" verned in a mode similar to that of a liv-
" ing and organised being; that, with re-
" spect

"spect to man, the knowledge of its laws is
"what constitutes his wisdom; that in their
"observance consist virtue and merit; and
"evil, sin, vice, in the ignorance and viola-
"tion of them; that happiness and misfor-
"tune are the respective result of this ob-
"servance or neglect, by the same necessity
"that occasions light substances to ascend,
"heavy ones to fall, and by a fatality of
"causes and effects, the chain of which ex-
"tends from the smallest atom to the stars of
"greatest magnitude and elevation (40)."

A crowd of Theologians of every sect instantly exclaimed, that this doctrine was rank materialism, and those who professed it impious Atheists, enemies both of God and man, who ought to be extirpated from the earth.—" Strange reasoning," replied the Chamans. " Supposing us to be mistaken,
"which is by no means impossible, since it
"is one of the attributes of the human mind
"to be subject to illusion, what right have
"you to deprive beings like yourselves of
"the life which God has given them? If
"heaven considers us as culpable, and looks
"upon us with horror, why does it dispense
"to

"to us the same blessings as to you! If it
"treats us with endurance, what right have
"you to be less indulgent? Pious men,
"who speak of God with so much certainty
"and confidence, condescend to tell us what
"he is; explain, so that we may compre-
"hend them, those abstract and metaphy-
"sical beings which you call God and the
"soul; substances without matter, exist-
"ence without body, life without organs or
"sensations. If you discover these beings
"by means of your senses, render them in
"like manner perceptible to us. If you
"speak of them only upon testimony and
"tradition, show us a uniform recital, and
"give an identical and determinate basis to
"your creed."

There now arose a warm controversy between the Theologians respecting the nature
of God and his mode of acting and manifesting himself; respecting the soul and its
union with the body, whether it has existence previous to the organs, or from the
time of their formation only; respecting the
life to come and another world; and every
sect, every school, every individual, differing

from the rest as to all these points, and assigning for its dissent plausible reasons and respectable but opposite authorities, they were all involved in an inextricable labyrinth of contradictions.

At length, the legislators having restored silence, recalled the dispute to its true object, and said: " Leaders and instructors of the
" people, you came hither for the purpose
" of investigating truth; and at first every
" one of you, confident in his own infalli-
" bility, demanded an implicit faith: pre-
" sently, however, you felt the contrariety
" of your opinions, and consented to submit
" them to a fair comparison and a common
" rule of evidence. You proceeded to ex-
" pose your proofs: you began with the
" allegation of facts; but it presently ap-
" peared that every religion and every sect
" had its miracles and its martyrs, and had
" an equal cloud of witnesses to boast, who
" were ready to prove the rectitude of their
" sentiments by the sacrifice of their lives.
" Upon this first point therefore the balance
" remained equal.

" You next passed to proofs of reasoning:
" the

"the same arguments were alternately ap-
"plied to the support of opposite proposi-
"tions; the same assertions, equally gratui-
"tous were successively advanced and re-
"pelled; every one was found to have an
"equal reason for denying his assent to the
"system of the others. A farther conse-
"quence that arose from thus confronting
"your systems was, that, notwithstanding
"their dissimilitude in some points, their
"resemblance in others was not less strik-
"ing. Each of you claimed the first de-
"posit and the original discovery; each of
"you taxed his neighbour with adulteration
"and plagiarism; and a previous question
"to the embracing of any of your doctrines
"appeared to result from the history of opi-
"nions.

"A still greater embarrassment arose
"when you entered into the explication of
"your doctrines: the more assiduous were
"your endeavours, the more confused did
"they appear; they rested upon a basis in-
"accessible to human understanding, of
"consequence you had no means to judge
"of their validity, and you readily admitted

"that,

"that, in afferting them, you were the echos
"of your fathers. Hence it became impor-
"tant to know how they had come into the
"hands of that former generation, who had
"no means of learning them different from
"yourfelves. Thus the tranfmiffion of theo-
"logical ideas from country to country, and
"their firft rife in the human underftanding,
"were equally myfterious, and the queftion
"became every moment more complicated
"with metaphyfical fubtlety and antiquarian
"refearch.

"But as thefe opinions, however extra-
"ordinary, have fome origin; as all ideas,
"even the moft abftracted and fantaftical,
"have in nature fome phyfical model, we
"muft afcend to that origin in order to dif-
"cover what this model is, and how the
"underftanding came by thofe ideas of
"Deity, the foul and immaterial beings,
"that are fo obfcure, and which form the
"foundation of fo many religious fyftems;
"we muft trace their lineal defcent and the
"alterations they have undergone in their
"various fucceffions and ramifications. If
"therefore there are in this affembly men
"who

"who have made these objects their pecu-
"liar study, let them come forward and en-
"deavour to dispel, in the presence of the
"nations of the earth, the obscurity of opi-
"nions in which for so long a period they
"have all wandered."

CHAP.

CHAP. XXII.

ORIGIN AND GENEALOGY OF RELIGIOUS IDEAS.

At these words a new groupe, formed in an instant of individuals from every standard, but undistinguished by any, advanced in the sand, and one of the members, speaking in the name of the general body, said:

"Legislators, friends of evidence and of truth!

"That the subject of which we treat should be involved in so many clouds, is by no means astonishing, since, beside the difficulties that are peculiar to it, thought itself has, till this moment, ever had shackles imposed upon it, and free enquiry, by the intolerance of every religious system, been interdicted. But now that thought is unrestrained, and may develope all its powers, we will expose in the face of day, and submit to the common judgment of assembled nations, such rational truths as unprejudiced minds

minds have by long and laborious study discovered: and this, not with the design of imposing them as a creed, but from a desire of provoking new lights, and obtaining better information.

"Chiefs and instructors of the people, you are not ignorant of the profound obscurity in which the nature, origin, and history of the dogmas you teach are inveloped. Imposed by force and authority, inculcated by education, maintained by the influence of example, they were perpetuated from age to age, and habit and inattention strengthened their empire. But if man, enlightened by experience and reflection, summon to the bar of mature examination the prejudices of his infancy, he presently discovers a multitude of incongruities and contradictions which awaken his sagacity, and call forth the exertion of his reasoning powers.

"At first, remarking the various and opposite creeds into which nations are divided, we are led boldly to reject the infallibility claimed by each; and arming ourselves alternately with their reciprocal pretensions, to conceive that the senses and the understanding

ing emanating directly from God, are a law not less sacred, and a guide not less sure than the indirect and contradictory codes of the prophets.

"If we proceed to examine the texture of the codes themselves, we shall observe that their pretended divine laws, that is to say, laws immutable and eternal, have risen from the complexion of times, of places, and of persons; that these codes issue one from another in a kind of a genealogical order, mutually borrowing a common and similar fund of ideas, which every institutor modifies agreeably to his fancy.

"If we ascend to the source of those ideas, we shall find that it is lost in the night of time, in the infancy of nations, in the very origin of the world, to which they claim alliance; and there, immersed in the obscurity of chaos, and the fabulous empire of tradition, they are attended with so many prodigies as to be seemingly inaccessible to the human understanding. But this prodigious state of things gives birth itself to a ray of reasoning, that resolves the difficulty; for if the miracles held out in systems of religion

have

have actually existed; if, for instance, metamorphoses, apparitions, and the conversations of one or more Gods, recorded in the sacred books of the Hindoos, the Hebrews, and the Parses, are indeed events in real history, it follows that nature in those times was perfectly unlike the nature that we are acquainted with now; that men of the present age are totally different from the men that formerly existed; and, consequently, that we ought not to trouble our heads about them.

"On the contrary, if those miraculous facts have had no real existence in the physical order of things, they must be regarded solely as productions of the human intellect: and the nature of man, at this day, capable of making the most fantastic combinations, explains the phenomenon of those monsters in history. The only difficulty is to ascertain how and for what purpose the imagination invented them. If we examine with attention the subjects that are exhibited by them, if we analize the ideas which they combine and associate, and weigh with accuracy all their concomitant circumstances, we shall find a solution perfectly conformable

able to the laws of nature. Those fabulous stories have a figurative sense different from their apparent one; they are founded on simple and physical facts: but these facts, being ill conceived and erroneously represented, have been disfigured and changed from their original nature by accidental causes dependent on the human mind, by the confusion of signs made use of in the representation of objects, by the equivocation of words, the defeat of language, and the imperfection of writing. These Gods, for example, who act such singular parts in every system, are no other than the physical powers of nature, the elements, the winds, the meteors, the stars, all which have been personified by the necessary mechanism of language, and the manner in which objects are conceived by the understanding. Their life, their manners, their actions, are only the operation of the same powers, and the whole of their pretended history no more than a description of their various phenomena, traced by the first naturalist that observed them, but taken in a contrary sense by the vulgar who did not understand it, or by succeeding genera-

tions who forgot it. In a word, all the
theological dogmas respecting the origin of
the world, the nature of God, the revelation of his laws, the manifestation of his
person, are but recitals of astronomical facts,
figurative and emblematical narratives of
the motion and influence of the heavenly
bodies. The very idea itself of the Divinity, which is at present so obscure, ab-
stracted, and metaphysical, was in its origin
merely a composit of the powers of the material universe, considered sometimes analy-
tically, as they appear in their agents and
their phenomena, and sometimes syntheti-
cally, as forming one whole, and exhibiting
an harmonious relation in all its parts. Thus
the name God has been bestowed sometimes
upon the wind, upon fire, water, and the
elements; sometimes upon the sun, the
stars, the planets, and their influences;
sometimes upon the universe at large, and
the matter of which the world is composed;
sometimes upon abstract and metaphysical
properties, such as space, duration, motion,
and intelligence; but in every instance, the
idea of a deity has not flowed from the miraculous revelation of an invisible world,

but

but has been the natural result of human reflection, has followed the progress and undergone the changes of the successive improvement of intellect, and has had for its subject the visible universe and its different agents.

"It is then in vain that nations refer the origin of their religion to heavenly inspiration; it is in vain that they pretend to describe a supernatural state of things as first in the order of events: the original barbarous state of mankind, attested by their own monuments (41), belies all their assertions. These assertions are still more victoriously refuted by considering this great principle, *that man receives no ideas but through the medium of his senses* (42): for from hence it appears, that every system which ascribes human wisdom to any other source than experience and sensation, includes in it a υςερον προ]ερον, and represents the last results of understanding as earliest in the order of time. If we examine the different religious systems which have been formed respecting the action of the Gods, and the origin of the world, we shall discover at every turn an anticipation in the order of narrating things,

which

which could only be suggested by subsequent reflection. Reason, then, emboldened by these contradictions, hesitates not to reject whatever does not accord with the nature of things, and accepts nothing for historical truth that is not capable of being established by argument and ratiocination. Its ideas and suggestions are as follow:

"Before any nation received from a neighbour nation dogmas already invented; before one generation inherited the ideas of another, none of these complicated systems had existence. The first men, the children of nature, whose consciousness was anterior to experience, and who brought no preconceived knowledge into the world with them, were born without any idea of those articles of faith which are the result of learned contention; of those religious rites which had relation to arts and practices not yet in existence; of those precepts which suppose the passions already developed; of those laws which have reference to a language and a social order hereafter to be produced; of that God, whose attributes are abstractions of the knowledge of nature, and the idea of whose conduct is suggested by the experience of a despotic government; in fine, of that soul and those spiritual existences which are said not to be the object of the senses, but which, however, we must for ever have remained unacquainted with, if our senses had not introduced them to us. Previously to arriving at these notions, an immense catalogue of existing facts must have been observed. Man, originally savage, must have learned from repeated trials the use of his organs. Successive generations must have invented and refined upon the means of subsistence; and the understanding, at liberty to disengage itself from the wants of nature, must have risen to the complicated art of comparing ideas, digesting reasonings, and seizing upon abstract similitudes.

SECT. I. *Origin of the idea of God: Worship of the elements, and the physical powers of nature.*

"IT was not till after having surmounted those obstacles, and run a long career in the night of history, that man, reflecting on his state, began to perceive his subjection to forces

forces superior to his own and independent of his will. The sun gave him light and warmth; fire burned, thunder terrified, the winds buffetted, water overwhelmed him; all the various natural existences acted upon him in a manner not to be resisted. For a long time, an automaton, he remained passive, without enquiring into the cause of this action; but the very moment he was desirous of accounting to himself for it, astonishment seized his mind; and passing from the surprise of a first thought to the reverie of curiosity, he formed a chain of reasoning.

' " At first, considering only the action of the elements upon him, he inferred, relatively to himself, an idea of weakness, of subjection, and relatively to them, an idea of power, of domination; and this idea was the primitive and fundamental type of all his conceptions of the Divinity.

" The action of the natural existences, in the second place, excited in him sensations of pleasure or pain, of good or evil; by virtue of his organization, he conceived love or aversion for them, he desired or dreaded their presence;

presence; and fear or hope was the principle of every idea of religion.

"Afterwards, judging every thing by comparison, and remarking in those beings a motion spontaneous like his own, he supposed there to be a will, an intelligence inherent in that motion, of a nature similar to what existed in himself; and hence, by way of inference, he started a fresh argument.— Having experienced that certain modes of behaviour towards his fellow-creatures wrought a change in their affections and governed their conduct, he applied those practices to the powerful beings of the universe. "When " my fellow-creature of superior strength," said he to himself, " is disposed to injure me, " I humble myself before him, and my prayer " has the art of appeasing him. I will pray " to the powerful beings that strike me. I " will supplicate the faculties of the winds, " the planets, the waters, and they will hear " me. I will conjure them to avert the ca- " lamities, and to grant me the blessings " which are at their disposal. My tears will " move, my offerings propitiate them, and I " shall enjoy complete felicity."

§ " And,

"And, simple in the infancy of his reason, man spoke to the sun and the moon, he animated with his understanding and his passions the great agents of nature; he thought by vain sounds and useless practices to change their inflexible laws. Fatal error! He desired that the water should ascend, the mountains be removed, the stone mount in the air; and substituting a fantastic to a real world, he constituted for himself beings of opinion, to the terror of his mind and the torment of his race.

"Thus the ideas of God and religion sprung, like all others, from physical objects, and were in the understanding of man the produce of his sensations, his wants, the circumstances of his life, and the progressive state of his knowledge.

"As these ideas had natural beings for their first models, it resulted from hence that the Divinity was originally as various and manifold as the forms under which he seemed to act: each being was a Power, a Genius, and the first men found the universe crowded with innumerable Gods.

"In like manner the ideas of the Divinity having had for motors the affections of

the human heart, they underwent an order
of division calculated from the sensations of
pain and pleasure, of love and hatred: the
powers of nature, the Gods, the Genii, were
classed into benign and maleficent, into good
and evil ones: and this constitutes the uni-
versality of these two ideas in every system
of religion.

"These ideas, analogous to the condition
of their inventors, were for a long time
confused and gross. Wandering in woods,
beset with wants, destitute of resources, men
in their savage state had no leisure to make
comparisons and draw conclusions. Suffering more ills than they tasted enjoyments,
their most habitual sentiment was fear, their
theology terror, their worship confined to
certain modes of salutation, of offerings
which they presented to beings whom they
supposed to be ferocious and greedy like
themselves. In their state of equality and
independence, no one took upon him the office of mediator with Gods as insubordinate
and poor as himself. No one having any superfluity to dispose of, there existed no pa-
rasite under the name of priest, nor tribute
under

under the name of victim, nor empire under the name of altar; their dogma and morality, jumbled together, were only self-preservation; and their religion, an arbitrary idea without influence on the mutual relations existing between men, was but a vain homage paid to the visible powers of nature.

"Such was the first and necessary origin of every idea of the Divinity."

The orator then addressing the savage nations, said: "We appeal to you, who have received no foreign fictitious ideas, whether your conceptions have not been formed precisely in this manner? We ask you also, learned theologians, if such be not the unanimous record of all the monuments of antiquity (43)?

SECT. II. *Second system: Worship of the Stars, or Sabeism.*

"BUT those same monuments offer us a more methodical and more complicated system, that of the worship of all the stars, adored at one time under their proper form, at another under emblems and figurative symbols.

symbols. This worship was also the effect of the knowledge of man in physics, and derived immediately from the first causes of the social state; that is to say, from wants and arts of the first degree, the elements as it were in the formation of society.

"When men began to unite in society, they found it necessary to enlarge the means of their subsistence, and consequently to apply themselves to agriculture; and the practice of agriculture required the observation and knowledge of the heavens (44). It was necessary to know the periodical return of the same operations of nature, the same phenomena of the skies; it was necessary to regulate the duration and succession of the seasons, months and year. In order to this it was requisite to become acquainted with the march of the sun, which in its zodiacal revolution showed itself the first and supreme agent of all creation; then of the moon, which by its changes and returns regulated and distributed time; finally of the stars, and even of the planets, which, by their appearance and disappearance on the horizon and the nocturnal hemisphere, formed the minutest divisions. In a word it was necessary to establish an entire system of astronomy, to form an almanac; and from this labour there quickly and spontaneously resulted a new manner of considering the dominant and governing powers. Having observed that the productions of the earth bore a regular and constant connection with the phenomena of the heavens; that the birth, growth, and decay of each plant, were allied to the appearance, exaltation and decline of the same planet, the same groupe of stars; in short, that the langour or activity of vegetation seemed to depend on celestial influences, men began to infer from this an idea of action, of power, in those bodies, superior to terrestrial beings; and the stars dispensing scarcity or abundance, became powers, Genii (45), Gods, authors of good and evil.

" As the state of society had already introduced a methodical hierarchy of ranks, employments and conditions, men, continuing to reason from comparison, transferred their new acquired notions to their theology, and the result was a complicated system of gradual Divinities, in which the sun, as the first God,

God, was a military chief, a political king; the moon, a queen, his consort; the planets, servants, bearers of commands, messengers: and the multitude of stars, a nation, an army of heroes, of Genii, appointed to govern the world under the command of their officers; every individual had a name, functions, attributes, drawn from its connections and influences, and even a sex derived from the gender of its appellation (46).

"As the state of society had introduced certain usages and complex practices, worship, leading the van, adopted similar ones. Ceremonies, simple and private at first, became public and solemn; offerings were more rich and more numerous; rites more methodical; places of assembly, chapels and temples were erected; officers, pontiffs, created to administer; forms and epochas were settled; and religion became a civil act, a political tie. But in this developement it altered not its first principles, and the idea of God was still that of physical beings, operating good or ill, that is to say, impressing sensations of pain or pleasure: the dogma was the knowledge of their laws or modes of acting; virtue and

and fin the obfervance or infringement of thofe laws; and morality, in its native fimplicity, a judicious practice of all that is conducive to the prefervation of exiftence, to the well-being of the individual and of his fellow-creatures (47).

"Should it be afked at what epoch this fyftem took birth, we fhall anfwer, fupported by the authority of the monuments of aftronomy itfelf, that its principles can be traced back with certainty to a period of nearly feventeen thoufand years (48). Should we farther be afked to what people or nation it ought to be attributed, we fhall reply, that thofe felf-fame monuments, feconded by unanimous tradition, attribute it to the firft tribes of Egypt. And when reafon finds in that region a concurrence of all the phyfical circumftances calculated to give rife to it; when it finds at once a zone of heaven, in vicinity of the tropic, equally free from the rains of the equator, and the fogs of the north (49); when it finds there the central point of the antique fphere; a falubrious climate; an immenfe yet manageable river; a land fertile without art, without fatigue;

inundated,

inundated, without pestilential exhalations; situate between two seas which lave the shores of the richest countries—it becomes manifest that the inhabitant of the districts of the Nile, inclined to agriculture from the nature of his soil; to commerce, from the facility of communication; to geometry, from the annual necessity of measuring his possessions; to astronomy, from the state of his heaven, ever open to observation, must first have passed from the savage to the social state, and consequently attained that physical and moral knowledge proper to civilized man.

"It was thus, upon the distant shores of the Nile, and among a nation of sable complexion, that the complex system of the worship of the stars, as connected with the produce of the soil and the labours of agriculture, was constructed. The worship of the stars under their proper forms, or their natural attributes, was a simple process of the human understanding; but in a short time the multiplicity of objects, their relations, their action and re-action, having confounded the ideas and the signs that represented them, a
consequence

consequence resulted as absurd in its nature as pernicious in its tendency.

Sect. III. *Third System: Worship of symbols, or idolatry.*

"From the instant this agricolar race had turned an eye of observation on the stars, they found it necessary to distinguish individuals or groupes, and to assign to each a proper name. A considerable difficulty here presented itself; for on the one hand, the celestial bodies, similar in form, offered no peculiar character by which to denominate them; and on the other hand, language, poor and in a state of infancy, had no expressions for so many new and metaphysical ideas. The usual stimulus of genius, necessity, conquered all obstacles. Having remarked that in the annual revolution, the renewal and periodical appearance of the productions of the earth were constantly connected with the rising and setting of certain stars, and with their position relatively to the sun, the mind, by a natural mechanism, associated in its thought terrestrial and celestial objects, which had in fact a certain alliance; and applying to them the same sign, it gave to the stars and the groupes it formed of them, the very names of the terrestrial objects to which they bore affinity (50).

"Thus the Ethiopian of Thebes called stars of inundation, or of *Aquarius*, those under which the river began to overflow *; stars of the ox or bull, those under which it was convenient to plough the earth; stars of the lion, those under which that animal, driven by thirst from the deserts, made his appearance on the banks of the Nile; stars of the sheaf, or of the harvest maid, those under which the harvests were got in; stars of the lambs, stars of the goat, those under which those valuable animals brought forth their young; and thus was a first part of the difficulty resolved.

"On the other hand, man, having remarked in the beings that surrounded him certain qualities peculiar to each species, and having invented a name by which to design them, speedily discovered an ingenious mode of generalizing his ideas, and transferring the name

* This must have been June. See Note (46).

already

already invented to every thing bearing a similar or analogous property or agency, enriched his language with a multiplicity of metaphors and tropes.

"Thus the same Ethiopian, having observed that the return of the inundation answered constantly to the appearance of a very beautiful star towards the source of the Nile, which seemed to warn the husbandman against being surprised by the waters, he compared this action with that of the animal who by barking gives notice of danger, and called this star the dog, the barker *(Syrius)*. In the same manner he called stars of the crab, those which showed themselves when the sun, having reached the bounds of the tropic, returned backwards and sideways like the crab or *Cancer*; stars of the wild goat, those which, the sun being arrived at its greatest altitude, at the top of the horary gnomon, imitated the action of that animal who delights in climbing the highest rocks; stars of the balance, those which, the days and nights being of the same length, seemed to observe an equilibrium like that instrument; stars of the scorpion, those which were perceptible when certain regular winds brought a burning vapour like

like the poison of the scorpion. In the same manner he called by the name of rings and serpents the figured traces of the orbits of the stars and planets (51); and this was the general means of appellation of all the heavenly bodies, taken in groupes or individually, according to their connection with rural and terrestrial operations, and the analogies which every nation found them to bear to the labours of the field and the objects of their climate and soil.

"From this proceeding it resulted, that abject and terrestrial beings entered into association with the superior and powerful beings of the heavens; and this association became more rivetted every day by the very constitution of language and the mechanism of the mind. Men would say, by a natural metaphor: " The bull spreads upon the earth the " germins of fecundity (in spring); and " brings back abundance by the revival of " vegetation. The lamb (or ram) delivers " the heavens from the malevolent Genii of " winter; and saves the world from the ser- " pent (emblem of the wet season). The " scorpion pours out his venom upon the " earth, and spreads diseases and death, &c."

This

"This language, understood by every body, was at first attended with no inconvenience; but, in process of time, when the almanac had been regulated, the people, who could do without further observation of the skies, lost sight of the motive which led to the adoption of these expressions; and the allegory still remaining in the practices of life, became a fatal stumbling-block to the understanding and reason. Habituated to join to symbols the ideas of their models, the mind finally confounded them; then those same animals which the imagination had raised to heaven, descended again on the earth; but in this return, decked in the livery and invested with the attributes of the stars, they imposed upon their own authors. The people, imagining that they saw their Gods before them, found it a more easy task to offer up their prayers. They demanded of the ram of their flock, the influence which they expected from the celestial ram; they prayed the scorpion not to pour out his venom upon Nature; they revered the fish of the river, the crab of the sea, and the scarabeus of the slime; and by a series of corrupt,

corrupt, but inseparable analogies, they lost themselves in a labyrinth of consequent absurdities.

"Such was the origin of this ancient and singular worship of animals; such the train of ideas by which the character of the Divinity became common to the meanest of the brute creation; and thus was formed the vast, complicated, and learned theological system which, from the banks of the Nile, conveyed from country to country by commerce, war, and conquest, invaded all the old world; and which, modified by times, by circumstances, and by prejudices, is still to be found among a hundred nations, and subsists to this day as the secret and inseparable basis of the theology of those even who despise and reject it."

At these words, murmurs being heard in various groupes: "I repeat it," continued the orator. "People of Africa! hence, for example, has arisen among you the adoration of your *Feteches*, plants, animals, pebbles, bits of wood, before which your ancestors would never have been so absurd as to prostrate themselves, if they had not seen feen in them talifmans, partaking of the nature of the ftars (52). Nations of Tartary! this is equally the origin of your *Marmouzets*, and of the whole train of animals with which your Chamans ornament their magic robes. This is the origin of thofe figures of birds and ferpents, which all the favage nations, with myftic and facred ceremonies, imprint on their fkin. Indians! it is in vain you cover yourfelves with the veil of myftery: the hawk of your God Vichenou is but one of the thoufand emblems of the fun in Egypt, and his incarnations in a fifh, boar, lion, turtle, together with all his monftrous adventures, are nothing more than the metamorphofes of the fame ftar, which, paffing fucceffively through the figns of the twelve animals *, was fuppofed to affume their forms, and to act their aftronomical parts (53). Japanefe! your bull which breaks the egg of the world, is merely that of the heavens, which, in times of yore, opened the age of the creation, the equinox of Spring. Rabbins, Jews! that fame bull is the *Apis* worfhipped in Egypt,

* The Zodiac.

and which your ancestors adored in the idol of the golden calf. It is also your bull, children of Zoroaster! that, sacrificed in the symbolic mysteries of Mithra, shed a blood fertilizing to the world. Lastly, your bull of the Apocalypse, Christians! with his wings, the symbol of the air, has no other origin: your lamb of God, immolated, like the bull of Mithra, for the salvation of the world, is the self-same sun in the sign of the celestial ram, which, in a subsequent age, opening the equinox in his turn, was deemed to have rid the world of the reign of evil, that is to say, of the serpent, of the large snake, the mother of winter and emblem of the Ahrimanes or Satan of the Persians, your institutors. Yes, vainly does your imprudent zeal consign idolaters to the torments of the Tartarus which they have invented: the whole basis of your system is nothing more than the worship of the star of day, whose attributes you have heaped upon your chief personage. It is the sun which, under the name of Orus, was born, like your God, in the arms of the celestial virgin, and passed through an obscure, indigent,

digent, and destitute childhood, answering to the season of cold and frost. It is the sun, which, under the name of Osiris, persecuted by Typhon and the tyrants of the air, was put to death, laid in a dark tomb, the emblem of the hemisphere of winter, and which, rising afterwards from the inferior zone to the highest point of the heavens, awoke triumphant over giants and the destroying angels. Ye priests! from whom the murmurs proceed, you wear yourselves its signs all over your bodies. Your tonsure is the disk of the sun; your stole its Zodiac (54); your rosaries the symbols of the stars and planets. Pontiffs and prelates! your mitre, your crosier, your mantle, are the emblems of Osiris; and that crucifix of which you boast the mystery, without comprehending it, is the cross of Serapis, traced by the hands of Egyptian priests on the plan of the figurative world, which, passing through the equinoxes and the tropics, became the emblem of future life and resurrection, because it touched the gates of ivory and horn through which the soul was to pass in its way to heaven."

Here the doctors of the different groupes looked with astonishment at one another, but none of them breaking silence, the orator continued.

"Three principal causes concurred to produce this confusion of ideas. First, the necessity, on account of the infant state of language, of making use of figurative expressions to depict the relations of things; expressions that, passing afterwards from a proper to a general, from a physical to a moral sense, occasioned, by their equivocal and synonymous terms, a multiplicity of mistakes.

"Thus having at first said, that the sun surmounted and passed in its course through the twelve animals, they afterwards supposed that it combated, conquered, and killed them, and from this was composed the historical life of Hercules.

"Having said that it regulated the period of rural operations, of seed time and of harvest; that it distributed the seasons, ran through the climates, swayed the earth, &c. it was taken for a legislative king, a conquering warrior, and hence they formed the stories

stories of Osiris, of Bacchus, and other similar Gods.

"Having said that a planet entered into a sign, the conjunction was denominated a marriage, adultery, incest (55): having farther said, that it was buried, because it sunk below the horizon, returned to light and gained its state of eminence, they gave it the epithet of dead, risen again, carried into heaven, &c.

"The second cause of confusion was the material figures themselves, by which thoughts were originally painted, and which, under the name of hieroglyphics, or sacred characters, were the first invention of the mind. Thus to denote an inundation, and the necessity of preserving one's-self from it, they painted a boat, the vessel Argo; to express the wind, they painted a bird's wing; to specify the season, the month, they delineated the bird of passage, insect, or animal, which made its appearance at that epoch; to express winter they drew a hog, or a serpent, which are fond of moist and miry places. The combination of these figures had also a meaning, and was substituted for words

words and phrases* (56). But as there was nothing fixed or precise in this sort of language, as the number of those figures and their combinations became excessive and burdensome to the memory, confusions and false interpretations were the first and obvious result. Genius having afterwards invented the more simple art of applying signs to sounds, of which the number is limited, and of painting the word instead of the thought, hieroglyphic pictures were, by means of alphabetical writing, brought into disuse; and from day to day their forgotten significations made way for a variety of illusions, equivoques, and errors.

" Lastly, the civil organization of the first states was a third cause of confusion. Indeed, when the people began to apply themselves to agriculture, the formation of the rural calendar requiring continual astronomical observations, it was necessary to chuse individuals whose province it should be to watch the appearance and setting of certain stars, to give notice of the return of the inundation, of particular winds and rains, and

* See the examples cited in note (45).

the

the proper time for sowing every species of grain. These men, on account of their office, were exempted from the common occupations, and the society provided for their subsistence. In this situation, solely occupied in making observations, they soon penetrated the great phenomena of nature, and dived into the secret of various of her operations. They became acquainted with the course of the stars and planets; the connection which their absence and return had with the productions of the earth and the activity of vegetation: the medicinal or nutritive properties of fruits and plants; the action of the elements, and their reciprocal affinities. But, as there were no means of communicating this knowledge otherwise than by the painful and laborious one of oral instruction, they imparted it only to their friends and kindred; and hence resulted a concentration of science in certain families, who, on this account assumed to themselves exclusive privileges, and a spirit of corporation and separate distinction fatal to the public weal. By this continued succession of the same labours and enquiries, the progress of knowledge it is true was hastened, but, by the mystery that

that accompanied it, the people, plunged daily in the thickest darkness, became more superstitious and more slavish. Seeing human beings produce certain phenomena, announce, as it were at will, eclipses and comets, cure diseases, handle noxious serpents, they supposed them to have intercourse with celestial powers; and, to obtain the good or have the ills averted which they expected from those powers, they adopted these extraordinary human beings as mediators and interpreters. And thus were established in the very bosom of states sacrilegious corporations of hypocritical and deceitful men, who arrogated to themselves every kind of power; and priests, being at once astronomers, divines, naturalists, physicians, necromancers, interpreters of the Gods, oracles of the people, rivals of kings or their accomplices, instituted under the name of religion an empire of mystery, which to this very hour has proved ruinous to the nations of mankind."

At these words the priests of all the groupes interrupted the orator; with loud cries, they accused him of impiety, irreligion, blasphemy, and were unwilling he should proceed: but the legislators having observed,

that

that what he related was merely a narrative of historical facts; that if those facts were false or forged, it would be an easy matter to refute them; and that if every one were not allowed the perfect liberty to declare his opinion, it would be impossible to arrive at truth—he thus went on with his discourse.

" From all these causes, and the perpetual association of dissimilar ideas, there followed a strange mass of disorders in theology, morality, and tradition. And first, because the stars were represented by animals, the qualities of the animals, their likings, their sympathies, their aversions, were transferred to the Gods and supposed to be their actions. Thus the God *Ichneumon* made war against the God crocodile; the God wolf wanted to eat the God sheep; the God stork devoured the God serpent; and the Deity became a strange, whimsical, ferocious being, whose idea misled the judgment of man, and corrupted both his morals and his reason.

" Again, as every family, every nation, in the spirit of its worship adopted a particular star or constellation for its patron, the affections and antipathies of the emblematical

brute

brute were transferred to the sectaries of this worship; and the partisans of the God dog were enemies to those of the God wolf; the worshippers of the God bull, abhorred those who fed upon beef, and religion became the author of combats and animosities, the senseless cause of frenzy and superstition (57).

"Farther, the names of the animal stars having, on account of this same patronage, been conferred on nations, countries, mountains, and rivers, those objects were also taken for Gods; and hence there arose a medley of geographical, historical, and mythological beings, by which all tradition was involved in confusion.

"In fine, from the analogy of their supposed actions the planetary gods having been taken for men, heroes, and kings; kings and heroes took in their turn the actions of the Gods for models, and became, from imitation, warlike, conquering, sanguinary, proud, lascivious, indolent; and religion consecrated the crimes of despots, and perverted the principles of governments.

SECT. IV. *Fourth system: Worship of two principles, or Dualism.*

"MEANWHILE the astronomical priests, enjoying in their temples peace and abundance, made every day fresh progress in the sciences; and the system of the world gradually displaying itself before their eyes, they started successively various hypotheses as to its agents and effects, which became so many systems of theology.

"The navigators of the maritime nations, and the caravans of the Asiatic and African Nomades, having given them a knowledge of the earth from the Fortunate Islands to Serica, and from the Baltic to the sources of the Nile, they discovered, by a comparison of the different Zones, the rotundity of the globe, which gave rise to a new theory. Observing that all the operations of Nature, during the annual period, were summed up in two principal ones, that of producing and that of destroying; that upon the major part of the globe, each of these operations was equally accomplished from one to the other equinox; that is to say, that during the six months

months of summer all was in a state of procreation and increase, and during the six months of winter all in a state of languor and nearly dead, they supposed nature to contain two contrary powers always struggling with and resisting each other; and considering in the same light the celestial sphere, they divided the pictures, by which they represented it into two halves or hemispheres, so that those constellations which appeared in the summer heaven formed a direct and superior empire, and those in the winter heaven an opposite and inferior one. Now as the summer constellations were accompanied with the season of long, warm, and unclouded days, together with that of fruits and harvests, they were deemed to be the powers of light, fecundity, and creation; and by transition from a physical to a moral sense, to be Genii, angels of science, beneficence, purity, virtue: in like manner the winter constellations, being attended with long nights and the polar fogs, were regarded as genii of darkness, destruction, death, and, by similar transition, as angels of wickedness, ignorance, sin, vice. By this disposal, fal, heaven was divided into two domains, two factions; and the analogy of human ideas opened already a vast career to the flights of imagination; but a particular circumstance determined, if it did not occasion the mistake and illusion. (Consult Plate II. at the end of the volume.)

"In the projection of the celestial sphere drawn by astronomical priests (58), the Zodiac and the constellations disposed in a circular order, presented their halves in diametrical opposition: the winter hemisphere was adverse, contrary, opposite to, being the Antipodes of, that of summer. By the continued metaphor these words were converted into a moral sense, and the adverse angels and Genii became rebels and enemies (59). From that period the whole astronomical history of the constellations was turned into a political history; the heavens became a human state, where every thing happened as it does on earth. Now as the existing states, for the most part despotic, had their monarchs, and as the sun was the apparent sovereign of the skies, the summer hemisphere (empire of light), and its constellations (a nation of white angels), had for king

king an enlightened, intelligent, creative, benign God; and as every rebellious faction muft have its chief, the hemifphere of winter (the fubterraneous empire of darknefs and woe), together with its ftars (a nation of black angels, giants, or demons), had for leader a malignant Genius, whofe part was affigned, by the different people of the earth, to that ftar which appeared to them the moft remarkable. In Egypt it was originally the Scorpion, the firft fign of the Zodiac after the Balance, and the hoary chief of the wintry figns: then it was the bear or the polar afs, called Typhon, that is to fay, deluge (60), on account of the rains which poured down upon the earth during the dominion of that ftar. In Perfia, at a fubfequent period (61), it was the ferpent, which, under the name of Ahrimanes, formed the bafis of the fyftem of Zoroafter; and it is the fame, Chriftians and Jews, that is become your ferpent of Eve (the celeftial origin), and that of the crofs; in both cafes the emblem of Satan, the great adverfary of the Ancient of Days, fung by Daniel. In Syria it was the hog or wild boar, enemy of Adonis, becaufe in that country the office of the

Northern

Northern bear was made to devolve upon the
animal whose fondness for mire and dirt is
emblematical of winter. And it is for this
reason that you, children of Moses and of
Mahomet, hold this animal in abhorrence, in
imitation of the priests of Memphis and Balbec, who detested him as the murderer of
their God the sun. This is likewise, O Indians! the type of your Chib-en, which was
once the Pluto of your brethren the Greeks
and Romans; your Brama also (God the creator), is only the Persian Ormuzd, and the
Osiris of Egypt, whose very name expresses
a creative power, producer of forms. And
these Gods were worshipped in a manner
analogous to their real or fictitious attributes;
and this worship, on account of the difference
of its objects, was divided into two distinct
branches. In one, the benign God received
a worship of joy and love; whence are derived all religious acts of a gay nature (62),
festivals, dances, banquets, offerings of
flowers, milk, honey, perfumes; in a word,
of every thing that delights the senses and
the soul. In the other, the malign God, on
the contrary, received a worship of fear and

S pain;

pain; whence originated all religious acts of the sombre kind (63), tears, grief, mourning, self-denial, blood-offerings, and cruel sacrifices.

"From the same source flowed the division of terrestrial beings into pure and impure, sacred or abominable, according as their species was found among the respective constellations of the two Gods, and made a part of their domains. This produced, on one hand, the superstitions of pollution and purification; and on the other, the pretended efficacious virtues of amulets and talismans.

"You now understand," continued the orator, addressing himself to the Indians, Persians, Jews, Christians and Mussulmans, "you now understand the origin of those ideas of combats and rebellion, which equally pervade your respective mythology. You perceive what is meant by white and black angels; by the cherubs and seraphs with heads of an eagle, a lion or a bull; the Deus, devils or demons with horns of goats and tails of snakes; the thrones and dominions, ranged in seven orders or gradations, like the seven spheres of the planets; all of them beings acting

acting the same parts, partaking of the same attributes in the Vedas, the Bibles, or the Zendavesta; whether their chief be Ormuzd or Brama, Typhon or Chib-en, Michael or Satan; whether their form be that of giants with a hundred arms and feet of serpents, or that of Gods metamorphosed into lions, storks, bulls and cats, as they appear in the sacred tales of the Greeks and Egyptians: you perceive the successive genealogy of these ideas, and how in proportion to their remoteness from their sources, and as the mind of man became refined, their gross forms were purified, and reduced to a state less shocking and repulsive.

"But, just as the system of two opposite principles or deities originated in that of symbols; in the same manner you will find a new system spring out of this, to which it served in its turn as a foundation and support."

SECT. V. *Mystical or moral worship, or the system of a future state.*

"IN reality, when the vulgar heard talk of a new heaven and another world, they soon gave a body to these fictions; they erected on it a solid stage and real scenes; and their notions of geography and astronomy served to strengthen, if they did not give rise to the allusion.

"On the one hand, the Phenician navigators, those who passed the pillars of Hercules to fetch the pewter of Thule and the amber of the Baltic, related that at the extremity of the world, the boundaries of the ocean (the Mediterranean), where the sun sets to the countries of Asia, there were fortunate Islands, the abode of an everlasting spring; and at a farther distance, hyperborean regions, placed under the earth (relatively to the tropics), where reigned an eternal night *. From these stories, badly understood, and no doubt confusedly related, the imagination of the people composed the Elysian Fields (64), delightful sports in a world below, having their heaven, their sun and their stars; and Tartarus, a place of darkness, humidity, mire, and chilling frost. Now, inasmuch as mankind, inquisitive about all that of which they

---

* Nights of six months duration.

are ignorant, and defirous of a protracted existence, had already exerted their faculties refpecting what was to become of them after death; inafmuch as they had early reafoned upon that principle of life which animates the body, and which quits it without changing the form of the body, and had conceived to themfelves airy fubftances, phantoms and fhades, they loved to believe that they fhould refume in the fubterranean world that life which it was fo painful to lofe; and this abode appeared commodious for the reception of thofe beloved objects which they could not prevail on themfelves to renounce.

"On the other hand, the aftrological and philofophical priefts told fuch ftories of their heavens as perfectly quadrated with thefe fictions. Having, in their metaphorical language, denominated the equinoxes and folftices the gates of heaven, or the entrance of the feafons, they explained the terreftrial phenomena by faying, that through the gate of horn (firft the bull, afterwards the ram), vivifying fires defcended, which, in fpring, gave life to vegetation, and aquatic Spirits, which caufed, at the folftice, the overflowing of the Nile: that through the gate of ivory (originally the Bowman, or Sagittarius, then the Balance) and through that of Capricorn, or the urn, the emanations or influences of the heavens returned to their source and reascended to their origin; and the milky Way which passed through the doors of the solstices, seemed to them to have been placed there on purpose to be their road and vehicle (65). The celestial scene farther presented, according to their Atlas, a river (the Nile, designated by the windings of the Hydra); together with a barge (the vessel Argo), and the dog Sirius, both bearing relation to that river of which they forboded the overflowing. These circumstances added to the preceding ones, increased the probability of the fiction; and thus, to arrive at Tartarus or Elysium, souls were obliged to cross the rivers Styx and Acheron, in the boat of Charon the ferryman, and to pass through the doors of horn and ivory, which were guarded by the mastiff Cerberus. At length a civil usage was joined to all these inventions, and gave them consistency.

"The

"The inhabitants of Egypt having remarked that the putrefaction of dead bodies became in their burning climate the source of pestilence and diseases, the custom was introduced in a great number of states, of burying the dead at a distance from the inhabited districts, in the desert which lies at the West. To arrive there it was necessary to cross the canals of the river in a boat, and to pay a toll to the ferryman, otherwise the body, remaining unburied, would have been left a prey to wild beasts. This custom suggested to her civil and religious legislators, a powerful means of affecting the manners of her inhabitants; and addressing savage and uncultivated men with the motives of filial piety and reverence for the dead, they introduced, as a necessary condition, the undergoing that previous trial which should decide whether the deceased deserved to be admitted upon the footing of his family honours into the *black city*. Such an idea too well accorded with the rest of the business not to be incorporated with it: it accordingly entered for an article into religious creeds, and hell had its Minos and its Radaman-

Radamanthus, with the wand, the chair, the guards and the urn, after the exact model of this civil transaction. The Divinity then, for the first time, became a subject of moral and political consideration, a legislator, by so much the more formidable as, while his judgment was final and his decrees without appeal, he was unapproachable to his subjects. This mythological and fabulous creation, composed as it was of scattered and discordant parts, then became a source of future punishments and rewards, in which divine justice was supposed to correct the vices and errors of this transitory state. A spiritual and mystical system, such as I have mentioned, acquired so much the more credit as it applied itself to the mind by every argument suited to it. The oppressed looked thither for an indemnification; and entertained the consoling hope of vengeance; the oppressor expected by the costliness of his offerings to secure to himself impunity, and at the same time employed this principle to inspire the vulgar with timidity: kings and priests, the heads of the people, saw in it a new source of power, as they reserved to themselves

themselves the privilege of awarding the favours or the censure of the great judge of all, according to the opinion they should inculcate of the odiousness of crimes and the meritoriousness of virtue.

"Thus, then, an invisible and imaginary world entered into competition with that which was real. Such, O Persians, was the origin of your renovated earth, your city of resurrection, placed under the equator, and distinguished from all other cities by this singular attribute, that the bodies of its inhabitants cast no shade (66). Such, O Jews and Christians, disciples of the Persians, was the source of your new Jerusalem, your paradise and your heaven, modelled upon the astrological heaven of Hermes. Meanwhile, your hell, O ye Mussulmans, a subterraneous pit surmounted by a bridge, your balance of souls and good works, your judgment pronounced by the angels Monkir and Nekir, derives its attributes from the mysterious ceremonies of the cave of Mithra (67); and your heaven is exactly coincident with that of Osiris, Ormudz and Brama."

SECT.

SECT. VI. *Sixth System: The animated world, or worship of the universe under different emblems.*

"WHILE the nations were losing themselves in the dark labyrinth of mythology and fables, the physiological priests, pursuing their studies and enquiries about the order and disposition of the universe, came to fresh results, and set up fresh systems of powers and moving causes.

"Long confined to simple appearances, they had only seen in the motion of the stars an unknown play of luminous bodies, which they supposed to roll round the earth, the central point of all the spheres; but from the moment they had discovered the rotundity of our planet, the consequences of this first fact led them to other considerations, and from inference to inference they rose to the highest conceptions of astronomy and physics.

"In truth, having conceived the enlightened and simple idea, that the celestial globe is a small circle inscribed in the greater circle of the heavens, the theory of the concentral circles

circles naturally presented itself to their hypothesis, to resolve the unknown circle of the terrestrial globe by known points of the celestial circle; and the measure of one or several degrees of the meridian, gave precisely the total circumference. Then taking for compass the diameter of the earth, a fortunate genius described with auspicious boldness the immense orbits of the heavens; and, by an unheard of abstraction, man, who scarcely peoples the grain of sand of which he is the inhabitant, embraced the infinite distances of the stars, and launched himself into the abyss of space and duration. There a new order of the universe presented itself, of which the petty globe that he inhabited no longer appeared to him to be the center: this important part was transferred to the enormous mass of the sun, which became the inflamed pivot of eight circumjacent spheres, the movements of which were henceforward submitted to exact calculation.

"The human mind had already done a great deal, by undertaking to resolve the disposition and order of the great beings of nature; but not contented with this first effort, it wished

also

also to resolve its mechanism, and discover its origin and motive principle. And here it is that, involved in the abstract and metaphysical depths of motion and its first cause, of the inherent or communicated properties of matter, together with its successive forms and extent, or, in other words, of boundless space and time, these physiological divines lost themselves in a chaos of subtle argument and scholastic controversy.

"The action of the sun upon terrestrial bodies, having first led them to consider its substance as pure and elementary fire, they made it the focus and reservoir of an ocean of igneous and luminous fluid, which, under the name of ether, filled the universe, and nourished the beings contained therein. They afterwards discovered, by the analysis of a more accurate philosophy, this fire, or a fire similar to it, entering into the composition of all bodies, and perceived that it was the grand agent in that spontaneous motion, which in animals is denominated life, and in plants vegetation. From hence they were led to conceive of the mechanism and action of the universe, as of a homogeneous WHOLE,

a single

a single body, whose parts, however distant
in place, had a reciprocal connection with
each other (69); and of the world as a living
substance, animated by the organical circulation of an ingneous or rather electrical
fluid (70), which, by an analogy borrowed
from men and animals, was supposed to have
the sun for its heart (71).

" Meanwhile, among the theological philosophers, one sect beginning from these principles, the result of experiment, said: That
nothing was annihilated in the world; that
the elements were unperishable; that they
changed their combinations, but not their
nature; that the life and death of beings
were nothing more than the varied modifi-
cations of the same atoms; that matter contained in itself properties, which were the
cause of all its modes of existing; that the
world was eternal (72), having no bounds
either of space or duration. Others said:
That the whole universe was God; and, according to them, God was at once effect and
cause, agent and patient, moving principle
and thing moved, having for laws the invariable properties which constitute fatality;

and

and they defignated their idea fometimes by the emblem of PAN (the GREAT ALL); or of Jupiter, with a ftarry front, a planetary body, and feet of animals; or by the fymbol of the Orphic egg *, whofe yolk fufpended in the middle of a liquid encompaffed by a vault, reprefented the globe of the fun fwimming in ether in the middle of the vault of heaven (73); or by the emblem of a large round ferpent, figurative of the heavens, where they placed the firft princicle of motion, and for that reafon of an azure colour, ftudded with gold fpots (the ftars), and devouring his tail, that is, re-entering into himfelf, by winding continually like the revolutions of the fpheres; or by the emblem of a man, with his feet preffed and tied together to denote immutable exiftence, covered with a mantle of all colours, like the appearance of nature, and wearing on his head a fphere of gold (74), figurative of the fphere of the planets; or by that of another man fometimes feated upon the flower of *Lotos*, borne upon the abyfs of the waters, at others reclined upon

* Vide Œdip. Ægypt. tom. II. p. 205.

a pile

a pile of twelve cushions, signifying the twelve celestial signs. And this, O nations of India, Japan, Siam, Thibet, and China, is the theology, which, invented by the Egyptians, has, been transmitted down and preserved among yourselves, in the pictures you give of Brama, Beddou, Sommanacodom, and Omito. This, O ye Jews and Christians, is the counterpart of an opinion, of which you have retained a certain portion, when you describe God as *the breath of life moving upon the face of the waters*, alluding to the wind (75), which at the origin of the world, that is, at the departure of the spheres from the sign of the Crab, announced the overflowing of the Nile, and seemed to be the preliminary of creation."

SECT. VII. *Seventh System: Worship of the* SOUL *of the* WORLD, *that is, the element of fire, the vital principle of the universe.*

" BUT a third set of the theological philosophers, disgusted with the idea of a being at once effect and cause, agent and patient, and uniting in one and the same nature all contrary attributes, distinguished the moving principle from the thing moved; and laying it down as a datum that matter was in itself inert, they pretended that it received its properties from a distinct agent of which it was only the envelope or case. Some made this agent the igneous principle, the acknowledged author of all motion; others made it the fluid called ether, because it was thought to be more active and subtile: now, as they denominated the vital and motive principle in animals, a soul, a spirit; and as they always reasoned by comparison, and particularly by comparison with human existence, they gave to the motive principle of the whole universe the name of soul, intelligence, spirit; and God was the vital spirit, which, diffused through all beings, animated the vast body of the world. This idea was represented sometimes by You-piter, essence of motion and animation, principle of existence, or rather existence itself (76); at other times by Vulcan, or *Phtha*, elementary principle of fire, or by the altar of Vesta, placed centrally in her temple, like the sun in the spheres; and again by *Kneph*, a human being dressed in deep blue, holding in his hands a sceptre and a girdle (the Zodiac), wearing on his

his head a cap with feathers, to express the fugacity of thought, and producing from his mouth the great egg (77).

"As a consequence from this system, every being containing in itself a portion of the igneous or etherial fluid, the universal and common mover, and that fluid, soul of the world, being the Deity, it followed that the souls of all beings were a part of God himself, partaking of all his attributes, that is, being an indivisible, simple, and immortal substance; and hence is derived the whole system of the immortality of the soul, which at first was eternity (78). Hence also its transmigrations known by the name of metempsychosis, that is to say, passage of the vital principle from one body to another; an idea which sprung from the real transmigration of the material elements. Such, O Indians, Budsoists, Christians, Mussulmans, was the origin of all your ideas of the spirituality of the soul! Such was the source of the reveries of Pythagoras and Plato, your institutors, and who were themselves but the echoes of another, the last sect of visionary philosophers that it is necessary to examine.

T SECT.

SECT. VIII. *Eighth system: The world a machine: worship of the Demi-ourgos, or supreme artificer.*

"HITHERTO the theologians, in exercising their faculties on the detached and subtile substances of ether and the igneous principle, had not however ceased to treat of existences palpable and perceptible to the senses, and their theology had continued to be the theory of physical powers, placed sometimes exclusively in the stars, and sometimes disseminated through the universe. But at the period at which we are arrived, some superficial minds, losing the chain of ideas which had directed these profound enquiries, or ignorant of the facts which served as their basis, rendered abortive all the results that had been obtained from them, by the introduction of a strange and novel chimera. They pretended that the universe, the heavens, the stars, the sun, differed in no respect from an ordinary machine; and applying to this hypothesis a comparison drawn from the works of art, they erected an edifice of the most whimsical sophisms. "A machine," said

said they, "cannot form itself, there must be "a workman to construct it; its very exist- "ence implies this. The world is a machine: "it has therefore an artificer (79)."

"Hence the *Demi-ourgos*, or supreme artificer, the autocrator and sovereign of the universe. It was in vain that the ancient philosophy objected to the hypothesis, that this artificer did not stand in less need of parents and an author, and that a scheme, which added only one link to the chain by taking the attribute of eternity from the world and giving it to the creator, was of little value. These innovators, not contented with a first paradox, added a second, and applying to their artificer the theory of human understanding, pretended that the *Demi-ourgos* fashioned his machine upon an archetype or idea extant in his mind. In a word, just as their masters, the natural philosophers, had placed the *primum mobile* in the sphere of the fixed stars, under the appellation of intelligence and reason, so their apes, the spiritualists, adopting the same principle, made it an attribute of the *Demi-ourgos*, representing this being as a distinct substance, necessarily existing, to which they

they applied the terms of *Mens* or *Logos*, in other words, understanding and speech. Separately from this being, they held the existence of a solar principle, or soul of the world, which, taken with the preceding, made three gradations of divine personages; first, the *Demi-ourgos*, or supreme artificer; secondly, the *Logos*, understanding or speech; and thirdly, the spirit or soul of the world (80). And this, O Christians, is the fiction on which you have founded your doctrine of the Trinity; this is the system, which, born a Heretic in the Egyptian temples, transmitted a Heathen to the schools of Greece and Italy, is now Catholic or Orthodox by the conversion of its partisans, the disciples of Pythagoras and Plato, to Christianity.

" Thus the Deity, after having been originally considered as the sensible and various action of meteors and the elements; then as the combined power of the stars, considered in their relation to terrestrial objects; then as those terrestrial objects themselves, in consequence of confounding symbols with the things they represented; then as the complex power of Nature, in her two principal operations

operations of production and destruction; then as the animated world without distinction of agent and patient, cause and effect; then as the solar principle or element of fire acknowledged as the sole cause of motion—the Deity, I say, considered under all these different views, became at last a chimerical and abstract being; a scholastic subtlety of substance without form, of body without figure; a true delirium of the mind beyond the power of reason at all to comprehend. But in this its last transformation, it seeks in vain to conceal itself from the senses: the seal of its origin is indelibly stamped upon it. All its attributes, borrowed from the physical attributes of the universe, as immensity, eternity, indivisibility, incomprehensibleness; or from the moral qualities of man, as goodness, justice, majesty; and its very names (81), derived from the physical beings which were its types, particularly the sun, the planets, and the world, present to us continually, in spite of those who would corrupt and disguise it, infallible marks of its genuine nature.

"Such is the chain of ideas through which the

the human mind had already run at a period anterior to the positive recitals of history; and since their systematic form proves them to have been the result of one scene of study and investigation, every thing inclines us to place the theatre of investigation, where its primitive elements were generated, in Egypt. There their progress was rapid, because the idle curiosity of the theological philosophers had, in the retirement of the temples, no other food than the enigma of the universe, which was ever present to their minds; and because, in the political dissentions which long disunited that country, each state had its college of priests, who, being in turns auxiliaries or rivals, hastened by their disputes the progress of science and discovery (82).

" On the borders of the Nile there happened at that distant period, what has since been repeated all over the globe. In proportion as each system was formed, it excited by its novelty quarrels and schisms: then, gaining credit even by persecution, it either destroyed anterior ideas, or incorporated itself with and modified them. But political institutions

institutions taking place, all opinions, by the aggregation of states and mixture of different people, were at length confounded; and the chain of ideas being lost, theology, plunged in a chaos, became a mere logogryph of old traditions no longer understood. Religion, losing its object, was now nothing more than a political expedient by which to rule the credulous vulgar; and was embraced either by men credulous themselves and the dupes of their own visions, or by bold and energetic spirits, who formed vast projects of ambition."

SECT. IX. *Religion of Moses, or worship of the soul of the world (You-piter).*

"OF this latter description was the Hebrew legislator, who, desirous of separating his nation from every other, and of forming a distinct and exclusive empire, conceived the design of taking for its basis religious prejudices, and of erecting round it a sacred rampart of rites and opinions. But in vain did he proscribe the worship of symbols, the reigning religion, at that time, in Lower Egypt and Phenicia (83): his God was not on that account the less an Egyptian God, of the invention of those priests whose disciple Moses had been; and *Yahouh* (84), detected by his very name, which means essence of beings, and by his symbol, the fiery bush, is nothing more than the soul of the world, the principle of motion, which Greece shortly after adopted under the same denomination in her *You-piter*, generative principle, and under that of *Ei*, existence (85); which the Thebans consecrated by the name of *Kneph*; which Sais worshipped under the emblem of *Isis veiled*, with this inscription, *I am all that has been, all that is, and all that will be, and no mortal has drawn aside my veil*; which Pythagoras honoured under the appellation of *Vesta*, and which the Stoic philosophy defined with precision, by calling it the principle of fire. In vain did Moses wish to blot from his religion whatever could bring to remembrance the worship of the stars; a multiplicity of traits in spite of his exertions still remained to point it out: the seven lamps of the great candlestick, the twelve stones or signs of the Urim of the high-priest, the feast of the two equinoxes, each of which at that

that epocha formed a year, the ceremony of the lamb or celestial ram, then at its fifteenth degree; lastly, the name of Osiris even preserved in his song (86), and the ark or coffer, an imitation of the tomb in which that God was inclosed; all these remain to bear record to the genealogy of his ideas, and their derivation from the common source."

SECT. X. *Religion of Zoroaster.*

"ZOROASTER was also a man of the same bold and energetic stamp, who, five centuries after Moses, and in the time of David, revived and moralized among the Medes and Bactrians the whole Egyptian system of Osiris, under the names of Ormuzd and Ahrimanes. He called the reign of summer, virtue and good; the reign of winter, sin and evil; the renovation of nature in spring, creation; the revival of the spheres in the secular periods of the conjunction, resurrection; and his future life, hell, paradise, were the Tartarus and Elysium of the ancient astrologers and geographers; in a word, he only consecrated the already existing reveries of the mystic system."

SECT.

Sect. XI. *Budoism, or religion of the Samaneans.*

In the same rank must be included the promulgators of the sepulchral doctrine of the Samaneans, who, on the basis of the metempsychosis, raised the misanthropic system of self-renunciation and denial, who, laying it down as a principle, that the body is only a prison where the soul lives in impure confinement; that life is but a dream, an illusion, and the world a place of passage to another country, to a life without end; placed virtue and perfection in absolute insensibility, in the abnegation of physical organs, in the annihilation of all being: whence resulted the fasts, penances, macerations, solitude, contemplations, and all the deplorable practices of the mad-headed Anchorets."

Sect. XII. *Braminism, or the Indian system.*

" Finally, of the same cast were the founders of the Indian system, who, refining after Zoroaster upon the two principles of creation and destruction, introduced an intermediate one, that of conservation, and upon their trinity in unity, of Brama, Chiven, and Bichenou,

Bichenou, accumulated a multitude of traditional allegories, and the alembicated subtleties of their metaphysics."

"These are the materials which, scattered through Asia, there existed for many ages, when, by a fortuitous course of events and circumstances, new combinations of them were introduced on the banks of the Euphrates, and on the shores of the Mediterranean."

SECT. XIII. *Christianity, or the allegorical worship of the Sun, under the cabalistical names of* CHRIS-EN *or* CHRIST, *and* YÊS-US *or* JESUS.

"IN constituting a separate people, Moses had vainly imagined that he should guard them from the influence of every foreign idea: but an invincible inclination, founded on affinity of origin, continually called back the Hebrews to the worship of the neighbouring nations; and the relations of commerce that necessarily subsisted between them, tended every day to strengthen the propensity. While the Mosaic institution maintained its ground, the coercion of government and the laws, was a considerable obstacle to the inlet of innovations; yet even then the principal places were full of idols, and God the sun had his chariot and horses painted in the palaces of kings, and in the very temple of Yahouh: but when the conquests of the kings of Nineveh and Babylon had dissolved the bands of public power, the people left to themselves, and solicited by their conquerors, no longer kept a restraint on their inclinations, and profane opinions were openly professed in Judea. At first the Assyrian colonies, placed in the situation of the old tribes, filled the kingdom of Samaria with the dogmas of the Magi, which soon penetrated into Judea. Afterwards Jerusalem having been subjugated, the Egyptians, Syrians and Arabs, entering this open country, introduced their tenets, and the religion of Moses thus underwent a second alteration. In like manner the priests and great men, removing to Babylon, and educated in the science of the Chaldeans, imbibed, during a residence of seventy years, every principle of their theology, and from that moment the dogmas of the evil Genius (Satan), of the archangel Michael (87), of the Ancient of Days

Days (Ormuzd), of the rebellious angels, the celeſtial combats, the immortality of the ſoul, and the reſurrection, dogmas unknown to Moſes, or rejected by him, ſince he obſerves a perfect ſilence reſpecting them, became naturalized among the Jews.

"On their return to their country, the emigrants brought back with them theſe ideas; and at firſt the innovations occaſioned diſputes between their partiſans, the Phariſees, and the adherents to the ancient national worſhip, the Sadducees: but the former, ſeconded by the inclination of the people, and the habits they had already contracted, and ſupported by the authority of the Perſians, their deliverers, finally gained the aſcendancy, and the theology of Zoroaſter was conſecrated by the children of Moſes (88).

"A fortuitous analogy between two leading ideas, proved particularly favourable to this coalition, and formed the baſis of a laſt ſyſtem, not leſs ſurpriſing in its fortune than in the cauſes of its formation.

"From the time that the Aſſyrians had deſtroyed the kingdom of Samaria, ſome ſa-
gacious

gacious spirits foresaw, announced, and predicted the same fate to Jerusalem: and all their predictions were stamped by this particularity, that they always concluded with prayers for a happy re-establishment and regeneration, which were in like manner spoken of in the way of prophesies. The enthusiasm of the Hierophants had figured a royal deliverer, who was to re-establish the nation in its ancient glory: the Hebrews were again to become a powerful and conquering people, and Jerusalem the capital of an empire that was to extend over the whole world.

" Events having realized the first part of those predictions, the ruin of Jerusalem, the people clung to the second with a firmness of belief proportioned to their misfortunes; and the afflicted Jews waited with the impatience of want and of desire for that victorious king and deliverer that was to come, in order to save the nation of Moses, and restore the throne of David.

" The sacred and mythological traditions of precedent times had spread over all Asia a tenet perfectly analogous. A great mediator, a final judge, a future saviour, was spoken of, who,

who, as king, God, and victorious legiflator, was to reftore the golden age upon earth (89), to deliver the world from evil, and regain for mankind the reign of good, the kingdom of peace and happinefs. Thefe ideas and expreffions were in every mouth, and they confoled the people under that deplorable ftate of real fuffering into which they had been plunged by fucceffive conquefts and conquerors, and the barbarous defpotifm of their governments. This refemblance between the oracles of different nations and the predictions of the prophets, excited the attention of the Jews; and the prophets had doubtlefs been careful to infufe into their pictures, the fpirit and ftyle of the facred books employed in the Pagan myfteries. The arrival of a great ambaffador, of a final faviour, was therefore the general expectation in Judea, when at length a fingular circumftance was made to determine the precife period of his coming.

"It was recorded in the facred books of the Perfians and the Chaldeans, that the world, compofed of a total revolution of twelve thoufand periods, was divided into two

two partial revolutions, of which one, the age and reign of good, was to terminate at the expiration of six thousand, and the other, the age and reign of evil, at the expiration of another six thousand.

"Their first authors had meant by these recitals, the annual revolution of the great celestial orb (a revolution composed of twelve months or signs each divided into a thousand parts), and the two systematic periods of winter and summer, each consisting equally of six thousand. But these equivocal expressions having been erroneously explained, and having received an absolute and moral, instead of their astrological and physical sense, the result was, that the annual was taken for a secular world, the thousand periods for a thousand years; and judging, from the appearance of things, that the present was the age of misfortune, they inferred that it would terminate at the expiration of the six thousand pretended years (90).

"Now, according to the Jewish computation, six thousand years had already nearly elapsed since the supposed creation of the world (91). This coincidence produced
considerable

considerable fermentation in the minds of the people. Nothing was thought of but the approaching termination. The Hierophants were interrogated, and their sacred books examined. The great Mediator and final Judge was expected, and his advent desired, that an end may be put to so many calamities. This was so much the subject of conversation, that some one was said to have seen him, and a rumour of this kind was all that was wanting to establish a general certainty. The popular report became a demonstrated fact; the imaginary being was realized; and all the circumstances of mythological tradition being in some manner connected with this phantom, the result was an authentic and regular history, which from henceforth it was blasphemy to doubt.

"In this mythological history the following traditions were recorded: " That, " *in the beginning, a man and a woman had,* " *by their fall, brought sin and evil into the* " *world.*" (Examine plate II.)

" By this was denoted the astronomical fact of the celestial Virgin, and the herdsman (Bootes)

(Bootes) who, setting heliacally at the autumnal equinox, resigned the heavens to the wintry constellations, and seemed, in sinking below the horizon, to introduce into the world the genius of evil, Ahrimanes, represented by the constellation of the Serpent (92.)

" *That the woman had decoyed and seduced*
" *the man* (93.)."

" And in reality, the Virgin setting first, appears to draw the Herdsman (Bootes) after her.

" *That the woman had tempted him, by*
" *offering him fruit pleasant to the sight and*
" *good for food, which gave the knowledge of*
" *good and evil.*"

" Manifestly alluding to the Virgin, who is depicted holding a bunch of fruit in her hand, which she appears to extend towards the Herdsman: in like manner the branch, emblem of autumn, placed in the picture of Mithra (94) on the front of winter and summer, seems to open the door, and to give the knowledge, the key, of good and evil.

" *That this couple had been driven from the*
" *celestial garden, and that a cherub with a*
" *flaming*

" flaming sword had been placed at the door to
" guard it."

" And when the Virgin and the Herdsman sink below the Western horizon, Perseus rises on the opposite side (95), and sword in hand, this Genius may be said to drive them from the summer heaven, the garden and reign of fruits and flowers.

" *That from this virgin would be born,*
" *would spring up a shoot, a child, that should*
" *crush the serpent's head, and deliver the*
" *world from sin.*"

" By this was denoted the Sun, which, at the period of the summer solstice, at the precise moment that the Persian Magi drew the horoscope of the new year, found itself in the bosom of the Virgin, and which, on this account, was represented in their astrological pictures in the form of an infant suckled by a chaste virgin (96), and afterwards became, at the vernal equinox the Ram or Lamb, conqueror of the constellation of the Serpent, which disappeared from the heavens.

" *That in his infancy, this restorer of the*
" *divine*

"*divine or celestial nature, would lead a mean,*
"*humble, obscure and indigent life.*"

"By which was meant, that the winter sun was humbled, depressed below the horizon, and that this first period of his four ages, or the seasons, was a period of obscurity and indigence, of fasting and privation.

"*That being put to death by the wicked, he* "*would gloriously rise again, ascend from hell* "*into heaven, where he would reign for* "*ever.*"

"By these expressions was described the life of the same Sun, who, terminating his career at the winter solstice, when Typhon and the rebellious angels exercised their sway, seemed to be put to death by them; but shortly after revived and rose again (97) in the firmament, where he still remains.

"These traditions went still farther, specifying his astrological and mysterious names, maintaining that he was called sometimes *Chris* or Conservator (98); and hence the Hindoo God, *Chris-en*, or *Christna*; and the Christian *Chris-tos*, the son of Mary. That at other times he was called *Yés*, by the union

union of three letters, which, according to their numerical value, form the number 608, one of the folar periods (99). And behold, O Europeans, the name which, with a Latin termination has become your *Yés-us* or Jefus; the ancient and cabaliftical name given to young Bacchus, the clandeftine fon of the virgin Minerva, who in the whole hiftory of his life, and even in his death, calls to mind the hiftory of the God of the Chriftians; that is, the ftar of day, of which they are both of them emblems."

At thefe words a violent murmur arofe on the part of the Chriftian groupes; but the Mahometans, the Lamas and the Hindoos having called them to order, the orator thus concluded his difcourfe.

"You are not to be told," faid he, "in what manner the reft of this fyftem was formed in the chaos and anarchy of the three firft centuries; how a multiplicity of opinions divided the people, all of which were embraced with equal zeal and retained with equal obftinacy, becaufe alike founded on ancient tradition, they were alike facred. You know how, at the end of three centuries,

turies, government having espoused one of these sects, made it the orthodox religion; that is to say, the predominant religion, to the exclusion of the rest, which, on account of their inferiority, were denominated heresies; how, and by what means of violence and seduction this religion was propagated and gained strength, and afterwards became divided and weakened; how, six centuries after the innovation of Christianity, another system was formed out of its materials and those of the Jews, and a political and theological empire was created by Mahomet at the expence of that of Moses and the vicars of Jesus.

"Now, if you take a retrospect of the whole history of the spirit of religion, you will find, that in its origin it had no other author than the sensations and wants of man: that the idea of God had no other type, no other model, than that of physical powers, material existences, operating good or evil, by impressions of pleasure or pain on sensible beings. You will find that in the formation of every system, this spirit of religion pursued the same track, and was uniform

form in its proceedings; that in all, the dogma never failed to represent, under the name God, the operations of nature, and the passions and prejudices of men; that in all, morality had for its sole end, desire of happiness and aversion to pain; but that the people and the majority of legislators, ignorant of the true road that led thereto, invented false, and therefore contrary ideas of virtue and vice, of good and evil; that is, of what renders man happy or miserable. You will find, that in all, the means and causes of propagation and establishment exhibited the same scenes, the same passions, and the same events, continual disputes about words, false pretexts for inordinate zeal, for revolutions, for wars, lighted up by the ambition of chiefs, by the chicanery of promulgators, by the credulity of proselytes, by the ignorance of the vulgar, and by the grasping cupidity and the intolerant pride of all. In short, you will find that the whole history of the spirit of religion, is merely that of the fallibility and uncertainty of the human mind, which, placed in a world that it does not comprehend, is yet desirous of solving the enigma; and which, the astonished spectator of this mysterious and visible prodigy, invents causes, supposes ends, builds systems; then, finding one defective, abandons it for another not less vicious; hates the error that it has renounced, is ignorant of the new one that it adopts; rejects the truth of which it is in pursuit, invents chimeras of heterogeneous and contradictory beings, and, ever dreaming of wisdom and happiness, loses itself in a labyrinth of torments and illusions."

CHAP. XXIII.

END OF ALL RELIGIONS THE SAME.

Thus spoke the orator, in the name of those who had made the origin and genealogy of religious ideas their peculiar study.

The theologians of the different systems now expressed their opinions of this discourse. " It is an impious representation," said some, " which aims at nothing less than the sub- " version of all belief, the introducing in- " subordination into the minds of men, and " annihilating our power and ministry."— " It is a romance," said others, " a tissue of " conjectures, fabricated with art, but desti- " tute of foundation."—The moderate and prudent said, " Supposing all this to be true, " where is the use of revealing these myste- " ries? Our opinions are doubtless pervaded " with errors, but those errors are a neces- " sary curb on the multitude. The world " has gone on thus for two thousand years; " why should we now alter its course?"

The murmur of disapprobation, which never fails to arise against every kind of innovation, already began to increase, when a numerous groupe of plebeians and untaught men of every country and nation, without prophets, without doctors, without religious worship, advancing in the sand, attracted the attention of the whole assembly; and one of them, addressing himself to the legislators, spoke as follows:

"Mediators and umpires of nations! The strange recitals that have been made during the whole of the present debate, we never till this day heard of; and our understanding, astonished and bewildered at such a multitude of doctrines, some of them learned, others absurd, and all unintelligible, remains in doubt and uncertainty. One reflection however has struck us: in reviewing so many prodigious facts, so many contradictory assertions, we could not avoid asking ourselves, Of what importance to us are all these discussions? Where is the necessity of our knowing what happened five or six thousand years ago, in countries of which we are ignorant, among men who will ever be be unknown to us? True or false, of what importance is it to us to know whether the world has existed six thousand years or twenty thousand; whether it was made of something or of nothing; of itself, or by an artificer, equally in his turn requiring an author? What! uncertain as we are of what is passing around us, shall we pretend to ascertain what is transacting in the sun, the moon, and imaginary spaces? Having forgotten our own infancy, shall we pretend to know the infancy of the world? Who can attest what he has never seen? Who can certify the truth of what no one comprehends?

"Beside, what will it avail as to our existence, whether we believe or reject these chimeras? Hitherto neither our fathers nor ourselves have had any idea of them, and yet we do not perceive that on that account we have experienced more or less sun, more or less subsistence, more or less good or evil.

"If the knowledge of these things be necessary, how is it that we have lived as happily without it as those whom it has so much disquieted? If it be superfluous, why should we now take upon ourselves the burthen?"

then?"—Then addressing himself to the doctors and theologians: "How can it be required of us, poor and ignorant as we are, whose every moment is scarcely adequate to the cares of our subsistence and the labours of which you reap the profit; how can it be required of us to be versed in the numerous histories you have related, to read the variety of books which you have quoted, and to learn the different languages in which they are written? If our lives were protracted to a thousand years, scarcely would it be sufficient for this purpose."

"It is not necessary," said the doctors, "that you should acquire all this science: we possess it in your stead."

"Meanwhile," replied these children of simplicity, "with all your science, do you agree among yourselves? What then is its utility? Besides, how can you answer for us? If the faith of one man may be the substitute of the faith of many, what need was there that you should believe? Your fathers might believe for you; and that would have been the more reasonable, since they were the eye-witnesses upon whose credit you depend. Lastly, what is this circumstance

circumstance which you call belief if it has no practical tendency? And what practical tendency can you discover in this question, whether the world be eternal or no?"

"To believe wrong respecting it would be offensive to God," said the doctors.

"How do you know that?" cried the children of simplicity?

"From our scriptures," replied the doctors.

"We do not understand them," rejoined the simple men.

"We understand them for you," said the doctors.

"There lies the difficulty," resumed the simple men. "By what right have you appointed yourselves mediators between God and us?"

"By the command of God," said the doctors.

"Give us the proof of that command," said the simple men.

"It is in our scriptures," said the doctors.

"We do not understand them," answered the simple men; nor can we understand how a just God can place you over our heads. Why does our common Father require us to believe the same propositions with a less degree of evidence? He has spoken to you; be it so; he is infallible, he cannot deceive you. But we are spoken to by you; and who will assure us that you are not deceived, or that you are incapable of deceiving? If we are mistaken, how can it consist with the justice of God, to condemn us for the neglect of a rule with which we were never acquainted?"

"He has given you the law of nature," said the doctors.

"What is the law of nature?" said the simple men. "If this law be sufficient, why does he give us another? If it be insufficient, why did he give us that?"

"The judgments of God," replied the doctors, "are mysterious; his justice is not restrained by the rules of human justice."

"If justice with him and with us," said the simple men, "mean a different thing, what criterion can we have to judge of his justice? And once more, to what purpose all these laws? What end does he propose by them?"

"To render you more happy," replied a doctor, "by rendering you better and more virtuous.

virtuous. God has manifested himself by so many oracles and prodigies to teach mankind the proper use of his benefits, and to dissuade them from injuring each other."

"If that be the case," said the simple men, "the studies and reasonings you told us of are unnecessary: we want nothing but to have it clearly made out to us, which is the religion that best fulfils the end that all propose to themselves."

Instantly, every groupe boasting of the superior excellence of its morality, there arose among the partisans of the different systems of worship, a new dispute more violent than any preceding one. "Ours," said the Mahometans, "is the purest morality, which teaches every virtue useful to men and acceptable to God. We profess justice, disinterestedness, resignation, charity, almsgiving, and devotion. We torment not the soul with superstitious fears; we live free from alarm, and we die without remorse."

"And have you the presumption," replied the Christian priests, "to talk of morality; you whose chief has practised licentiousness, and preached doctrines that are a scandal to all purity, and the leading principle of

whose religion is homicide and war. For
the truth of this we appeal to experience.
For twelve centuries past your fanaticism
has never ceased to spread desolation and
carnage through the nations of the earth;
and that Asia, once so flourishing, now
languishes in insignificance and barbarism,
is ascribable to your doctrine; to that doctrine, the friend of ignorance, the enemy
of all instruction, which, on the one hand,
consecrating the most absolute despotism
in him who commands, and on the other,
imposing the most blind and passive obedience on those who are governed, has be-
numbed all the faculties of man, and plunged nations in a state of brutality.

"How different is the case with our sublime
and celestial morality! It is she that drew
the earth from its primitive barbarity, from
the absurd and cruel superstitions of idolatry,
from human sacrifices (100), and the orgies
of Pagan mystery: it is she that has purified
the manners of men, proscribed incest and
adultery, polished savage nations, abolished
slavery, introduced new and unknown virtues
to the world, universal charity, the equality

of

of mankind in the eyes of God, forgiveness and forgetfulness of injuries, extinction of the passions, contempt of worldly greatness, and, in short, taught the necessity of a life perfectly holy and spiritual."

"We admire," said the Mahometans, "the ease with which you can reconcile that evangelical charity and meekness of which you so much boast, with the injuries and outrages that you are continually exercising towards your neighbour. When you criminate with so little ceremony the morals of the great character revered by us, we have a fair opportunity of retorting upon you in the conduct of him whom you adore: but we disdain such advantages, and, confining ourselves to the real object of the question, we maintain, that your gospel morality is by no means characterised by the perfection which you ascribe to it. It is not true, that it has introduced into the world new and unknown virtues: for example, the equality of mankind in the eyes of God, and the fraternity and benevolence which are the consequence of this equality, were tenets formerly professed by the sect of Hermetics and Samaneans (101), from whom you have your descent. As to forgiveness of injuries, it had been taught by the Pagans themselves; but in the latitude you give to it, it ceases to be a virtue, and becomes an immorality and a crime. Your boasted precept, *to him that strikes thee on thy right cheek turn the other also*, is not only contrary to the feelings of man, but a flagrant violation of every principle of justice; it emboldens the wicked by impunity, degrades the virtuous by the servility to which it subjects them; delivers up the world to disorder and tyranny, and dissolves the bands of society: such is the true spirit of your doctrine. The precepts and parables of your gospel also never represent God other than as a despot, acting by no rule of equity; than as a partial father, treating a debauched and prodigal son with greater favour than his obedient and virtuous children; than as a capricious master, giving the same wages to him who has wrought but one hour, as to those who have borne the burthen and heat of the day, and preferring the last comers to the first. In short, your morality throughout is unfriendly to human intercourse,

intercourse, a code of misanthropy, calculated to give men a disgust for life and society, and attach them to solitude and celibacy.

"With respect to the manner in which you have practised your boasted doctrine, we in our turn appeal to the testimony of fact, and ask: Was it your evangelical meekness and forbearance which excited those endless wars among your sectaries, those atrocious persecutions of what you called heretics, those crusades against the Arians, the Manicheans and the Protestants; not to mention those which you have committed against us, nor the sacrilegious associations still subsisting among you, formed of men who have sworn to perpetuate them *? Was it the charity of your gospel that led you to exterminate whole nations in America, and to destroy the empires of Mexico and Peru; that makes you still desolate Africa, the inhabitants of which you sell like cattle, notwithstanding the abolition of slavery that you pretend your religion has effected; that makes you ravage

* The Oath taken by the Knights of the Order of Malta, is to kill, or make the Mahometans prisoners, for the glory of God.

India whose domains you usurp; in short, is it charity that has prompted you for three centuries past to disturb the peaceable inhabitants of three continents, the most prudent of whom, those of Japan and China, have been constrained to banish you from their country, that they might escape your chains and recover their domestic tranquillity?"

Here the Bramins, the Rabbins, the Bonzes, the Chamans, the priests of the Molucca Islands and of the coast of Guinea, overwhelming the Christian doctors with reproaches, cried: "Yes, these men are robbers and hypocrites, preaching simplicity to enveigle confidence; humility, the more easy to enslave; poverty, in order to appropriate all riches to themselves; they promise another world the better to invade this; and, while they preach toleration and charity, they commit to the flames, in the name of God, those who do not worship him exactly as they do."

"Lying priests," retorted the missionaries, "it is you who abuse the credulity of ignorant nations, that you may bend them to your yoke: your ministry is the art of imposture and deception: you have made religion a system of avarice and cupidity: you feign to have correspondence with spirits, and the oracles they issue are your own wills; you pretend to read the stars, and your desires only are what destiny decrees: you make idols speak, and the Gods are the mere instruments of your passions: you have invented sacrifices and libations for the sake of the profit you would thus derive from the milk of the flocks, and the flesh and fat of victims; and under the cloak of piety you devour the offerings made to Gods who cannot eat, and the substance of the people, obtained by industry and toil."

"And you," replied the Bramins, the Bonzes, and the Chamans, "sell to the credulous survivor vain prayers for the souls of his dead relatives. With your indulgences and absolutions you have arrogated to yourselves the power and functions of God himself: and making a traffic of his grace, you have put heaven up to auction, and have founded, by your system of expiation, a tariff of crimes that has perverted the consciences of men (102)."

"Add

"Add to this," said the Imans, "that with these men has originated the most insidious of all wickedness, the absurd and impious obligation of recounting to them the most impenetrable secrets of actions, of thoughts, of *velléités*, (confession); by means of which their insolent curiosity has carried its inquisition even to the sacred sanctuary of the nuptial bed (103), and the inviolable asylum of the heart."

By thus reproaching each other, the chiefs of the different worships revealed all the crimes of their ministry, all the hidden vices of their profession, and it appeared that the spirit, the system of conduct, the actions and manners of priests were, among all nations, uniformly the same: that, every where they had formed secret associations, corporations of individuals, enemies to the rest of the society (104) :— that they had attributed to themselves certain prerogatives and immunities, in order to be exempt from the burthens which fell upon the other classes:—that they shared neither the toil of the labourer, nor the perils of the soldier, nor the vicissitudes of the merchant:—that they led a life of celibacy,

to avoid domestic inconveniences and cares:
—that, under the garb of poverty, they found
the secret of becoming rich, and of procuring
every enjoyment:—that under the name of
mendicants, they collected imposts more considerable than those paid to princes:—that
under the appellation of gifts and offerings,
they obtained a certain revenue unaccompa-
nied with trouble or expence:—that upon
the pretext of seclusion and devotion, they
lived in indolence and licentiousness:—
that they had made alms a virtue, that they
might subsist in comfort upon the labour of
other men:—that they had invented the ceremonies of worship to attract the reverence
of the people, calling themselves the mediators and interpreters of the Gods, with the
sole view of assuming all his power; and that
for this purpose, according to the knowledge
or ignorance of those upon whom they had
to work, they made themselves, by turns,
astrologers, casters of planets, augurers, magicians (106), necromancers, quacks, courtiers, confessors of princes, always aiming at
influence for their own exclusive advantage:
—that sometimes they had exalted the prerogative

rogative of kings, and held their persons to be sacred, to obtain their favour or participate in their power:—that at others they had decried this doctrine and preached the murder of tyrants (reserving it to themselves to specify the tyranny), in order to be revenged of the slights and disobedience they had experienced from them:—that at all times they had called by the name of impiety what proved injurious to their interest; had opposed public instruction, that they might monopolize science; and, in short, had universally found the secret of living in tranquillity amidst the anarchy they occasioned; secure, under the despotism they sanctioned; in indolence, amidst the industry they recommended; and in abundance, in the very bosom of scarcity; and all this, by carrying on the singular commerce of selling words and gestures to the credulous, who paid for them as for commodities of the greatest value (107).

Then the people, seized with fury, were upon the point of tearing to pieces the men who had deceived them; but the legislators, arresting this sally of violence, and addressing the chiefs and doctors, said: "And is it thus,

O in-

O institutors of the people, that you have misled and abused them?"

And the terrified priests replied: " O legislators, we are men, and the people are so superstitious! their weakness excited us to take advantage of it *."

And the kings said: " O legislators, the people are so servile and so ignorant! they have prostrated themselves before the yoke which we scarcely had the boldness to show to them †."

Then the legislators, turning towards the people, said to them: " Remember what you have just heard; it contains two important truths. Yes, it is yourselves that cause the evils of which you complain; it is you that encourage tyrants by a base flattery of their power, by an absurd admiration of their pretended beneficence, by converting obedience into servility, and liberty into licentiousness, and receiving every imposition with credulity.

---

* Consider in this view the Brabanters.

† The inhabitants of Vienna, for example, who harnessed themselves like cattle, and drew the chariot of Leopold.

Can you think of punishing upon them the errors of your own ignorance and selfishness?"

And the people, smitten with confusion, remained in a melancholy silence.

CHAP. XXIV.

SOLUTION OF THE PROBLEM OF CONTRADICTIONS.

The legiflators then refumed their addrefs. "O nations!" faid they, "we have heard the difcuffion of your opinions; and the difcord that divides you has fuggefted to us various reflections, which we beg leave to propofe to you as queftions which it is neceffary you fhould folve.

"Confidering, in the firft place, the numerous and contradictory creeds you have adopted, we would afk on what motives your perfuafion is founded? Is it from deliberate choice that you have enlifted under the banners of one prophet rather than under thofe of another? Before you adopted this doctrine in preference to that, did you firft compare, did you maturely examine them? Or has not your belief been rather the chance refult of birth, and of the empire of education and habit? Are you not

not born Christians on the banks of the
Tiber, Mahometans on those of the Euphrates, Idolaters on the shores of India, in
the same manner as you are born fair in
cold and temperate regions, and of a sable
complexion under the African sun! And if
your opinions are the effect of your position
on the globe, of parentage, of imitation, are
such fortuitous circumstances to be regarded as grounds of conviction and arguments
of truth?

"In the second place, when we reflect
on the proscriptive spirit and the arbitrary
intolerance of your mutual claims, we are
terrified at the consequences that flow from
your principles. Nations! who reciprocally
doom each other to the thunder-bolts of
celestial wrath, suppose the universal Being,
whom you revere, were at this moment to
descend from heaven among this crowd of
people, and, clothed in all his power, were
to sit upon this throne to judge you: suppose
him to say—" Mortals! I consent to adopt
" your own principles of justice into my ad-
" ministration. Of all the different reli-
" gions you profess, a single religion shall
" now

"now be preferred to the rest; all the others,
"this vast multitude of standards, of nations,
"of prophets, shall be condemned to ever-
"lasting destruction. Nor is this enough:
"among the different sects of the chosen re-
"ligion one only shall experience my favour,
"and the rest be condemned. I will go
"farther than this: of this single sect of
"this one religion, I will reject all the in-
"dividuals whose conduct has not corre-
"sponded to their speculative precepts. O
"man! few indeed will then be the number
"of the elect you assign me! Penurious
"hereafter will be the stream of beneficence
"which will succeed to my unbounded
"mercy? Rare and solitary will be the ca-
"talogue of admirers that you henceforth
"destine to my greatness and my glory."

And the legislators arising said: "It is enough; you have pronounced your will. Ye nations, behold the urn in which your names shall be placed; one single name shall be drawn from the multitude; approach and conclude this terrible lottery."—But the people, seized with terror, cried: "No, no; we are brethren and equals, we cannot consent to to condemn each other."—Then the legiſlators having reſumed their ſeats, continued: "O men! who diſpute upon ſo many ſubjects, lend an attentive ear to a problem we ſubmit to you, and decide it in the exerciſe of your own judgments."—The people accordingly lent the ſtricteſt attention; and the legiſlators lifting one hand towards heaven, and pointing to the ſun, ſaid: "O nations, is the form of this ſun which enlightens you triangular or ſquare?"—And they replied with one voice, "It is neither, it is round."

Then taking the golden balance that was upon the altar, "This metal," aſked the legiſlators, "which you handle every day, is a maſs of it heavier than another maſs of equal dimenſions of braſs?"—"Yes," the people again unanimouſly replied; "gold is heavier than braſs."

The legiſlators then took the ſword. "Is this iron leſs hard than lead?"—"No," ſaid the nations.

"Is ſugar ſweet and gall bitter?—"Yes."

"Do you love pleaſure, and hate pain?"—"Yes."

"Reſpecting theſe objects and a multiplicity

plicity of others of a similar nature, you have then but one opinion. Now tell us, is there an abyss in the centre of the earth, and are there inhabitants in the moon?"

At this question a general noise was heard, and every nation gave a different answer. Some replied in the affirmative, others in the negative; some said it was probable, others that it was an idle and ridiculous question, and others that it was a subject worthy of enquiry; in short there prevailed among them a total disagreement.

After a short interval, the legislators having restored silence: " Nations," said they, " how is this to be accounted for? We proposed to you certain questions, and you were all of one opinion without distinction of race or sect: fair or black, disciples of Mahomet or of Moses, worshippers of Bedou or of Jesus, you all gave the same answer. We now propose another question, and you all differ! whence this unanimity in one case, and this discordance in the other."

And the groupe of simple and untaught men replied: " The reason is obvious. Respecting the first questions, we see and feel

the

the objects; we speak of them from sensation: respecting the second, they are above the reach of our senses, and we have no guide but conjecture."

"You have solved the problem," said the legislators; "and the following truth is thus by your own confession established: Whenever objects are present and can be judged of by your senses, you invariably agree in opinion; and your differ in sentiment only when they are absent and out of your reach.

"From this truth flows another equally clear and deserving of notice. Since you agree respecting what you with certainty know, it follows, that when you disagree, it is because you do not know, do not understand, are not sure of the object in question: or in other words, that you dispute, quarrel and fight among yourselves, for what is uncertain, for that of which you doubt. But is this wise; is this the part of rational and intelligent beings?

"And is it not evident, that it is not truth for which you contend; that it is not her cause you are jealous of maintaining, but the cause of your own passions and prejudices;
that

that it is not the object as it really exists that you wish to verify, but the object as it appears to you; that it is not the evidence of the thing that you are anxious should prevail, but your personal opinion, your mode of seeing and judging? There is a power that you want to exercise, an interest that you want to maintain, a prerogative that you want to assume; in short, the whole is a struggle of vanity. And as every individual, when he compares himself with every other, finds himself to be his equal and fellow, he resists by a similar feeling of right; and from this right, which you all deny to each other, and from the inherent consciousness of your equality, spring your disputes, your combats and your intolerance.

" Now, the only way of restoring unanimity is by returning to nature, and taking the order of things which she has established for your director and guide; and this farther truth will then appear from your uniformity of sentiment:

" That real objects have in themselves an identical, constant, and invariable mode of existence, and that in your organs exists a similar

similar mode of being affected and impressed by them.

"But at the same time, inasmuch as these organs are liable to the direction of your will, you may receive different impressions, and find yourselves under different relations towards the same objects; so that you are with respect to them, as it were a sort of mirror, capable of reflecting them such as they are, and capable of disfiguring and misrepresenting them.

"As often as you perceive the objects, such as they are, your feelings are in accord with the objects, and you agree in opinion; and it is this accord that constitutes truth.

"On the contrary, as often as you differ in opinion, your dissentions prove that you do not see the objects such as they are, but vary them.

"Whence it appears, that the cause of your dissentions is not in the objects themselves, but in your minds, in the manner in which you perceive and judge.

"If therefore we would arrive at uniformity of opinion, we must previously establish certainty, and verify the resemblance

blance which our ideas have to their models. Now this cannot be obtained, except so far as the objects of our enquiry can be referred to the testimony and subjected to the examination of our senses. Whatever cannot be brought to this trial is beyond the limits of our understanding; we have neither rule to try it by, nor measure by which to institute a comparison, nor source of demonstration and knowledge concerning it.

"Whence it is obvious, that, in order to live in peace and harmony, we must consent not to pronounce upon such objects, nor annex to them importance; we must draw a line of demarcation between such as can be verified and such as cannot, and separate by an inviolable barrier, the world of fantastic beings from the world of realities: that is to say, all civil effect must be taken away from theological and religious opinions.

"This, O nations, is the end that a great people, freed from their fetters and prejudices, have proposed to themselves; this is the work in which, by their command, and under their immediate auspices, we were engaged,

gaged, when your kings and your priests came to interrupt our labours.... Kings and priests, you may yet for a while suspend the solemn publication of the laws of nature; but it is no longer in your power to annihilate or to subvert them."

A loud cry was then heard from every quarter of the general assembly of nations; and the whole of the people, unanimously testifying their adherence to the sentiments of the legislators, encouraged them to resume their sacred and sublime undertaking. "Investigate," said they, "the laws which nature, for our direction, has implanted in our breasts, and form from thence an authentic and immutable code. Nor let this code be calculated for one family, or one nation only, but for the whole without exception. Be the legislators of the human race, as ye are the interpreters of their common nature. Shew us the line that separates the world of chimeras, from that of realities; and teach us, after so many religions of error and delusion, the religion of evidence and truth."

Upon this, the legislators resuming their enquiry into the physical and constituent

attributes

attributes of man, and the motives and affections which govern him in his individual and social capacity, unfolded in the following terms the laws on which Nature herself has founded his felicity.

END OF THE FIRST PART.

NOTES.

Page 1. (*) *Eleventh year of Abd-ul Hâmid.* That is, 1784 of the Christian æra, and 1198 of the Hegira. The emigration of the Tartars took place in March, immediately on the manifesto of the empress declaring the Crimea to be incorporated with Russia.... *A Mussulman prince of the name of Gengis Khan.* It was Châhin Guerai. Gengis Khan was borne and served by the kings whom he conquered: Châhin, on the contrary, after selling his country for a pension of eighty thousand roubles, accepted the commission of captain of guards to Catherine II. He afterwards returned home, and, according to custom was strangled by the Turks.

Page 7. (a). *The precious thread of Serica.* That is the silk originally derived from the mountainous country where the *great wall* terminates, and which appears to have been the cradle of the Chinese empire.... The *tissues of Cassimere.* The shawls which Ezekiel seems to have described under the appellation of Choud-choud.... *The gold of Ophir.* This country, which was one of the twelve Arab cantons,

cantons, and which has so much and so unsuccessfully been sought for by the antiquaries, has left however some trace of itself in Ofor, in the province of Oman, upon the Persian Gulph, neighbouring on one side to the Sabeans, who are celebrated by Strabo for their plenty of gold, and on the other to Aula or Hevila where the pearl fishery was carried on. See the 27th chapter of Ezekiel, which gives a very curious and extensive picture of the commerce of Asia at that period.

Page 8. (*b*). *This Syria contained a hundred flourishing cities.* According to Josephus and Strabo, there were in Syria twelve millions of souls; and the traces that remain of culture and habitation confirm the calculation.

Page 12. (*c*). *A blind fatality.* This is the universal and rooted prejudice of the East. "It was written," is there the answer to every thing. Hence result an unconcern and apathy, the most powerful impediments to instruction and civilization.

Page 28. (*d*). *The too famous peninsula of India.* Of what real good has been the commerce of India to the mass of the people? On the contrary, how great the evil occasioned by the superstition of this country having been added to the general superstition?

Page 29. (*e*). *Ancient kingdom of Ethiopia.* In the next volume of the Encyclopedia will appear a memoir respecting the chronology of the twelve ages anterior to the passing of Xerxes into Greece, in which I conceive myself to have proved, that Upper Egypt formerly composed a distinct kingdom, known to the Hebrews by the name of *Kous*, and to which the appellation of Ethiopia was specially given. This kingdom preserved its independence to the time of Psammeticus, at which period, being united

united to the Lower Egypt, it lost its name of Ethiopia, which thenceforth was bestowed upon the nations of Nubia, and upon the different hordes of Blacks, including Thebes, their metropolis.

Page id. (*f*). *Thebes with its hundred palaces.* The idea of a city with a hundred gates, in the common acceptation of the word, is so absurd, that I am astonished the equivoque has not before been felt.

It has ever been the custom of the East to call palaces and houses of the great by the name of gates, because the principal luxury of these buildings consists in the singular gate leading from the street into the court, at the farthest extremity of which the palace is situated. It is under the vestibule of this gate that conversation is held with passengers, and a sort of audience and hospitality given. All this was doubtless known to Homer; but poets make no commentaries, and readers love the marvellous.

This city of Thebes, now Lougsor, reduced to the condition of a miserable village, has left astonishing monuments of its magnificence. Particulars of this may be seen in the plates of Norden, in Pocock, and in the recent travels of Bruce. These monuments give credibility to all that Homer has related of its splendour, and led us to infer of its political power and external commerce.

Its geographical position was favourable to this twofold object. For, on one side, the valley of the Nile, singularly fertile, must have early occasioned a numerous population; and, on the other, the Red Sea giving communication with Arabia and India, and the Nile with Abyssinia and the Mediterranean, Thebes was thus naturally allied to the richest countries on the globe; an

alliance

alliance that procured it an activity so much the greater, as Lower Egypt, at first a swamp, was nearly, if not totally, uninhabited. But when at length this country had been drained by the canals and dikes which Sesostris constructed, population was introduced there, and wars arose which proved fatal to the power of Thebes. Commerce then took another route, and descended to the point of the Red Sea, to the canals of Sesostris (See Strabo) and wealth and activity were transformed to Memphis. This is manifestly what Diodorus means, when he tells us (Lib. I. sect. 2.) that as soon as Memphis was established and made a wholesome and delicious abode, kings abandoned Thebes to fix themselves there. Thus Thebes continued to decline, and Memphis to flourish till the time of Alexander, who, building Alexandria on the border of the sea, caused Memphis to fall in its turn; so that prosperity and power seem to have descended historically step by step along the Nile: whence it results, both physically and historically, that the existence of Thebes was prior to that of the other cities. The testimony of writers is very positive in this respect. " The " Thebans," says Diodorus, " consider themselves as the " most ancient people of the earth, and assert, that with " them originated philosophy and the science of the " stars. Their situation, it is true, is infinitely favourable " to astronomical observation, and they have a more accu- " rate division of time into months and year than other " nations, &c."

What Diodorus says of the Thebans, every author and himself elsewhere, repeat of the Ethiopians, which tends more firmly to establish the identity of place of which I have spoken. " The Ethiopians conceive themselves (says

† " he

" he, Lib. III.) to be of greater antiquity than any other
" nation: and it is probable that, born under the sun's path,
" its warmth may have ripened them earlier than other
" men. They suppose themselves also to be the inventors
" of divine worship, of festivals, of solemn assemblies,
" of sacrifices, and every other religious practice. They
" affirm that the Egyptians are one of their colonies, and
" that the Delta, which was formerly sea, became land
" by the conglomeration of the earth of the higher
" country, which was washed down by the Nile. They
" have, like the Egyptians, two species of letters, hiero-
" glyphics and the alphabet; but among the Egyptians
" the first was known only to the priests, and by them
" transmitted from father to son, whereas both species are
" common among the Ethiopians."

" The Ethiopians," says Lucian, page 985, " were the
" first who invented the science of the stars, and gave
" names to the planets, not at random and without mean-
" ing, but descriptive of the qualities which they con-
" ceived them to possess; and it was from them that
" this art passed, still in an imperfect state, to the Egyp-
" tians."

It would be easy to multiply citations upon this subject; from all which it follows, that we have the strongest reason to believe that the country neighbouring to the tropic, was the cradle of the sciences, and of consequence that the first learned nation was a nation of Blacks, for it is incontrovertible, that by the term Ethiopians, the ancients meant to represent a people of black complexion, thick lips, and woolly hair. I am therefore inclined to believe, that the inhabitants of Lower Egypt were originally a foreign colony imported from Syria and Arabia, a

medley

medley of different tribes of Savages, originally shepherds and fishermen, who by degrees formed themselves into a nation, and who, by nature and descent, were enemies of the Thebans, by whom they were no doubt despised and treated as barbarians.

I have suggested the same ideas in my Travels into Syria, founded upon the black complexion of the Sphinx. I have since ascertained, that the antique images of Thebais have the same characteristic; and Mr. Bruce has offered a multitude of analogous facts: but this traveller, of whom I heard some mention at Cairo, has so interwoven these facts with certain systematic opinions, that we should have recourse to his narratives with caution.

It is singular that Africa, situated so near us, should be the country on earth which is the least known. The English are at this moment making attempts, the success of which ought to excite our emulation.

Page 30. (*g*). *Here were the ports of the Idumeans*, Ailah (Eloth), and Atsiom-Gaber (Hesion-Geber). The name of the first of these towns still subsists in its ruins, at the point of the gulph of the Red Sea, and in the route which the pilgrims take to Mecca. Hesion has at present no trace, any more than Qolzoum and Faran: it was, however, the harbour for the fleets of Solomon. The vessels of this prince, conducted by the Tyrians, sailed along the coast of Arabia to Ophir in the Persian Gulph, thus opening a communication with the merchants of India and Ceylon. That this navigation was entirely of Tyrian invention, appears both from the pilots and shipbuilders employed by the Jews, and the names that were given to the trading islands, viz. Tyrus and Aradus, now Barhain. The voyage was performed in two diffent modes, either in canoes of osier and rushes, covered on the outside with skins done over with pitch: these vessels were unable to quit the Red Sea, or so much as to leave the shore. The second mode of carrying on the trade was by means of vessels with decks of the size of our long boats, which were able to pass the strait and to weather the dangers of the ocean: but for this purpose it was necessary to bring the wood from Mount Lebanus and Cilicia, where it is very fine and in great abundance. This wood was first conveyed in floats from Tarsus to Phenicia, for which reason the vessels were called ships of Tarsus: from whence it has been ridiculously inferred, that they went round the promontary of Africa as far as Tortosa in Spain. From Phenicia it was transported on the backs of camels to the Red Sea, which practice still continues, because the shores of this sea are absolutely unprovided with wood even for fuel. These vessels spent a complete year in their voyage, that is, sailed one year, sojourned another, and did not return till the third. This tediousness was owing, first to their cruizing from port to port, as they do at present; secondly, to their being detained by the Monsoon currents; and thirdly, because, according to the calculations of Pliny and Strabo, it was the ordinary practice among the ancients to spend three years in a voyage of twelve hundred leagues. Such a commerce must have been very expensive, particularly as they were obliged to carry with them their provisions and even fresh water. For this reason Solomon made himself master of Palmyra, which was at that time inhabited, and was already the magazine and high road of merchants by the way of the Euphrates.

This

This conquest brought Solomon much nearer to the country of gold and pearls. This alternative of a route either by the Red Sea or by the river Euphrates was to the ancients, what in later times has been the alternative in a voyage to the Indies, either by crossing the Isthmus of Suez or doubling the Cape of Good Hope. It appears that till the time of Moses this trade was carried on across the desert of Syria and Theais; that afterwards it fell into the hands of the Phenicians, who fixed its site upon the Red sea, and that it was mutual jealousy that induced the kings of Nineveh and Babylon to undertake the destruction of Tyre and Jerusalem. I insist the more upon these facts, because I have never seen any thing reasonable upon the subject.

Page 31. (*h*). *Babylon, the ruins of which are trodden under foot of men.* It appears that Babylon occupied on the Eastern Bank of the Euphrates a space of ground six leagues in length. Throughout this space bricks are found, by means of which daily additions are made to the town of Hellé. Upon many of these are characters written with a nail similar to those of Persepolis. I am indebted for these facts to M. de Beauchamp, grand vicar of Babylon, a traveller equally distinguished for his knowledge of astronomy and his veracity.

Page 59. (*i*). *Those wells of Tyre.* See respecting these monuments, my Travels into Syria, vol. ii. p. 214.

Those artificial banks of the Euphrates. From the town or village of Samaouat the course of the Euphrates is accompanied with a double bank, which descends as far as its junction with the Tygris, and from thence to the sea, being a length of about a hundred leagues French measure. The heighth of these artificial banks is not uniform,

form, but increases as you advance from the sea; it may be estimated at from twelve to fifteen feet. But for them, the inundation of the river would bury the country around, which is flat, to an extent of twenty or twenty-five leagues; and even, notwithstanding these banks, there has been in modern times an overflow which has covered the whole triangle formed by the junction of this river to the Tigris, being a space of country of 130 square leagues. By the stagnation of these waters an epidemical disease of the most fatal nature was occasioned. It follows from hence, 1. That all the flat country bordering upon these rivers was originally a marsh; 2. That this marsh could not have been inhabited previously to the construction of the banks in question; 3. That these banks could not have been the work but of a population prior as to date: and the elevation of Babylon therefore must have been posterior to that of Nineveh, as I think I have chronologically demonstrated in the memoir above cited. See Encyclopedie, vol. xiii. of Antiquities.

Page id. (k). *Those conduits of Medea.* The modern Aderbidjan, which was a part of Medea, the mountains of Kourdestan, and those of Diarbekr, abound with subterranean canals, by means of which the ancient inhabitants conveyed water to their parched soil in order to fertilize it. It was regarded as a meritorious act, and a religious duty prescribed by Zoroaster, who, instead of preaching celibacy, mortifications, and other pretended virtues of the Monkish sort, repeats continually in the passages that are preserved respecting him in the Sad-der and the Zend-avesta, " That the action most pleasing to " God is to plough and cultivate the earth, to water it " with running streams, to multiply vegetation and living
" beings,

"beings, to have numerous flocks, young and fruitful "virgins, a multitude of children, &c. &c."

Page 62. *(l). This inequality, the result of accident, was taken for the law of nature.* Almost all the ancient philosophers and politicians have laid it down as a principle, that men are born unequal, that nature has created some to be free, and others to be slaves. Expressions of this kind are to be found in Aristotle, and even in **Plato**, called the divine, doubtless in the same sense as the mythological reveries which he promulgated. With all the people of antiquity, the Gauls, the Romans, the Athenians, the right of the strongest was the right of nations; and from the same principle are derived all the political disorders and public national crimes that at present exist.

Page id. *(m). Paternal tyranny laid the foundation of political despotism.* Upon this single expression it would be easy to write a long and important chapter. We might prove in it, beyond contradiction, that all the abuses of national governments have sprung from those of domestic government, from that government called patriarchal, which superficial minds have extolled without having analyzed it. Numberless facts demonstrate, that with every infant people, in every savage and barbarous state, the father, the chief of the family, is a despot, and a cruel and insolent despot. The wife is his slave, the children his servants. This king sleeps or smokes his pipe, while his wife and daughters perform all the drudgery of the house, and even that of tillage and cultivation, as far as occupations of this nature are practised in such societies; and no sooner have the boys acquired strength, than they are allowed to beat the females and make

make them serve and wait upon them as they do upon their fathers. Similar to this is the state of our own uncivilized peasants. In proportion as civilization spreads, the manners become milder, and the condition of the women improves, till, by a contrary excess, they arrive at dominion, and then a nation becomes effeminate and corrupt. It is remarkable, that parental authority is great according as the government is despotic. China, India, and Turkey are striking examples of this. One would suppose that tyrants gave themselves accomplices, and interested subaltern despots to maintain their authority. In opposition to this the Romans will be cited; but it remains to be proved that the Romans were men truly free; and their quick passage from their republican despotism to their abject servility under the emperors, gives room at least for considerable doubts as to that freedom.

Page 67. (n). *Always tending to concenter the power in a single hand.* It is remarkable, that this has in all instances been the constant progress of societies: beginning with a state of anarchy or democracy, that is, with a great division of power, they have passed to aristocracy, and from aristocracy to monarchy. Does it not hence follow, that those who constitute states under the democratic form, destine them to undergo all the intervening troubles between that and monarchy; and that the supreme administration by a single chief is the most natural government, as well as that best calculated for peace?

Page 69. (o). *And kings followed the dictates of every depraved taste.* It is equally worthy of remark, that the conduct and manners of princes and kings of every country and every age, are found to be precisely the same at

Z

similar

similar periods, whether of the formation or dissolution of empires. History every where presents the same pictures of luxury and folly; of parks, gardens, lakes, rocks, palaces, furniture, excess of the table, wine, women, concluding with brutality.

The absurd rock in the garden of Versailles has alone cost three millions. I have sometimes calculated what might have been done with the expence of the three pyramids of Gizah, and I have found that it would easily have constructed, from the Red Sea to Alexandria, a canal 150 feet wide and 30 deep, completely covered in with cut stones and a parapet, together with a fortified and commercial town, consisting of 400 houses furnished with cisterns. What difference in point of utility between such a canal and these pyramids?

Page 79. (*p*). *By their led horses, &c.* A Tartar horseman has always two horses, of which he leads one in hand. . . . The *Kalpak* is a bonnet made of the skin of a sheep or other animal. The part of the head covered by this bonnet is shaved, with the exception of a tuft about the size of a crown-piece, and which is suffered to grow to the length of seven or eight inches, precisely where our priests place their tonsure. It is by this tuft of hair, worn by the majority of Mussulmans, that the angel of the tomb is to take the elect and carry them into Paradise.

Page 80. (*q*). *Infidels are in possession of a consecrated land.* It is not in the power of the sultan to cede to a foreign power a province inhabited by TRUE BELIEVERS. The people, instigated by the lawyers, would not fail to revolt. This is one reason which has led those who know the

Turks,

Turks, to regard as chimerical the ceding of Candia, Cyprus, and Egypt, projected by certain European potentates.

Page 86. (r). *Pronouncing mysteriously the word Aûm.* This word is in the religion of the Hindoos a sacred emblem of the Divinity. It is only to be pronounced in secret, without being heard by any one. It is formed of three letters, of which the first, *a*, signifies the principle of all, the creator, Brama; the second, *u*, the conservator, Vichenou; and the last, *m*, the destroyer, who puts an end to all, Chiven. It is pronounced like the monosyllable ôm, and expresses the unity of those three Gods. The idea is precisely that of the Alpha and Omega mentioned in the New Testament.

Page id. (s). *Whether he ought to begin the ceremony at the elbow, &c.* This is one of the grand points of schism between the partizans of Omar and those of Ali. Suppose two Mahometans to meet on a journey, and to accost each other with brotherly affection: the hour of prayer arrives; one begins his ablution at his fingers, the other at the elbow, and instantly they are mortal enemies. O sublime importance of religious opinions! O profound philosophy of the authors of them!

Page 99. (t). *The horde of Oguzians.* Before the Turks took the name of their chief Othman I. they bore that of Oguzians; and it was under this appellation that they were driven out of Tartary by Gengis, and came from the borders of Gihoun to settle themselves in Anatolia.

Page 100. (u). *A general anarchy take place, as happened in the empire of the Sophis.* In Persia, after the death of Thamas-Koulikan, each province had its chief, and for

forty

forty years these chiefs were in a constant state of war. In this view the Turks do not say without reason: "Ten years of a tyrant are less destructive than a single night of anarchy."

Page 107. (x). *From people to people barbarous wars were prevalent.* Read the history of the wars of Rome and Carthage, of Sparta and Messina, of Athens and Syracuse, of the Hebrews and the Phenicians: yet these are the nations of which antiquity boasts as being most polished!

Page 114. (y). *The decision of their disputes.* What is a people? An individual of the society at large. What a war? A duel between two individual people. In what manner ought a society to act when two of its members fight? Interfere and reconcile, or repress them. In the days of the Abbe de Saint-Pierre this was treated as a dream, but happily for the human race it begins to be realized.

Page 119. (z). *The Chinese subjected to an insolent despotism.* The emperor of China calls himself the son of heaven, that is, of God; for in the opinion of the Chinese, the material heaven, the arbiter of fatality, is the Deity himself. "The emperor only shows himself once in ten months, lest the people, accustomed to see him, might lose their respect; for he holds it as a maxim, that power can only be supported by force, that the people have no idea of justice, and are not to be governed but by coercion." *Narrative of two Mahometan Travellers in* 851 *and* 877, translated by the Abbe Renaudot in 1718.

Notwithstanding what is asserted by the missionaries, this situation has undergone no change. The bamboo still reigns in China, and the son of heaven bastinades, for the moſt trivial fault, the Mandarin, who, in his turn, baſtinades the people. The Jeſuits may tell us that this is the beſt governed country in the world, and its inhabitants the happieſt of men: but a ſingle letter from Amyot has convinced me, that China is a truly Turkiſh government, and the account of Sonnerat confirms it. See Vol. II. of *Voyage aux Indes*, in 4to.

The irremediable vice of their language. As long as the Chineſe ſhall in writing make uſe of their preſent characters, they can be expected to make no progreſs in civilization. The neceſſary introductory ſtep muſt be the giving them an alphabet like our own, or the ſubſtituting in the room of their language that of the Tartars: the improvement made in the latter by M. de Lengles, is calculated to introduce this change. See the *Mantchou alphabet*, the production of a mind truly learned in the formation of language.

Page 119. (1.) *In the North I ſee nothing but ſerfs reduced to the level of cattle.* When this was written the revolution in Poland had not taken place. I beg leave to apologiſe to the virtuous nobles and the enlightened prince by whom it was effected.

Page 128. (2.) *And govern yourſelves.* This dialogue between the people and the indolent claſſes, is applicable to every ſociety; it contains the ſeeds of all the political vices and diſorders that prevail, and which may thus be defined; men who do nothing, and who devour the ſubſtance of others; and men who arrogate to themſelves particular rights and excluſive privileges of wealth and indolence. Compare the Mamlouks of Egypt, the nobility of Europe, the Nairs of India, the Emirs of Arabia, the Patricians of Rome, the Chriſtian clergy, the Imans, the Bramins, the Bonzes, the Lamas, &c. &c. and you will find in all the same characteristic feature,—" Men " living in idleness at the expence of those who labour."

Page 138. (3). *Equality and liberty constitute the physical basis.* In the declaration of rights there is an inversion of ideas in the first article, liberty being placed before equality from which it in reality springs. This defect is not to be wondered at; the science of the rights of man is a new science; it was invented yesterday by the Americans, to-day the French are perfecting it, but there yet remains a great deal to be done. In the ideas that constitute it there is a genealogical order which, from its basis, physical equality, to the minutest and most remote branches of government, ought to proceed in an uninterrupted series of inferences. This will be demonstrated in the second part of this work.

Page 147. (4.) *A vast hat of the leaves of the palm-tree.* This species of the palm-tree is called *Latanier*. Its leaf, similar to a fan-mount, grows upon a stalk issuing directly from the earth. A specimen may be seen in the botanic garden.

Page 148. (5.) *The contemplation of one species thus infinitely varied.* A hall of costumas in one of the galleries of the Louvre, would in every point of view be an interesting establishment: it would furnish an admirable treat to the curiosity of a great number of men, excellent models to the artist, and useful subjects of meditation to the physician, the philosopher, and the legislator. Picture to yourself a collection of the various faces and figures of every country and nation, exhibiting accurately colour, features and form: what a field for investigation and enquiry as to the influence of climate, manners, aliment,
&c.!

&c.! It might truly be ftyled the fcience of man! Buffon has attempted a chapter of this nature, but it only ferves to exhibit more ftrikingly our actual ignorance. Such a collection it is faid is begun at Peterfburg, but it is faid at the fame time, to be as imperfect as the vocabulary of the 300 languages. The enterprize would be worthy of the French nation.

Page 157. (6). *Thus are there fects to the number of feventy-two.* The Muffulmans enumerate in common feventy-two fects; but I read, while I refided among them, a work which gave an account of more than eighty, all equally wife and important.

Page id. (7). *Has never ceafed for twelve hundred years.* Read the hiftory of Iflamifm by its own writers, and you will be convinced that one of the principal caufes of the wars which have defolated Afia and Africa fince the days of Mahomet, has been the apoftolical fanaticifm of its doctrine. Cæfar has been fuppofed to have deftroyed three millions of men: it would be interefting to make a fimilar calculation refpecting every founder of a religious fyftem.

Page 161. (8). *The Neftorians, the Eutycheans, and a hundred others.* Confult upon this fubject *Dictionnaire des Herefies par l'Abbé Pluquet,* in two volumes, 8vo; a work admirably calculated to infpire the mind with philofophy, in the fenfe that the Lacedemonians taught their children temperance, by fhewing to them the drunken Heliotes.

Page 163. (9). *Difciples of Zoroafter.* They are the Parfes, better known by the opprobrious name of Gaures or Guebres, another word for infidels. They are in Afia

Z 4   what

what the Jews are in Europe. The name of their pope or high priest is Mobed.

Page 164. (10). *Their Destours*; that is to say, their priests. See, respecting the rites of this religion, *Henry Lord*, *Hyde*, and the *Zendavesta*. Their costuma is a robe with a belt of four knots, and a veil over the mouth for fear of polluting the fire with their breath.

Page id. (11). *The resurrection of the body, or the soul, or both*. The Zoroastrians are divided between two opinions, one party believing that both soul and body will rise, the other, that it will be the soul only. The Christians and Mahometans have embraced the most solid of the two.

Page 165. (12). *They wear a net over their mouths, &c.* According to the system of the Metempsychosis, a soul, to undergo purification, passes into the body of some insect or animal. It is of importance not to disturb this penance, as the work must in that case begin afresh.... *Paria*. This is the name of a cast or tribe reputed unclean, because they eat of what has enjoyed life.

Page id. (13). *Brama.—reduced to serve as a pedestal to the Lingam.* See *Sonnerat, Voyage aux Indes.* Vol. I.

Page 166. (14). *Hideous forms of a boar, a lion, &c.* These are the incarnations of Vichenou, or metamorphoses of the sun. He is to come at the end of the world, that is, at the expiration of the great period, in the form of a horse, like the four horses of the apocalypse.

Page id. (15). *In their devotion, &c.* When a sectary of Chiven hears the name of Vichenou pronounced, he stops his ears, flies, and purifies himself.

Page 167. (16). *The Chinese worship him under the name*

of Fôt. The original name of this God is *Baits*, which in Hebrew signifies an egg. The Arabs pronounce it *Baidh*, giving to the *dh* an emphatic sound which makes it approach to *dz*. Kempfer, an accurate traveller, writes it *Budso*, which must be pronounced *Boudso*, whence is derived the name of Budsoist and of Bonze, applied to the priests. Clement of Alexandria, in his Stromata, writes it *Bedou*, as it is pronounced also by the Chingulais; and Saint Jerome, *Boudda* and *Boutta*. At Thibet they call it Budd: and hence the name of the country called *Boud-tan* and *Ti-budd*: it was in this province that this system of religion was first inculcated in Upper Asia; *La* is a corruption of *Allah*, the name of God in the Syriac language, from which many of the Eastern dialects appear to be derived. The Chinese having neither *b* nor *d*, have supplied their place by *f* and *t*, and have therefore said *Fout*.

Page 168. (17). *That the soul can exist independently of the senses.* See in Kempfer the doctrine of the Sintoists, which is a mixture of that of Epicurus and of the Stoics.

Page id. (18). *Talipat screen.* It is a leaf of the *Latanier* species of the palm tree. Hence the Bonzes of Siam take the appellation of *Talapoin*. The use of this screen is an exclusive privilege.

Page 169. (19). *Conjunction of the stars.* The sectaries of Confucius are no less addicted to astrology than the Bonzes. It is indeed the malady of every eastern nation.

Page id. (20). *The Grand Lama.* The *Delai-La-Ma*, or immense high priests of *La*, is the same person whom we find mentioned in our old books of travels, by the name

name of Prester John, from a corruption of the Persian word *Djehan*, which signifies the world, to which has been prefixed the French word prestre or prêtre, priest. Thus the *priest world* and the *God world* are in the Persian idiom the same.

Page id. (21). *The excrements of their pontiff.* In a recent expedition, the English have found certain idols of the Lamas filled in the inside with sacred pastils from the close-stool of the high-priest. Mr. Hastings, and Colonel Pollier who is now at Lausanne, are living witnesses of this fact, and undoubtedly worthy of credit. It will be very extraordinary to observe, that this disgusting ceremony is connected with a profound philosophical system, to wit, that of the metempsychosis, admitted by the Lamas. When the Tartars swallow these sacred relics, which they are accustomed to do, they imitate the laws of the universe, the parts of which are incessantly absorbed and pass into the substance of each other. It is upon the model of the serpent who devours his tail, and this serpent is Budd and the world.

Page 170. (22). *The inhabitant of Juida, &c.* It frequently happens, that the swine devour the very species of serpents which the negroes adore, which is a source of great desolation in the country. President de Brosses has given us in his history of the *Fetiche*, a curious collection of absurdities of this nature.... *The Teleutean dresses, &c.* The Teleuteans, a Tartar nation, paint God as wearing a vesture of all colours, particularly red and green; and as these constitute the uniform of the Russian dragoons, they compare him to this description of soldiers. The Egyptians also dress the God World in a

garment

garment of every colour. *Eusebius Præp. Evang. p.* 115. *l.* 3. The Teleuteans call God *Bou*, which is only an alteration of Boudd, the God Egg and World.

Page *id.* (23). *The Kamchadale represents God under the figure of an ill-natured and arbitrary old man.* Consult upon this subject a work entitled, *Description des Peuples soumis à la Russe,* and it will be found that the picture is not overcharged.

Page 179. (24.) *His son-in-law Ali, or his vicars Omar and Aboubekre.* These are the two grand parties into which the Mussulmans are divided. The Turks have embraced the second, the Persians the first.

Page 182. (25). *To make war upon infidels.* Whatever the advocates for the philosophy and civilization of the Turks may assert, to make war upon infidels is considered by them as an obligatory precept and an act of religion. See *Reland de Relig. Moham.*

Page 190. (26). *Your system rests entirely on mystical interpretations.* When we read the fathers of the church, and see upon what arguments they have built the edifice of religion, we are inexpressibly astonished with their credulity, or their knavery; but allegory was the rage of that period: the Pagans employed it to explain the actions of their Gods, and the Christians acted in the same spirit when they employed it after their fashion.

Page 195. (27). *It was not till four hundred years after.* See the Chronology of the Twelve Ages, in which I conceive myself to have clearly proved that Moses lived about 1400 years before Jesus Christ, and Zoroaster about a thousand.

Page 196. (28). *In the corrected publication of their sacred books.* In the first periods of the Christian church, not only

only the most learned of those who have since been denominated heretics, but many of the orthodox, conceived Moses to have written neither the law nor the Pentateuch, but that the work was a compilation made by the elders of the people and the Seventy, who, after the death of Moses, collected his scattered ordinances, and mixed with them things that were extraneous; similar to what happened as to the Koran of Mahomet. See *Les Clémentines*, Homel. 2. sect. 51. and Homel. 3. sect. 42.

Modern critics, more enlightened or more attentive than the ancients, have found in Genesis in particular, marks of its having been composed on the return from the captivity; but the principal proofs have escaped them. These I mean to exhibit in an analysis of the book of Genesis, in which I shall demonstrate that the tenth chapter, among others, which treats of the pretended generations of the Man called Noah, is a real geographical picture of the world, as it was known to the Hebrews at the epoch of the captivity, which was bounded by Greece or Hellas at the West, mount Caucasus at the North, Persia at the East, and Arabia and Upper Egypt at the South. All the pretended personages from Adam to Abraham or his father Terah, are mythological beings, stars, constellations, countries. Adam is Bootes; Noah is Osyris, Xisuthrus Janus, Saturn; that is to say Capricorn, or the celestial Genius that opened the year. The Alexandrian Chronicle says expressly, page 85, that Nimrod was supposed by the Persians to be their first king, as having invented the art of hunting, and that he was translated into heaven, where he appears under the name of Orion.

Page 197. (29). *Creation of the world in six gahans*, or periods,

periods, or into six *gahan-bars*, that is, six periods of time. These periods are what Zoroaster calls the *thousands of God* or of *light*, meaning the six summer months. In the first, say the Persians, God created (arranged in order) the heavens; in the second the waters; in the third the earth; in the fourth trees; in the fifth animals; and in the sixth man: corresponding with the account in Genesis. For particulars see *Hyde*, ch. 9. and *Henry Lord*, ch. 2. *On the religion of the ancient Persians*. It is remarkable, that the same tradition is found in the sacred books of the Etrurians, which relate, " that the " Fabricator of all things had comprised the duration of " his work in a period of twelve thousand years, which " period was distributed to the twelve houses of the sun." In the first thousand, God made heaven and earth; in the second, the firmament; in the third, the sea and the waters; in the fourth, the sun, moon, and stars; in the fifth, the soul of animals, birds, and reptiles; in the sixth, man. See *Suidas*, at the word *Tyrrhena*; which shows first, the identity of their theological and astrological opinions; and secondly, the identity, or rather confusion of ideas, between absolute and systematical creation, that is, the periods assigned for renewing the face of nature, which were at first the period of the year, and afterwards periods of 60, of 600, of 25,000, of 36,000, and of 432,000 years.

Page 198. (30). *Auricular confession, &c.* The modern Parses and the ancient Mithriacs, who are the same sect, observe all the Christian sacraments, even the laying on of hands in confirmation. " The priest of Mithra," says Tertullian (de Præscriptione, c. 40.) " promises ab-
" solution from sin on confession and baptism; and, if I
" rightly

"rightly remember, Mithra marks the soldiers in the fore-
"head (with the chrism, called in Egyptian *Kouphi*); he
"celebrates the sacrifice of bread, which is the resurrec-
"tion, and presents the crown to his followers, menacing
"them at the same time with the sword, &c."

In these mysteries they tried the courage of the initiated with a thousand terrors, presenting fire to his face, a sword to his breast, &c.; they also offered him a crown which he refused, saying, God is my crown: and this crown is to be seen in the celestial sphere by the side of Bootes. The personages in these mysteries were distinguished by the names of the animal constellations. The ceremony of mass is nothing more than an imitation of these mysteries and those of Eleusis. The benediction *the Lord be with you*, is a literal translation of the formular of admission *chen-k. am, p-ak*. See *Beausob. Hist. Du Manicheisme*, vol. ii.

Page 199. (31). *The Vedes, the Chastres, and the Pourans.* These are the sacred volumes of the Hindoos; they are sometimes written *Vedams, Pouranams, Chastrans,* because the Hindoos, like the Persians, are accustomed to give a nasal sound to the terminations of their words, which we represent by the affixes *on* and *an*, and the Portuguese by the affixes *om* and *am*. Many of these books have been translated, thanks to the liberal spirit of Mr. Hastings, who has founded at Calcutta a literary society and a printing press. At the same time, however, that we express our gratitude to this society, we must be permitted to complain of its exclusive spirit, the number of copies printed of each book being such as it is impossible to purchase them even in England; they are wholly in the hands of the East India proprietors.

Scarcely

Scarcely even is the Afiatic Mifcellany known in Europe, and a man muft be very learned in oriental antiquity before he fo much as hears of the Jones's, the Wilkins's and the Halhed's, &c. As to the facred books of the Hindoos, all that are yet in our hands are the Bhagvat Geeta, the Ezour-Vedam, the Bagavadam, and certain fragments of the Chaftres printed at the end of the Bhagvat Geeta. Thefe books are in Indoftan what the Old and New Teftament are in Chriftendom, the Koran in Turkey, the Sad-der and the Zendavefta among the Parfes, &c. When I have taken an extenfive furvey of their contents, I have fometimes afked myfelf, what would be the lofs to the human race if a new Omar condemned them to the flames; and unable to difcover any mifchief that would enfue, I call the imaginary cheft that contains them, the box of Pandora.

Page 201. (32). *Brama, Bichen or Vichenou, Chib or Chiven.* Thefe names are differently pronounced according to the different dialects: thus they fay *Birmak, Bremma, Brouma. Bichen* has been turned into *Vichen* by the eafy exchange of a *B* for a *V*, and into *Vichenou* by means of a grammatical affix. In the fame manner *Chib*, which is fynonymous with Satan, and fignifies adverfary, is frequently written *Chib-a* and *Chiv-en*; he is called alfo *Rouder* and *Routr-en*, that is, the deftroyer.

Page id. (33). *In the fhape of a tortoife.* This is the conftellation *teftudo*, or the *lyre*, which was at firft a tortoife, on account of its flow motion round the Pole; then a lyre, becaufe it is the fhell of this reptile on which the ftrings of the lyre are mounted. See an excellent memoir of *M. Dupuis, fur l'Origine des Conftellations,* in 4to.

Page 204. (34). *That you have borrowed the ancient Paganifm*

Paganism of the Western world. All the ancient opinions of the Egyptian and Grecian theologians are to be found in India, and they appear to have been introduced, by means of the commerce of Arabia and the vicinity of Persia, time immemorial.

Page 205. (35). *Breathed upon the face of the waters.* This cosmogony of the Lamas, the Bonzes, and even the Bramins, as Henry Lord asserts, is literally that of the ancient Egyptians. "The Egyptians," says Porphyry, "call "*Kneph*, intelligence, or efficient cause of the universe. "They relate that this God vomitted an egg, from which "was produced another God named *Phtha* or Vulcan, "(igneous principle, or the sun,) and they add, that this "egg is the world." *Euseb. Præp. Evang.* p. 115.

"They represent," says the same author in another place, "the God *Kneph*, or efficient cause, under the form "of a man in deep blue (the colour of the sky), having "in his hand a sceptre, a belt round his body, and a small "bonnet royal of light feathers on his head, to denote "how very subtile and fugacious the idea of that being "is." Upon which I shall observe, that *Kneph* in Hebrew signifies a wing, a feather, and that this colour of sky-blue is to be found in the majority of the Indian Gods, and is, under the name of Narayan, one of their most distinguishing epithets.

Page 208. (36). *That the Lamas were a degenerate sect of the Nestorians.* This is asserted by our missionaries, and among others by Georgi in his unfinished work of the Thibetan alphabet: but if it can be proved that the Manicheans were but plagiarists, and the ignorant echo of a doctrine that existed fifteen hundred years before them, what becomes of the declarations of Georgi? See upon this subject *Beausob. Hist. du Manicheisme.*

But

NOTES. 353

But the Lama demonstrated, &c. The eastern writers in general agree in placing the birth of *Bedou* 1027 years before Jesus Christ, which makes him the cotemporary of Zoroaster, with whom, in my opinion, they confound him. It is certain that his doctrine notoriously existed at that epoch: it is found entire in that of Orpheus, Pythagoras, and the Indian gymnosophists. But the gymnosophists are cited at the time of Alexander as an ancient sect already divided into Brachmans and Samaneans. See *Bardesanes en Saint Jerome, Epitre à Joviem.* Pythagoras lived in the ninth century before Jesus Christ; See *Chronology of the Twelve Ages*; and Orpheus is of still greater antiquity. If, as is the case, the doctrine of Pythagoras and that of Orpheus are of Egyptian origin, that of Bedou goes back to the common source; and in reality the Egyptian priests recite that Hermes, as he was dying, said: " I have hitherto lived an exile from my " country, to which I now return. Weep not for me, " I ascend to the celestial abode, where each of you will " follow in his turn: there God is: this life is only " death." *Chalcidius in Thimæum.* Such was the profession of faith of the Samaneans, the sectaries of Orpheus, and the Pythagoreans. Farther, Hermes is no other than Bedou himself; for among the Indians, Chinese, Lamas, &c. the planet Mercury, and the corresponding day of the week (Wednesday) bear the name of Bedou: and this accounts for his being placed in the rank of mythological beings, and discovers the illusion of his pretended existence as a man, since it is evident that Mercury was not a human being, but the Genius or Decan, who, placed at the summer solstice, opened the

A a   Egyptian

Egyptian year: hence his attributes taken from the constellation Syrius, and his name of Anubis, as well as that of Esculapius, having the figure of a man and the head of a dog: hence his serpent, which is the Hydra, emblem of the Nile (Hydor, humidity); and from this serpent he seems to have derived his name of Hermes, as *Remes* (with a *schin*), in the oriental languages, signifies serpent. Now Bedou and Hermes being the same names, it is manifest of what antiquity is the system ascribed to the former. As to the name of Samanean, it is precisely that of Chaman preserved in Tartary, China, and India. The interpretation given to it is, *man of the woods*, a *hermit mortifying the flesh*, such being the characteristic of this sect; but its literal meaning is *celestial* (Samâoui), and explains the system of those who are called by it. This system is the same as that of the sectaries of Orpheus, of the Essenians, of the ancient Anchorets of Persia and the whole Eastern country. See *Porphyry, de Abstin. Animal.* These celestial and penitent men, carried in India their insanity to such an extreme, as to wish not to touch the earth, and they accordingly lived in cages suspended to trees, where the people, whose admiration was not less absurd, brought them provisions. During the night there were frequent robberies, rapes and murders, and it was at length discovered that they were committed by those men, who, descending from their cages, thus indemnified themselves for their restraint during the day. The Bramins, their rivals, embraced the opportunity of exterminating them; and from that time their name in India has been synonymous with hypocrite. See *Hist. de la Chine*, in 5 vols. 4to.

4to. at the note page 50; *Hist. de Huns*, 2 vols.; and Preface to the *Ezour-Vedam*.

Page 209. (37). *Demonstrate his existence, &c.* There are absolutely no other monuments of the existence of Jesus Christ as a human being, than a passage in Josephus (*Antiq. Jud. lib.* 18. c. 3.), a single phrase in Tacitus, (*Annal. lib.* 15. c. 44.), and the Gospels. But the passage in Josephus is unanimously acknowledged to be apocryphal, and to have been interpolated towards the close of the third century, (*See Trad. de Josephe, par M. Gillet*); and that of Tacitus is so vague, and so evidently taken from the deposition of the Christians before the tribunals, that it may be ranked in the class of evangelical records. It remains to enquire of what authority are these records. "All the world knows," says Faustus, who, though a Manichean, was one of the most learned men of the third century, "All the world knows, that the Gospels "were neither written by Jesus Christ, nor his apostles, "but by certain unknown persons, who, rightly judging "that they should not obtain belief respecting things "which they had not seen, placed at the head of their "recitals the names of contemporary apostles." See *Beausob.* vol. i. and *Hist. des Apologistes de la Relig. Chret. par Burigni*, a sagacious writer, who has demonstrated the absolute uncertainty of those foundations of the Christian religion; so that the existence of Jesus is no better proved than that of Osiris and Hercules, or that of Fôt or Bedou, with whom, says M. de Guignes, the Chinese continually confound him, for they never call Jesus by any other name than Fôt. *Hist. de Huns*.

Page *id.* (38.) *Your Gospels are taken from the books of the Mithriacs.* That is to say, from the pious romances formed

formed out of the sacred legends of the Mysteries of Mithra, Ceres, Isis, &c.; from whence are equally derived the books of the Hindoos and the Bonzes. Our missionaries have long remarked a striking resemblance between those books and the Gospels. M. Wilkins expressly mentions it in a note in the Bhagvat-Geeta. All agree that Krisna, Fôt, and Jesus, have the same characteristic features; but religious prejudice has stood in the way of drawing from this circumstance the proper and natural inference. To time and reason must it be left to display the truth.

Page 210. (39). *The interior and secret doctrine.* The Budsoists have two doctrines, the one public and ostensible, the other interior and secret, precisely like the Egyptian priests. It may be asked, why this distinction? It is, that as the public doctrine recommends offerings, expiations, endowments, &c. the priests find their profit in teaching it to the people; whereas the other, teaching the vanity of worldly things, and attended with no lucre, it is thought proper to make it known only to adepts. Can the teachers and followers of this religion, be better classed than under the heads of knavery and credulity?

Page 212. (40). *That happiness and misfortune, &c.* These are the expressions of La Loubere, in his description of the kingdom of Siam and the theology of the Bonzes. Their dogmas, compared with those of the ancient philosophers of Greece and Italy, give a complete representation of the whole system of the Stoics and Epicureans, mixed with astrological superstitions, and some traits of Pythagorism.

Page 224. (41). *The original barbarous state of mankind.*

It

It is the unanimous testimony of history, and even of legends, that the first human beings were every where savages, and that it was to civilize them, and teach them *to make bread*, that the Gods manifested themselves.

Page *id.* (42). *Man receives no ideas but through the medium of his senses.* The rock on which all the ancients have split, and which has occasioned all their errors, has been their supposing the idea of God to be innate and co-eternal with the soul; and hence all the reveries developed in Plato and Jamblicus. See the *Timæus*, the *Phedon*, and *De Myst. Ægyptiorum*, sect. 1. c. 3.

Page 231. (43). *Record of all the monuments of antiquity.* It clearly results, says Plutarch, from the verses of Orpheus and the sacred books of the Egyptians and Phrygians, that the ancient theology, not only of the Greeks, but of all nations, was nothing more than a system of physics, a picture of the operations of nature, wrapped up in mysterious allegories and enigmatical symbols, in a manner that the ignorant multitude attended rather to their apparent than to their hidden meaning, and even in what they understood of the latter, supposed there to be something more deep than what they perceived. *Fragment of a work of Plutarch now lost, quoted by Eusebius, Præpar. Evang. lib.* 3. *ch.* 1. *p.* 83.

The majority of philosophers, says Porphyry, and among others Chæremon (who lived in Egypt in the first age of Christianity), imagine there never to have been any other world than the one we see, and acknowledge no other Gods of all those recognized by the Egyptians, than such as are commonly called planets, signs of the Zodiac, and constellations; whose aspects, that is, rising and setting, are supposed to influence the fortunes of men; to which they add, their divisions of the signs into decans and dispensers of time, whom they style lords of the ascendant, whose names, virtues in the relieving distempers, rising, setting, and presages of future events, are the subjects of almanacks; (for be it observed, that the Egyptian priests had almanacks the exact counterpart of Matthew Lansberg's) for when the priests affirmed that the sun was the architect of the universe, Chæremon presently concludes that all their narratives respecting Isis and Osiris, together with their other sacred fables, referred in part to the planets, the phases of the moon, and the revolution of the sun, and in part to the stars of the daily and nightly hemispheres and the river Nile; in a word, in all cases to physical and natural existences, and never to such as might be immaterial and incorporeal.... All these philosophers believe, that the acts of our will, and the motion of our bodies, depend upon those of the stars to which they are subjected, and they refer every thing to the laws of physical necessity, which they call destiny or *Fatum*, supposing a chain of causes and effects which binds, by I know not what connection, all beings together, from the meanest atom to the supreme power and primary influence of the Gods; so that, whether in their temples or in their idols, the only subject of worship is the power of destiny. *Porphyr. Epist. ad Janebonem.*

Page 232. (44). *The practice of agriculture required the observation and knowledge of the heavens.* It continues to be repeated every day, on the indirect authority of the book of Genesis, that astronomy was the invention of the children of Noah. It has been gravely said, that, while wandering shepherds in the plains of Shinar, they employed their leisure in composing a planetary system: as if shepherds had occasion to know more than the Polar star, and if necessity was not the sole motive of every invention! If the ancient shepherds were so studious and sagacious, how does it happen that the modern ones are so stupid, ignorant, and inattentive? And it is a fact, that the Arabs of the desert know not so many as six constellations, and understand not a word of astronomy.

Page 233. (45). *Genii, Gods, authors of good and evil.* It appears that by the words genius, the ancients denoted a quality, a generative power; for the following words, which are all of one family, convey this meaning: *generary, genos, genesis, genus, gens.*

The Sabeans, ancient and modern, says Maimonides, acknowledge a principal God, the maker and inhabitant of heaven; but on account of his great distance they conceive him to be inaccessible; and in imitation of the conduct of people towards their kings, they employ as mediators with him, the planets and their angels, whom they call princes and potentates, and whom they suppose to reside in those luminous bodies as in palaces or tabernacles, &c. *More-Nebuchim,* pars 3. c. 29.

Page 234. (46). *And even a sex derived from the gender of its appellation.* According as the gender of the object was in the language of the nation masculine or feminine, the Divinity who bore its name was male or female. Thus the Cappadocians called the moon God, and the sun Goddess; a circumstance which gives to the same beings a perpetual variety in ancient mythology.

Page 235. (47). *Morality was a judicious practice of all that is conducive to the preservation of existence.* We may add, says Plutarch, that these Egyptian priests always regarded the preservation of health as a point of first importance, and as indispensably necessary to the practice of piety and the service of the Gods. See his account of *Isis and Osiris*, towards the end.

Page *id.* (48). *That its principles* (those of astronomy), *can be traced back to a period of* 17,000 *years*. The historical orator follows here the opinion of Mr. Dupuis, who, in his learned memoir concerning the origin of the constellations, has assigned many plausible reasons to prove that *Libra* was formerly the sign of the vernal, and *Aries* of the nocturnal equinox; that is, that since the origin of the actual astronomical system, the procession of the equinoxes has carried forward by seven signs the primitive order of the Zodiac. Now estimating the procession at about seventy years and a half to a degree, that is 2,115 years to each sign; and observing that *Aries* was in its fifteenth degree, 1,447 years before Christ, it follows, that the first degree of *Libra* could not have coincided with the vernal equinox more lately than 15,194 years before Christ, to which if you add 1790 years since Christ, it appears that 16,984 have elapsed since the origin of the Zodiac. The vernal equinox coincided with the first degree of *Aries* 2,504 years before Christ, and with the first degree of *Taurus* 4,619 years before Christ. Now it is to be observed, that the worship of the Bull is the principal article in the theological creed of the Egyptians, Persians, Japanese, &c.; from whence it clearly follows, that some general revolution took place among those nations at that time. The chronology of five or six thousand years in Genesis is little agreeable to this hypothesis; but as the book of Genesis cannot claim to

be

be considered as a history farther back than Abraham, we are at liberty to make what arrangements we please in the eternity that preceded.

Page *id*. (49). *When reason finds there a zone of heaven equally free from the rains of the equator and the fogs of the North.* Mr. Bailli, in placing the first astronomers at Selingenskoy, near the lake Baikal, paid no attention to this twofold circumstance: it equally argues against their being placed at Axoum on account of the rains, and the *Zimb fly* of which Mr. Bruce speaks.

Page 238. (50). *Men gave to the stars, &c.* "The "ancients," says Maimonides, "directing all their at- "tention to agriculture, gave names to the stars derived "from their occupation during the year." *More Neb. pars* 3.

Page 240. (51). *They call by the name of serpents the figured traces of the orbits.* The ancients had verbs from the substantives *crab, goat, tortoise,* as the French have at present the verbs *serpenter, coquetier.* The history of all languages is nearly the same.

Page 243. (52). *If they had not seen in them talismans partaking of the nature of the stars.* The ancient astrologers, says the most learned of the Jews (Maimonides), having sacredly assigned to each planet a colour, an animal, a tree, a metal, a fruit, a plant, formed from them all a figure or representation of the star, taking care to select for the purpose a proper moment, a fortunate day, such as the conjunction of the star, or some other favourable aspect. They conceived, that by their magic ceremonies they could introduce into those figures or idols the influences of the superior beings after which they were modelled. These were the idols that the Chaldean-

Sabeans

Sabeans adored; and in the performance of their worship they were obliged to be dressed in the proper colour.... The astrologers, by their practices, thus introduced idolatry, desirous of being regarded as the dispensers of the favours of heaven; and as agriculture was the sole employment of the ancients, they succeeded in persuading them, that the rain and other blessings of the seasons were at their disposal. Thus the whole art of agriculture was exercised by rules of astrology, and the priests made talismans or charms which were to drive away locusts, flies, &c. See *Maimonides, More, Nebuchim, pars* 3. *c*. 29.

The priests of Egypt, Persia, India, &c. pretended to bind the Gods to their idols, and to make them come from heaven at their pleasure. They threatened the sun and moon, if they were disobedient, to reveal the secret mysteries, to shake the skies, &c. &c. *Euseb. Præcep. Evang. p.* 198, *and Iamblicus de Mysteriis Ægypt.*

Page *id.* (53). *The sun was supposed to assume their forms* (the forms of the twelve animals). These are the very words of Iamblicus de Symbolis Ægyptiorum, c. 2. sect. 7. The sun was the grand Proteus, the universal metamorphist.

Page 245. (54). *Your tonsure is the disk of the sun.* The Arabs, says Herodotus, shave their heads in a circle and about the temples, in imitation of Bacchus (that is the sun,) who shaves himself, they say, in this manner. Jeremiah speaks also of this custom. The tuft of hair which the Mahometans preserve, is taken also from the sun, who was painted by the Egyptians at the winter solstice, as having but a single hair on his head.... *Your stole its Zodiac.* The robes of the goddess of Syria and of Diana of Ephesus, from whence are borrowed the dress of priests, have the twelve animals of the Zodiac painted on them..... *Rosaries* are found upon all the Indian idols, constructed more than four thousand years ago; and their use in the East has been universal for time immemorial..... The *crosier* is precisely the staff of Bootes or Osiris (See Plate II.) All the Lamas wear the *mitre* or cap in the shape of a cone, which was an emblem of the sun.

Page 247. (55.) *Having said that a planet entered into a sign, their conjunction was denominated a marriage*, &c. These are the very words of Plutarch in his account of Isis and Osiris. The Hebrews say, in speaking of the generations of the Patriarchs, *et ingressus est in eam*. From this continual equivoque of ancient language, proceeds every mistake.

Page 248. (56). *The combination of these figures had also a meaning.* The reader will doubtless see, with pleasure, some examples of ancient hieroglyphics.

"The Egyptians (says Hor-appolo) represent eternity by the figure of the sun and moon. They designate the world by a blue serpent with yellow scales (stars, it is the Chinese Dragon). If they were desirous of expressing the year, they drew a picture of Isis, who is also in their language called *Sothis*, or dog-star, one of the first constellations, by the rising of which the year commences: its inscription at Sais was, *It is I that rise in the constellation of the Dog*.

"They also represent the year by a palm-tree, and the month by one of its branches; because it is the nature of this tree to produce a branch every month. They farther represent it by the fourth part of an acre of land." (The
whole

whole acre divided into four denotes the bissextile period of four years. The abbreviation of this figure of a field in four divisions, is manifestly the letter *bâ* or *bêt*, the seventh in the Samaritan alphabet; and in general all the letters of the alphabet are merely astronomical hieroglyphics: and it is for this reason that the mode of writing is from right to left, like the march of the stars).
— "They denote a prophet by the image of a dog, because the dog-star (*Anoubis*) by its rising gives notice of the inundation. *Noubi* in Hebrew signifies prophet.— They represent inundation by a lion, because it takes place under that sign: and hence, says Plutarch, the custom of placing at the gates of temples figures of lions with water issuing from their mouths.—They express the idea of God and Destiny by a star. They also represent God, says Porphyry, by a black stone, because his nature is dark and obscure. All white things express the celestial and luminous Gods: all circular ones the world, the moon, the sun, the destinies: all semicircular ones, as bows and crescents, are also descriptive of the moon. Fire and the Gods of Olympus, they represent by pyramids and obelisks: (the name of the sun *Baal* is found in this latter word): the sun, by a cone (the mitre of Osiris): the earth, by a cylinder (which revolves): the generative power of the air, by the *phalus*, and that of the earth, by a triangle, emblem of the female organ. *Euseb. Præcep. Evang. p.* 98.

"Clay (says Iamblicus de Symbolis, sect. 7. c. 2.) denotes matter, the generative and nutrimental power, every thing which receives the warmth and fermentation of life.

"A man sitting upon the *Lotos* or *Nenuphar*, represents the moving spirit (the sun), which, in like manner as the

the plant lives in the water without any communication with clay, exists equally distinct from matter, swimming in empty space, resting on itself: it is round also in all its parts like the leaves, the flowers and the fruit of the Lotos. (Brama has the eyes of the Lotos, says Chaster Neadirsen, to denote his intelligence: his eye swims over every thing, like the flowers of the Lotos on the waters). A man at the helm of a ship, adds Iamblicus, is descriptive of the sun which governs all. And Porphyry tells us, that the sun is also represented by a man in a ship resting upon an amphibious crocodile (emblem of air and water).

" At Elephantine they worshipped the figure of a man in a sitting posture, painted blue, having the head of a ram, and the horns of a goat which encompassed a disk: all which represented the sun and moon's conjunction at the sign of the ram; the blue colour denoting the power of the moon at the period of junction, to raise water into clouds. *Euseb. Præcep. Evang. p.* 116.

" The hawk is an emblem of the sun and of light, on account of his rapid flight, and his soaring into the highest regions of the air where light abounds.

" A fish is the emblem of aversion, and the *Hippopotamus* of violence, because it is said to kill its father and ravish its mother. Hence, says Plutarch, the emblematical inscription of the temple of Sais, where we see painted on the vestibule, 1. A child. 2. An old man. 3. A hawk. 4. A fish. 5. A hippopotamus; which signify, 1. Entrance (into life). 2. Departure. 3. God. 4. Hatred. 5. Injustice. (See *Isis & Osiris*).

" The Egyptians, adds he, represent the world by a Scarabeus, because this insect pushes, in a direction contrary

trary to that in which it proceeds, a ball containing its eggs, juft as the heaven of the fixed ftars caufes the revolution of the fun (the yolk of an egg) in an oppofite direction to its own.

"They reprefent the world alfo by the number *five*, being that of the elements, which, fays Diodorus, are earth, water, air, fire, and ether or *fpiritus*. The Indians have the fame number of elements, and according to Macrobius's Myftics they are the fupreme God, or *primum mobile*, the intelligence, or *mens*, born of him, the foul of the world which proceeds from him, the celeftial fpheres and all things terreftrial. Hence, adds Plutarch, the analogy between the Greek *pente*, five, and *pan*, all.

"The afs," fays he again, "is the emblem of Typhon, becaufe like that animal he is of a reddifh colour. Now Typhon fignifies whatever is of a mirey or clayey nature; (and in Hebrew I find the three words, *clay*, *red*, and *afs*, to be formed from the fame root, *hamr*. Iamblicus has farther told us, that clay was the emblem of matter; and he elfewhere adds, that all evil and corruption proceeded from matter: which, compared with the phrafe of Macrobius, *all is perifhable*, liable to change in the celeftial fphere, gives us the theory, firft phyfical, then moral, of the fyftem of good and evil of the ancients."

Page 252. (57). *The fenfelefs caufe of fuperftition.* Thefe are properly the words of Plutarch, who relates, that thofe various worfhips were given by a king of Egypt to the different towns to difunite and enflave them (and thefe kings had been taken from the caft of priefts). See *Ifis & Ofiris.*

Page 255. (58). *In the projection of the celestial sphere.* The ancient priests had three kind of spheres, which it may be useful to make known to the reader.

"We read in Eusebius," says Porphyry, "that Zoroaster was the first who, having fixed upon a cavern pleasantly situated in the mountains adjacent to Persia, formed the idea of consecrating it to Mithra (the sun) creator and father of all things: that is to say, having made in this cavern several geometrical divisions, representing the seasons and the elements, he imitated on a small scale the order and disposition of the universe by Mithra. After Zoroaster, it became a custom to consecrate caverns for the celebration of mysteries: so that in like manner as temples were dedicated to the Gods, rural altars to heroes and terrestrial deities, &c. subterraneous abodes to infernal deities, so caverns and grottoes were consecrated to the world, to the universe, and to the nymphs: and from hence Pythagoras and Plato borrowed the idea of calling the earth a cavern, a cave, *de Antro Nympharum.*"

Such was the first projection of the sphere in relief: though the Persians give the honour of the invention to Zoroaster, it is doubtless due to the Egyptians: for we may suppose, from this projection being the most simple, that it was the most ancient; the caverns of Thebes, full of similar pictures, tend to strengthen this opinion.

The following was the second projection, "The prophets or hierophants," says Bishop Synnesius, "who had been initiated in the mysteries, do not permit the common workmen to form idols or images of the Gods; but they descend themselves into the sacred caves, where
they

they have concealed coffers containing certain spheres, upon which they construct those images secretly and without the knowledge of the people, who despise simple and natural things, and wish for prodigies and fables." (*Syn. in Calvit.*) That is, the ancient priests had armillary spheres like ours; and this passage, which so well agrees with that of Chæremon, gives us the key to all their theological astrology.

Lastly, they had *flat models* of the nature of Plate II. with this difference, that they were of a very complicated nature, having every fictitious division of decan and subdecan, with the hieroglyphic signs of their influence. Kircher has given us a copy of one of them in his Egyptian Œdipus, and Gybelin a figured fragment in his book of the calendar (under the name of the Egyptian Zodiac). The ancient Egyptians, says the astrologer Julius Firmicus (*Astron. lib.* ii. and *lib.* iv. c. 16). divide each sign of the Zodiac into three sections; and each section was under the direction of an imaginary being, whom they called *Decan*, or *chief of ten*; so that there were three Decans a month, and thirty-three a year. Now these Decans, who were also called Gods (*Thoi*), regulate the destinies of mankind—and they were placed particularly in certain stars. They afterwards imagined in every *ten* three other Gods, whom they called *arbiters*; so that there were nine for every month, and these were farther divided into an infinite number of powers. (The Persians and Indians made their spheres on similar plans; and if a picture thereof were to be drawn from the description given by Scaliger at the end of Manilius, we should find in it a complete explanation of their hieroglyphics, for every article forms one).

Page

NOTES.

Page *id.* (59.) *The adverse Genii.* It was for this reason the Persians always wrote the name of Ahrimanes inverted thus: ˙sǝuɐɯıɹɥA

Page 256. (60). *Typhon, that is to say deluge.* Typhon, pronounced Touphon by the Greeks, is precisely the *touphan* of the Arabs, which signifies deluge; and these deluges in mythology are nothing more than winter and the rains, or the overflowing of the Nile; as their pretended fires which are to destroy the world, are simply the summer season. And it is for this reason that Aristotle (*De Meteor. lib.* I. *c.* xiv.), says, that the winter of the great cyclic year is a deluge; and its summer a conflagration. " The Egyptians, says Porphyry, " employ every year a talisman in remembrance of the world: at the summer solstice they mark their houses, flocks and trees with red, supposing that on that day the whole world had been set on fire. It was also at the same period that they celebrated the pyrric or fire dance." (And this illustrates the origin of purifications by fire and by water: for having denominated the tropic of Cancer the gate of heaven, and of genial heat or celestial fire, and that of Capricorn the gate of deluge or of water, it was imagined that the spirits or souls who passed through these gates in their way to and from heaven, were *roasted* or *bathed*: hence the baptism of Mithra, und the passage through flames, observed throughout the East long before Moses).

Page *id.* (61). *In Persia in a subsequent period.* That is, when the ram became the equinoxial sign, or rather when the alteration of the skies shewed that it was no longer the Bull. See Note 48.

Page 257. (62). *Whence are derived all religious acts of a gay nature.* All the ancient festivals respecting the return and exaltation of the sun were of this description: hence the *hilaria* of the Roman calendar at the period of the passage (Pascha) of the vernal equinox. The dances were imitations of the march of the planets. Those of the Dervises still represent it to this day.

Page 258. (63). *All religious acts of the sombre kind.* " Sacrifices of blood," says Porphyry, " were only offered to Demons and evil Genii to avert their wrath... Demons are fond of blood, humidity, stench." *Apud. Euseb. Præp. Ev. p.* 173.

" The Egyptians," says Plutarch, "only offer bloody victims to Typhon. They sacrifice to him a red ox, and the animal immolated is held in execration, and loaded with all the sins of the people." (The goat of Moses). See *Isis and Osiris.*

Division of terrestrial beings into pure and impure, sacred and abominable. Strabo says, speaking of Moses and the Jews, " Circumcision and the prohibition of certain kinds of meat sprung from superstition."—And I observe, respecting the ceremony of circumcision, that its object was to take from the symbol of Osiris (*Phallus*) the pretended obstacle to fecundity; an obstacle which bore the seal of Typhon, " whose nature," says Plutarch, " is made up of all that *hinders, opposes, causes obstruction.*"

Page 260. (64). *Elysian-fields. Aliz,* in the Phenician or Hebrew language signifies dancing and joyous.

Page 262. (65). *The Milky way.* See *Macrob. Som. Scip.* c. 12; and Note (78).

Page 265. (66). *The bodies of its inhabitants cast no shade.* There is on this subject a passage in Plutarch, so interesting and explanatory of the whole of this system, that we shall cite it entire. Having observed that the theory of good and evil had at all times occupied the attention of philosophers and theologians, he adds: "Many suppose there to be two Gods of opposite inclinations, one delighting in good the other in evil; the first of these is called particularly by the name of God, the second by that of Genius or Demon. Zoroaster has denominated them Oromaze and Ahrimanes, and has said that, of whatever falls under the cognizance of our senses, light is the best representation of the one, and darkness and ignorance of the other. He adds, that Mithra is an intermediate being, and it is for this reason the Persians call Mithra the *mediator* or *intermediator*. Each of these Gods has distinct plants and animals consecrated to him; for example, dogs, birds and hedge-hogs belong to the good Genius, and all aquatic animals to the evil one.

"The Persians also say, that Oromaze was born or formed out of the purest light; Ahrimanes, on the contrary, out of the thickest darkness: that Oromaze made six Gods as good as himself, and Ahrimanes opposed to them six wicked ones: that Oromaze afterwards multiplied himself threefold (Hermes trismegistus), and removed to a distance as remote from the sun as the sun is remote from the earth; that he there formed stars, and, among others, *Syrius*, which he placed in the heavens as a guard and centinel. He made also twenty-four other Gods, which he inclosed in an egg; but Ahrimanes created an equal number on his part, who broke the egg, and from that moment good and evil were mixed (in the universe). But Ahrimanes is one day to be conquered, and the earth to be made *equal* and *smooth*, that all men may live happy.

Theopompus adds, from the books of the Magi, that one of these Gods reigns in turn every three thousand years, during which the other is kept in subjection; that they afterwards contend with equal weapons during a similar portion of time, but that in the end the evil Genius will fall (never to rise again). Then men will become happy, and their bodies cast no shade. The God who mediates all these things reclines at present in repose, waiting till he shall be pleased to execute them." See *Isis and Osiris*.

There is an apparent allegory through the whole of this passage. The egg is the fixed sphere, the world; the six Gods of Oromaze are the six signs of summer, those of Ahrimanes the six signs of winter. The forty-eight other Gods are the forty-eight constellations of the ancient sphere, divided equally between Ahrimanes and Oromaze. The office of *Syrius*, as guard and centinel, tells us that the origin of these ideas was Egyptian: finally, the expression that the earth is to become *equal* and *smooth*, and that the bodies of happy beings are to cast no shade, proves that the equator was considered as their true paradise.

Page 265. (67). *The cave of Mithra*. See Note (58). In the caves which priests every where constructed, they celebrated mysteries which consisted (says Origen against Celsus) in imitating the motion of the stars, the planets, and the heavens. The initiated took the name of constellations and assumed the figures of animals. One was a lion, another a raven, and a third a ram. Hence the use of masks in the first representation of the drama. See *Ant. Devoilé*, vol. ii. p. 244. " In the mysteries of Ceres the chief in the procession called himself the creator; the bearer of the torch was denominated the sun: the person nearest to the altar, the moon; the herald or deacon, Mercury. In Egypt there was a festival in which the men and women represented the year, the age, the seasons, the different parts of the day, and they walked in procession after Bacchus. *Athen. lib.* v. *c.* 7. In the cave of Mithra was a ladder with seven steps, representing the seven spheres of the planets, by means of which souls ascended and descended. This is precisely the ladder in Jacob's vision, which shows that at that epocha the whole system was formed. There is in the French king's library a superb volume of pictures of the Indian Gods, in which the ladder is represented with the souls of men mounting it."

Page 267. (68). *Exact calculation.* Consult the ancient astronomy of M. Bailly, and you will find our assertions respecting the knowledge of the priests amply proved.

Page 269. (69). *A reciprocal connection.* These are the very words of Jamblicus. *De Myst. Ægypt.*

Page id. (70.) *Or rather electrical fluid.* The more I consider what the ancients understood by *ether*, and *spirit*, and what the Indians call *akache*, the stronger do I find the analogy between it and electrical fluid. A luminous fluid, principle of warmth and motion, pervading the universe, forming the matter of the stars, having small round particles, which insinuate themselves into bodies, and fill them by dilating itself, be their extent what it will, what can more strongly resemble electricity?

Page id. (71.) *Was supposed to have the sun for its heart.* Natural philosophers, says Macrobius, call the sun the heart of the world. *Som. Scip. c.* 20. The Egyptians, says Plutarch, call the East the *face*, the North the *right-*

side,

side, and the South the *left-side* of the world, becaufe there the heart is placed. They continually compare the univerfe to a man; and hence the celebrated *microcofm* of the Alchymifts. We obferve by the by, that the Alchymifts, Cabalifts, Free-mafons, Magnetifers, Martinifts, and every other fuch fort of vifionaries, are but the miftaken difciples of this ancient fchool: we fay miftaken, becaufe, in fpite of their pretenfions, the thread of the occult fcience is broken.

Page *id*. (72). *That the world was eternal.* See the Pythagorean *Ocellus Lucanus*.

Page 270. (73). *The Orphic egg.* This comparifon of the fun with the yolk of an egg refers, 1. To its round and yellow figure; 2. To its central fituation; 3. To the germ or principle of life contained in the yolk. May not the oval form of the egg allude to the elipfis of the orbs? I am inclined to this opinion. The word Orphic offers a farther obfervation. Macrobius fays (*Som. Scip. c.* 14. and *c.* 20), that the fun is the brain of the univerfe, and that it is from analogy that the fkull of a human being is round, like the planet, the feat of intelligence. Now the word Orph (with *ain*) fignifies in Hebrew the brain and its fens (*cervix*): Orpheus, then, is the fame as Bedou, or Bairs; and the Bonzes are thofe very Orphies which Plutarch reprefents as quacks, who ate no meat, vended talifmans, and little ftones, and deceived individuals, and even governments themfelves. See a learned Memoir of *Freret fur les Orphiques, Acad. des Infcrip. vol.* 23. *in* 4to.

Page *id*. (74). *Wearing on his head a fphere of gold.* See *Porphyry in Eufebius, Præp. Evang. lib.* 3. *p.* 115.

Page 271. (75). *Alluding to the wind.* The Northern

or *Elesian* wind, which commences regularly at the solstice, with the inundation.

Page 272. (76). *You-piter.* This is the true pronunciation of the Jupiter of the Latins. . . . *Existence itself.* This is the signification of the word *You.* See Note (84).

Page 273. (77). *Producing the great egg.* See Note (35).

Page id. (78). *The immortality of the soul, which at first was eternity.* In the system of the first spiritualists, the soul was not created with, or at the same time as the body, in order to be inserted in it: its existence was supposed to be anterior and from all eternity. Such, in a few words, is the doctrine of Macrobius on this head. *Som. Scip. passim.*

"There exists a luminous, igneous, subtle fluid, which, under the name of ether and spiritus, fills the universe. It is the essential principle and agent of motion and life, it is the Deity. When an earthly body is to be animated, a small round particle of this fluid gravitates through the milky way towards the lunar sphere, where, when it arrives, it unites with a grosser air, and becomes fit to associate with matter: it then enters and entirely fills the body, animates it, suffers, grows, increases, and diminishes with it; lastly, when the body dies, and its gross elements dissolve, this incorruptible particle takes its leave of it, and returns to the grand ocean of ether, if not retained by its union with the lunar air: it is this air or gas, which, retaining the shape of the body, becomes a phantom or ghost, the perfect representation of the deceased. The Greeks called this phantom the image or idol of the soul; the Pythagoreans, its chariot, its frame; and the Rabbinical school, its vessel, or boat. When a man had conducted himself well in this world, his whole soul, that is, its chariot and ether, ascended to the moon, where a separation took place: the chariot lived in the lunar Elysium, and the ether returned to the fixed sphere, that is, to God: for the fixed heaven, says Macrobius, was by many called by the name of God (c. 14.) If a man had not lived virtuously, the soul remained on earth to undergo purification, and was to wander to and fro, like the ghosts of Homer, to whom this doctrine must have been known, since he wrote after the time of Pherecydes and Pythagoras, who were is promulgators in Greece. Heredotus, upon this occasion, says, that the whole romance of the soul and its transmigrations was invented by the Egyptians, and propagated in Greece by men, who pretended to be its authors. I know their names, adds he, but shall not mention them (*lib.* 2.). Cicero, however has positively informed us, that it was Pherecydes, master of Pythagoras. *Tuscul. lib.* 1. *sect.* 16. Now admitting that this system was at that period a novelty, it accounts for Solomon's treating it as a fable, who lived 130 years before Pherecydes. " Who knoweth," says he, " the spirit of a man that it goeth upwards? I said in my heart concerning the estate of the sons of men, that God might manifest them, and that they might see that they themselves are beasts. For that which befalleth the sons of men, befalleth beasts; even one thing befalleth them; as the one dieth, so dieth the other; yea they have all one breath, so that a man hath no pre-eminence above a beast: for all is vanity." Eccles. c. iii. v. 18.

And such had been the opinion of Moses, as a translator of Herodotus (M. Archer of the Academy of Inscriptions), justly observes in note 389 of the second book, where

where he says also, that the immortality of the soul was not introduced among the Hebrews till their intercourse with the Assyrians. In other respects, the whole Pythagorean system, properly analysed, appears to be merely a system of physics badly understood.

Page 275. (79). *The world is a machine; it has therefore an artificer.* All the arguments of the spiritualists are founded on this. See *Macrobius*, at the end of the second book, and *Plato*, with the comments of *Marcilius Ficinus*.

Page 276. (80). *The demi-ourgos, the logos, and the spirit.* These are the real types of the Christian Trinity. See Note (99).

Page 277. (81). *Its very names.* In our last analysis we found all the names of the Deity to be derived from some material object in which it was supposed to reside. We have given a considerable number of instances; let us add one more relative to our word *God*. This is known to be the *Deus* of the Latins, and the *Theos* of the Greeks. Now by the confession of Plato (*in Cratylo*), of Macrobius (*Saturn, lib.* 1. *c.* 24), and of Plutarch (*Isis & Osiris*), its root is *thein*, which signifies to wander, like *planein*, that is to say, it is synonimous with planets; because, all our authors, both the ancient Greeks and barbarians particularly worshipped the planets. I know that such enquiries into etymologies have been much decried: but if, as is the case, words are the representative signs of ideas, the genealogy of the one becomes that of the other, and a good etymological dictionary would be the most perfect history of the human understanding. It would only be necessary in this enquiry to observe certain precautions, which have hitherto

hitherto been neglected, and particularly to make an exact comparison of the value of the letters of the different alphabets. But, to continue our subject, we shall add, that in the Phenician language, the word *thab* (with *ain*) signifies also to wander, and appears to be the derivation of *theïn*. If we suppose *Deus* to be derived from the Greek *Zeus*, a proper name of *You-piter*, having *zaw*, I live, for its root, its sense will be precisely that of *you*, and will mean *soul* of the world, *igneous* principle. See Note (84). *Div-us*, which only signifies Genius, God of the second order, appears to me to come from the oriental word *div* substituted for *dib*, wolf and chacal, one of the emblems of the sun. At Thebes, says Macrobius, the sun was painted under the form of a wolf or chacal, for there are no wolves in Egypt. The reason of this emblem, doubtless, is that the chacal, like the cock, announces by its cries the sun's rising; and this reason is confirmed by the analogy of the words *lykos*, wolf, and *lykè*, light of the morning, whence comes *lux*.

Dius, which is to be understood also of the sun, must be derived from *dib*, a hawk. " The Egyptians," says Porphyry (*Euseb. Præep. Evang. p.* 92.) " represent the sun under the emblem of a hawk, because this bird soars to the highest regions of air where light abounds." And in reality we continually see at Cairo large flights of these birds, hovering in the air, from whence they descend not but to stun us with their shrieks, which are like the monosyllable *dib*: and here, as in the preceding example, we find an analogy between the word *dies*, day, light, and *Dius*, God, Sun.

Page 278. (82). *The progress of science and discovery.* One of the proofs that all these systems were invented in Egypt,

Egypt, is, that this is the only country where we see a complete body of doctrine formed from the remotest antiquity.

Clemens Alexandrinus has transmitted to us (*Stromat. lib.* 6.), a curious detail of the 42 volumes which were borne in the procession of Isis. "The priest," says he, "or chanter, carries one of the symbolic instruments of "music, and two of the books of Mercury; one contain-"ing hymns of the Gods, the other the list of kings. "Next to him the *horoscope* (the regulator of time), "carries a palm and a dial, symbols of astrology; he "must know by heart the four books of Mercury which "treat of astrology: the first on the order of the planets; "the second on the risings of the sun and moon, and "the two last on the rising and aspect of the stars. "Then comes the sacred author, with feathers on his "head (like *Kneph*) and a book in his hand, together "with ink, and a reed to write with (as is still the "practice among the Arabs). He must be versed in "hieroglyphics, must understand the description of the "universe, the course of the sun, moon, stars, and "planets, be acquainted with the division of Egypt into "36 *nomes*, with the course of the Nile, with instru-"ments, measures, sacred ornaments, and sacred places. "Next comes the stole bearer, who carries the cubit of "justice, or measure of the Nile, and a cup for the liba-"tions; he bears also in the procession ten volumes on "the subject of sacrifices, hymns, prayers, offerings, "ceremonies, festivals. Lastly arrives the prophet, bear-"ing in his bosom a pitcher, so as to be exposed to view; "he is followed by persons carrying bread (as at the "marriage of Cana). This prophet, as president of the
"mysteries,

"mysteries, learns ten other sacred volumes, which treat
"of the laws, the Gods, and the discipline of the priests.
"Now there are in all forty-two volumes, thirty-six of
"which are studied and got by heart by these personages,
"and the remaining six are set apart to be consulted by
"the *pastophores*: they treat of medicine, the construction
"of the human body (anatomy), diseases, remedies, in-
"struments, &c. &c."

We leave the reader to deduce all the consequences of such an Encyclopedia. It is ascribed to Mercury; but Jamblicus tells us that each book, composed by priests, was dedicated to that God, who, on account of his title of Genius or *decan* opening the zodiac, presided over every enterprise. He is the *Janus* of the Romans, and the *Guianesa* of the Indians, and it is remarkable that *Yanus* and *Guianes* are homonymous. In short, it appears that these books are the source of all that has been transmitted to us by the Greeks and Latins in every science, even in alchymy, necromancy, &c. What is most to be regretted in their loss, is that part which related to the principles of medicine and diet, in which the Egyptians appear to have made a considerable progress, and to have delivered many useful observations.

Page 279. (83). *The reigning religion in Lower Egypt.* "At a certain period," says Plutarch (*de Iside*) "all the Egyptians have their animal Gods painted. The Thebans are the only people who do not employ painters, because they worship a God whose form comes not under the senses, and cannot be represented. And this is the God whom Moses, educated at Heliopolis, adopted; but the idea was not of his invention.

Page 280. (84). *And Yahouh.* Such is the true pronunciation

nunciation of the Jehovah of the moderns, who violate in this respect every rule of criticism; since it is evident that the ancients, particularly the Eastern Syrians and Phenicians, were acquainted neither with the *Je* nor the *V*, which are of Tartar origin. The subsisting usage of the Arabs, which we have re-established here, is confirmed by Diodorus, who calls the God of Moses *Iaw*, (*lib.* 1.), and *Iaw* and *Iahouh* are manifestly the same word: the identity continues in that of *Iou-piter*; but in order to render it more complete, we shall demonstrate the signification to be the same.

In Hebrew, that is to say, in one of the dialects of the common language of Lower Asia, *Yahouh* is the participle of the verb *hih*, to exist, to be, and signifies existing; in other words, the principle of life, the mover or even motion (the universal soul of beings). Now what is Jupiter? Let us hear the Greeks and Latins explain their theology. "The Egyptians," says Diodorus, after Manatho, priest of Memphis, "in giving names to the five elements, called *spirit*, or ether, *Youpiter*, on account of the true meaning of that word: for *spirit* is the source of life, author of the vital principle in animals; and for this reason they considered him as the father, the generator of beings." For the same reason Homer says, father, and king of men and gods (*Diod. lib.* 1. *sect.* 1.)

"Theologians," says Macrobius, "consider You-piter as the soul of the world." Hence the words of Virgil: "Muses let us begin with You-piter; the world is full of You-piter" (*Somn. Scip. ch.* 17.) And in the Saturnalia he says, "Jupiter is the sun himself." It was this also which made Virgil say: "The Spirit nourishes the "life (of beings), and the soul diffused through the vast
"members

" members (of the universe), agitates the whole mass,
" and forms but one immense body."

"Ioupiter," says the ancient verses of the Orphic sect, which originated in Egypt; verses collected by Onomacritus in the days of Pisistratus, " Ioupiter, repre-
" sented with the thunder in his hand, is the beginning,
" origin, end, and middle of all things: a single and
" universal power, he governs every thing; heaven,
" earth, fire, water, the elements, day, and night.
" These are what constitute his immense body: his eyes
" are the sun and moon: he is space and eternity; in
" fine," adds Porphyry, " Jupiter is the world, the uni-
" verse, that which constitutes the essence and life of all
" beings. Now," continues the same author, " as phi-
" losophers differed in opinion respecting the nature and
" constituent parts of this God, and as they could invent
" no figure that should represent all his attributes, they
" painted him in the form of man.... He is in a sitting
" posture, in allusion to his immutable essence; the
" upper part of his body is uncovered, because it is in
" the upper regions of the universe, (the stars) that he
" most conspicuously displays himself. He is covered
" from the waist downwards, because respecting ter-
" restrial things he is more secret and concealed. He
" holds a sceptre in his left hand, because on the left
" side is the heart, and the heart is the seat of the under-
" standing, which (in human beings) regulates every
" action." *Euseb. Præper. Evang. p.* 100.

The following passage of the geographer and philosopher Strabo, removes every doubt as to the identity of the ideas of Moses and those of the heathen theologians.

" Moses,

"Moses, who was one of the Egyptian priests, taught his followers, that it was an egregious error to represent the Deity under the form of animals, as the Egyptians did, or in the shape of man, as was the practice of the Greeks and Africans. That alone is the Deity, said he, which constitutes heaven, earth, and every living thing; that which we call the *world*, the *sum of all things, nature*; and no reasonable person will think of representing such a being by the image of any one of the objects around us. It is for this reason, that, rejecting every species of images or idols, Moses wished the Deity to be worshipped without emblems, and according to his proper nature; and he accordingly ordered a temple worthy of him to be erected, &c." *Geograph. lib.* 16. *p.* 1104, edition of 1707.

The theology of Moses has, then, differed in no respect from that of his followers, that is to say, from that of the Stoics and Epicureans, who consider the Deity as the soul of the world. This philosophy appears to have taken birth, or to have been disseminated when Abraham came into Egypt (200 years before Moses), since he quitted his system of idols for that of the God *Yahouh*; so that we may place its promulgation about the seventeenth or eighteenth century before Christ; which corresponds with what we have said, Note (78).

As to the history of Moses, Diodorus, properly represents it when he says, *lib.* 34 & 40, "That the Jews were driven out of Egypt at a time of dearth, when the country was full of foreigners, and that Moses, a man of extraordinary prudence and courage, seized this opportunity of establishing his religion in the mountains of Judea." It will seem paradoxical to assert, that the 600,000 armed men whom he conducted thither

ought

ought to be reduced to 6,000; but I can confirm the assertion by so many proofs drawn from the books themselves, that it will be necessary to correct an error which appears to have arisen from the mistake of the transcribers.

Page 280. (85). *Ei, existence.* This was the monosyllable written on the gate of the temple of Delphos. Plutarch has made it the subject of a dissertation.

Page 281. (86). *The name of Osiris preserved in his song.* These are the literal expressions of the book of Deuteronomy, ch. 32. "The works of *Tsour* are perfect." Now *Tsour* has been translated by the word creator; its proper signification is to give *forms*, and this is one of the definitions of Osiris in Plutarch.

Page 284. (87). *Of the Archangel Michael.* "The " names of the angels and of the months, such as Gabriel, " Michael, Yar, Nisan, &c. came from Babylon with " the Jews;" says expressly the Talmud of Jerusalem. See *Beausob. Hist. du Manich.* Vol. II. p. 624, where he proves that the saints of the Almanac are an imitation of the 365 angels of the Persians; and Jamblicus in his Egyptian Mysteries, *sect.* 2. *c.* 3. speaks of angels, archangels, seraphim, &c. like a true Christian.

Page 285. (88). *Theology of Zoroaster.* "The whole phi-" losophy of the gymnosophists," says Diogenes Laertius on the authority of an ancient writer, " is derived from " that of the Magi, and many assert that of the Jews to " have the same origin." *Lib.* 1. *c.* 9. Magasthenes, an historian of repute in the days of Seleucus Nicanor, and who wrote particularly upon India, speaking of the philosopy of the ancients respecting natural things, puts the Brachmans and the Jews precisely on the same footing.

Page 287. (89). *To restore the golden age upon earth.* This is the reason of the application of the many Pagan oracles to Jesus, and particularly the fourth eclogue of Virgil, and the Sybilline verses so celebrated among the ancients.

Page 288. (90). *At the expiration of the six thousand pretended years.* We have already seen, note 29, this tradition current among the Tuscans; it was disseminated through most nations, and shows us what we ought to think of all the pretended creations and terminations of the world, which are merely the beginnings and endings of astronomical periods invented by astrologers. That of the year or solar revolution, being the most simple and perceptible, served as a model to the rest, and its comparison gave rise to the most whimsical ideas. Of this description is the idea of the four ages of the world among the Indians. Originally these four ages were merely the four seasons; and as each season was under the supposed influence of a planet, it bore the name of the metal appropriated to that planet: thus spring was the age of the sun, or of gold; summer the age of the moon, or of silver; autumn the age of Venus, or of brass; and winter the age of Mars, or of iron. Afterwards when astronomers invented the great year of 25 and 36 thousand common years, which had for its object the bringing back all the stars to one point of departure and a general conjunction, the ambiguity of the terms introduced a similar ambiguity of ideas; and the myriads of celestial signs and periods of duration which were thus measured, were easily converted into so many revolutions of the sun. Thus the different periods of creation which have been so great a source of difficulty and misapprehension to curious enquirers,

quirers, were in reality nothing more than hypothetical calculations of astronomical periods. In the same manner the creation of the world has been attributed to different seasons of the year, just as these different seasons have served for the fictitious period of these conjunctions; and of consequence has been adopted by different nations for the commencement of an ordinary year. Among the Egyptians this period fell upon the summer solstice, which was the commencement of their year; and the departure of the spheres, according to their conjectures, fell, in like manner, upon the period when the sun enters Cancer. Among the Persians the year commenced at first in the spring, or when the sun enters Aries; and from thence the first Christians were led to suppose that God created the world in the spring: this opinion is also favoured by the book of Genesis; and it is farther remarkable, that the world is not there said to be created by the God of Moses *(Yahouh)*, but by the *Elohim* or gods in the plural, that is, by the *angels* or *genii*, for so the word constantly means in the Hebrew books. If we farther observe that the root of the word *Elohim* signifies strong or powerful, and that the Egyptians called their *decans* strong and powerful leaders, attributing to them the creation of the world, we shall presently perceive that the book of Genesis affirms neither more nor less than that the world was created by the *decans*, by those very genii whom, according to Sanchoniathon, Mercury excited against Saturn, and who were called *Elohim*. It may be farther asked, why the plural substantive *Elohim* is made to agree with the singular verb *bara* (the Elohim creates). The reason is, that after the Babylonish captivity the unity of the Supreme Being was the prevailing opinion of the Jews; it was

therefore

therefore thought proper to introduce a pious solecism in language, which it is evident had no existence before Moses: thus in the names of the children of Jacob many of them are compounded of a plural verb, to which Elohim is the nominative case understood, as *Raouben* (Reuben), *they have looked upon me*, and *Samaonni* (Simeon), *they have granted me my prayer*, to wit, the Elohim. The reason of this etymology is to be found in the religious creeds of the wives of Jacob, whose gods were the *taraphim* of Laban, that is, the angels of the Persians, and the Egyptian decans.

Page id. (91). *Six thousand years had already nearly elapsed since the supposed creation of the world.* According to the computation of the Seventy, the period elapsed consisted of about 5,600 years, and this computation was principally followed. It is well known how much, in the first ages of the church, this opinion of the end of the world agitated the minds of men. In the sequel, the general councils, encouraged by finding that the general conflagration did not come, pronounced the expectation that prevailed heretical, and its believers were called Millenarians; a circumstance curious enough, since it is evident from the history of the Gospels that Jesus Christ was a Millenarian, and of consequence a heretic.

Page 290. (92). *Constellation of the serpent.* " The " Persians," says Chardin, " call the constellation of the " serpent *Ophiucus*, serpent of Eve: and this serpent *Ophi-* " *ucus* or *Ophioneus* plays a similar part in the theology of " the Phenicians," for Pherecydes, their disciple, and the master of Pythagoras, said " that *Ophioneus serpentinus* had " been chief of the rebels against Jupiter." See Marf. Ficin.

Ficin. Apol. Socrat. p. m. 797. col. 2. I shall add that *æphah* (with aïn) signifies in Hebrew serpent.

Page *id.* (93). *Seduced the man.* In a physical sense to seduce, *seducere*, means only to attract, to draw after us.

Page *id.* (94). *Picture of Mithra.* See this picture in Hyde, page 111, edition of 1760.

Page 291. (95). *Perseus rises on the opposite side.* Rather the head of Medusa; that head of a woman once so beautiful, which Perseus cut off, and which he holds in his hand, is only that of the virgin, whose head sinks below the horizon at the very moment that Perseus rises; and the serpents which surround it are Ophiucus and the Polar Dragon, who then occupy the zenith. This shews us in what manner the ancients composed all their figures and fables. They took such constellations as they found at the same time on the circle of the horizon, and collecting the different parts, they formed groupes which served them as an almanac in hieroglyphic characters. Such is the secret of all their pictures, and the solution of all their mythological monsters. The Virgin is also Andromeda, delivered by Perseus from the whale that *pursues* her *(pro-sequitur.)*

Page *id.* (96). *By a chaste virgin.* Such was the picture of the Persian sphere, cited by Aben Ezra in the *Cælum Poeticum* of Blaeu, p. 71. " The picture of the first " decan of the Virgin," says that writer, " represents a " beautiful virgin with flowing hair, sitting in a chair, " with two ears of corn in her hand, and suckling an infant, " called Jesus by some nations, and Christ in Greek."

In the library of the king of France is a manuscript in Arabic, marked 1165, in which is a picture of the twelve

signs;

figns; and that of the Virgin represents a young woman with an infant by her side: the whole scene indeed of the birth of Jesus is to be found in the adjacent part of the heavens. The stable is the constellation of the charioteer and the goat, formerly Capricorn; a constellation called *præsepe Jovis Heniochi, stable of Iou*; and the word *Iou* is found in the name Iou-seph (Joseph). At no great distance is the ass of Typhon (the great she-bear), and the ox or bull, the ancient attendants of the manger. Peter the porter, is Janus with his keys and bald forehead: the twelve apostles are the genii of the twelve months, &c. This Virgin has acted very different parts in the various systems of mythology: she has been the Isis of the Egyptians, who said of her in one of their inscriptions cited by Julian, *the fruit I have brought forth is the sun*. The majority of traits drawn by Plutarch apply to her, in the same manner as those of Osiris apply to Bootes: also the seven principal stars of the she-bear, called David's chariot, were called the chariot of Osiris (See *Kirker*); and the crown that is situated behind, formed of ivy, was called *Chen Osiris*, the tree of Osiris. The Virgin has likewise been Ceres, whose mysteries were the same with those of Isis and Mithra; she has been the Diana of the Ephesians; the great goddess of Syria, Cybele, drawn by lions; Minerva, the mother of Bacchus; Astræa, a chaste virgin taken up into heaven at the end of the golden age; Thems, at whose feet is the balance that was put in her hands; the Sybil of Virgil, who descends into hell, or sinks below the hemisphere with a branch in her hand, &c.

Page 292. (97). *Rose again in the firmament. Resurgere*, to rise a second time, cannot signify to return to life, but in a metaphorical sense; but we see continually mistakes of this kind result from the ambiguous meaning of the words made use of in ancient tradition.

Page *id.* (98). *Chris, or conservator.* The Greeks used to express by X, or Spanish iota, the aspirated *há* of the Orientals, who said *háris.* In Hebrew *heres* signifies the sun, but in Arabic the meaning of the radical word is, to guard, to preserve, and of *háris,* guardian, preserver. It is the proper epithet of Vichenou, which demonstrates at once the identity of the Indian and Christian Trinities, and their common origin. It is manifestly but one system, which, divided into two branches, one extending to the east, and the other to the west, assumed two different forms: its principal trunk is the Pythagorean system of the soul of the world, or *Iou-piter.* The epithet *piter,* or father, having been applied to the demi-ourgos of Plato, gave rise to an ambiguity which caused an enquiry to be made respecting the son of this father. In the opinion of the philosophers the son was understanding, *Nous* and *Logos,* from which the *Latins* made their *Verbum.* And thus we clearly perceive the origin of the *eternal father* and of the *Verbum* his son, proceeding from him *(Mens ex Deo nata,* says Macrobius): the *anima* or *spiritus mundi* was the Holy Ghost; and it is for this reason that Manes, Basilides, Valentinius, and other pretended heretics of the first ages, who traced things to their source, said, that God the Father was the supreme inaccessible light (that of the heaven, the *primum mobile,* or the *aplanes*); the Son the secondary light resident in the sun, and the Holy Ghost the atmosphere of the earth (See *Beauseb.* Vol. II. p. 586): hence, among the Syrians, the representation of the Holy Ghost by a dove, the bird of Venus Urania, that is, of the

the air. The Syrians (says *Nigidius de Germanico*) assert that a dove sat for a certain number of days on the egg of a fish, and that from this incubation Venus was born: Sextus Empiricus also observes (*Inst. Pyrrh. lib.* 3. c. 23.) that the Syrians abstain from eating doves; which intimates to us a period commencing in the sign *Pisces*, in the winter solstice. We may farther observe, that if *Chris* comes from *Harisch* by a *chin*, it will signify *artificer*, an epithet belonging to the sun. These variations, which must have embarrassed the ancients, prove it to be the real type of Jesus, as had been already remarked in the time of Tertullian. " Many," says this writer, " suppose with " greater probability that the sun is our God, and they re- " fer us to the religion of the Persians." *Apologet.* c. 16.

Page 293. (99). *One of the solar periods.* See a curious ode to the Sun, by Martianus Capella, translated by Gebelin.

Page 304. (100). *Human sacrifices.* Read the cold declaration of Eusebius (*Præp. Evang. lib.* 1. p. 11.) who pretends that, since the coming of Christ, there have neither been wars, nor tyrants, nor cannibals, nor sodomites, nor persons committing incest, nor savages devouring their parents, &c. When we read these fathers of the church, we are astonished at their insincerity or infatuation.

Page 306. (101). *Sect of Samaneans.* The equality of mankind in a state of nature, and in the eyes of God, was one of the principal tenets of the Samaneans, and they appear to be the only ancients that entertained this opinion.

Page 309. (102.) *Perverted the consciences of men.* As long as it shall be possible to obtain purification from crimes, and exemption from punishment by means of money or other frivolous practices; as long as kings and great men shall suppose that building temples or instituting foundations, will absolve them from the guilt of oppression and homicide; as long as individuals shall imagine that they may rob and cheat, provided they observe fast during Lent, go to confession, and receive extreme unction, it is impossible there should exist in society any morality or virtue; and it is from a deep conviction of truth, that a modern philosopher has called the doctrine of expiations *la vérole des sociétés*.

Page 310. (103). *Has carried its inquisition even to the sacred sanctuary of the nuptial bed.* The Mussulmans, who suppose women to have no souls, are shocked at the idea of confession, and say; How can an honest man think of listening to the recital of the actions or the secret thoughts of a woman? May we not also ask, on the other hand, how can an honest woman consent to reveal them?

Page id. (104). *That every where they had formed secret associations, enemies to the rest of the society.* That we may understand the general feelings of priests respecting the rest of mankind, whom they always call by the name of the people, let us hear one of the doctors of the church. " The people," says Bishop Synnesius, *in Calvit. page* 315, " are desirous of being deceived, we cannot act otherwise " respecting them. The case was similar with the ancient " priests of Egypt, and for this reason they shut them-" selves up in their temples, and there composed their " mysteries out of the reach of the eye of the people." And forgetting what he has just before said, he adds, " For had the people been in the secret, they might have " been offended at the deception played upon them. In

" the

"the mean time how is it possible to conduct oneself otherwise with the people so long as they are the people? For my own part, to myself I shall always be a philosopher, but in dealing with the mass of mankind I shall be a priest."

"A little jargon," says Gregory Nazianzen to St. Jerome *(Hieron. ad Nep.)* "is all that is necessary to impose on the people. The less they comprehend, the more they admire. Our forefathers and doctors of the church have often said, not what they thought, but what circumstances and necessity dictated to them."

"We endeavour," says Sanchoniathon, "to excite admiration by means of the marvellous." *(Præp. Evang. lib. 3.)*

Such was the conduct of all the priests of antiquity, and is still that of the Bramins and Lamas, who are the exact counterpart of the Egyptian priests. Such was the practice of the Jesuits, who marched with hasty strides in the same career. It is useless to point out the whole depravity of such a doctrine. In general every association which has mystery for its basis, or an oath of secrecy, is a league of robbers against society, a league divided in its very bosom into knaves and dupes, or in other words agents and instruments. It is thus we ought to judge of those modern clubs, which, under the name of Illuminatists, Martinists, Caglioftronifts, Free-masons and Mesmerites, infest Europe. These societies ape the follies and deceptions of the ancient Cabalists, Magicians, Orphics, &c. who, says Plutarch, led into errors of considerable magnitude not only individuals, but kings and nations.

Page 311. (106). *They made themselves in turns astrologers,*

logers, casters of planets, magicians, &c. What is a magician, in the sense in which the people understand the word? a man who by words and gestures pretends to act on supernatural beings, and compel them to descend at his call and obey his orders. Such was the conduct of the ancient priests, and such is still that of all priests in idolatrous nations, for which reason we have given them the denomination of magicians.

And when a Christian priest pretends to make God descend from heaven, to fix him to a morsel of leaven, and to render, by means of this talisman, souls pure and in a state of grace, what is all this but a trick of magic? And where is the difference between a Chaman of Tartary who invokes the genii, or an Indian Bramin, who makes his Vichenou descend in a vessel of water to drive away evil spirits? Yes, the identity of the spirit of priests in every age and country is fully established! Every where it is the assumption of an exclusive privilege, the pretended faculty of moving at will the powers of nature; and this assumption is so direct a violation of the right of equality, that whenever the people shall regain their importance, they will for ever abolish this sacrilegious kind of nobility, which has been the type and parent stock of the other species of nobility.

Page 312. (107). *Who paid for them as for commodities of the greatest value.* A curious work would be the comparative history of the *agnuses* of the pope and the *pastils* of the grand Lama. It would be worth while to extend this idea to religious ceremonies in general, and to confront, column by column, the analogous or contrasting points of faith and superstitious practices in all nations. There is one more species of superstition which it would

be

be equally falutary to cure, blind veneration for the great; and for this purpofe it would be alone fufficient to write a minute detail of the private life of kings and princes. No work could be fo philofophical as this; and accordingly we have feen what a general outcry was excited among kings and the panders of kings, when the Anecdotes of the Court of Berlin firft appeared. What would be the alarm were the public put in poffeffion of the fequel of this work? Were the people fairly acquainted with all the crimes and all the abfurdities of this fpecies of idol, they would no longer be expofed to covet their fpecious pleafures, of which the plaufible and hollow appearance difturbs their peace, and hinders them from enjoying the much more folid happinefs of their own condition.

INDEX.

INDEX.

A.

	Page
Age, new	125
Aristocracy	64
Astronomy, origin of the study of	232, 258
————— antiquity of	360
————— source of mythology	360, 372, 385, 387, 388
Authority, paternal, remarks on	336

B.

Babylon	334
————— built after Nineveh	335
Books, borne in the procession of Isis	379
Brama, religion of	165, 199, 282
Budoism	282

C.

Celestial bodies, invention of names for	237
Chacal, animal like the fox	4
China, government of	340
————— obstacle to the improvement of	341
Christ, etymology of the name of	292, 390
————— on the proofs of the existence of	355
Christianity	158, 186, 283, 304
Circumcision, origin of	370
Civil war	65
Confession, remarks on	310, 392

D.

Demi-ourgos, worship of the	274
Democracy	63
Despotism	65, 336
Doubt not a crime	117
Dualism	253

E.

Egypt, first civilized country	235
————— Lower, whence peopled	331
————— various religions originated from	353
Empires, revolutions of	2
————, causes of the prosperity of	51, 57
————————— revolutions of	53, 61
Ethiopia, ancient	328, 330
————— the cradle of science	331
Etymology, observations on	377

Euphrates,

INDEX.

                                      Page

Euphrates, banks of the, artificial - - - - 334
Evils occasioned by man, not by God - - - 14

F.

Fatalism, remarks on - - - - - 328
French about to engage in a war for the Turks, *note* - 101
———— revolution - - - - - 125

G.

Genesis, remarks on some parts of - - 348, 386
God not the cause of our evils - - - - 14
——— origin of the idea of - - - - 226
——— mysterious name of - - - - 339
——— on the name of - - - - - 377
Government, origin of - - - - - 48
——————— various kinds of - - - 63, 340
——————— corruptions of - - - - 92
——————— progress of - - - 336, 337
Guebres - - - - - - 163, 194

H.

Hieroglyphics - - - - - 363

I. J.

Idolatry - - - - - - - 237
———— source of - - - - - 361
Improvement, grand obstacle to - - - 117
Indian sects - - - - 164, 169, 282
Isis, books borne in the procession of - - - 379
Jesus, etymology of the name of - - - - 292
Judaism - - - - - 162, 190, 279

K.

Kings, observations on - - - - 337, 395

L.

Lama, religion of the - - - - 169, 204
Laws, origin of - - - - - 48
——— observations on - - - - - 50
Liberty originates from equality - - - 342

M.

Mahometanism - - - 155, 180, 303, 339
Man, the cause of his own misfortunes - - 17, 313
——— condition of, in the universe - - - 35
——— original state of - - - - - 37
——— how brought into a state of society - - 40
——— source of the evils attendant on, in society - 44
——— in a state of improvement - - - 104
——— grand obstacle to the improvement of - - 117
——— rights of - - - - - 136, 348

                                              Man,

INDEX.

	Page
Man, natural equality of	137, 336
Mithriacs, ancient, the same with the modern Parses	349
Monarchy	64, 337
Moses, religion of	162, 190, 279, 381
——— on the antiquity of the books ascribed to	347
Mysteries, ancient	372
——— modern	374, 393
Mystical, or moral worship	259

O.

Ophir, situation of	327
Opinion, whence arise difference and agreement of	315
Orphics, who	374

P.

Parses	163, 194, 281
People, free and legislative	132
——— rights of the	136
Persia, unfortunate state of, after the death of Thamas Koulikan	339
Priestcraft, origin of	248
——— every where the same	310, 392
Privileged orders	127, 248, 341

R.

Religions, various	155
——— derived from Egypt	353
——— end of all, the same	297
Religious ideas, origin of	218, 294
Revolutions of empires	2
——————— causes of	53, 61
Romans, on the freedom of the	337

S.

Sabeism	231
Samaneans, religion of the	282, 391
Science, cradle of	235, 331
Self-love, the principle of society	40
——— effects of	40, 45, 50
Slavery, observations on	62
Societies, secret, remarks on	393
Society, origin of	40
——— source of the evils of	44
——— evils of, how to be avoided	100
——— on privileged orders in	127, 341
Solomon, trade of	332
Soul of the world, worship of the	271, 279, 381
——— ancient opinions concerning the	375

Soul,

INDEX.

	Page
Soul, immortality of the, not taught by Moses	376
Spheres of the ancients	367
State, future, origin of the doctrine of a	259
States, causes of the revolutions of	53, 61
———— rise of	54, 90
———— ancient, causes of the prosperity of	57
———————————— revolutions and ruin of	61
———— weakened by enlargement	67
———— causes of the fall of	92
Syria, populousness of	328

T.

Talismans	361
Tartars, evacuate the Crimea on its being incorporated with Russia	327
———— dress, &c. of	338
Thebes	329
Theocracy	64
Trade of the ancients	332
Trinity, origin of the doctrine of the	276
Truth, inquiry into	172
Turks, Sultan of the, cannot cede land to unbelievers	338

U. V.

Universe, worship of the, under different emblems	266
Venality	94

W.

War, observations on	340
World, on the creation of the	348
———— antiquity of the	360, 385
Worship of the elements, and the physical powers of nature,	227
———————— stars	231
———————— symbols	237
———————— two principles	253
———————— mystical or moral	259
———————— of the universe under different emblems	266
———————————————— soul of the world, or of the element of fire	271, 279
———————————————— Demi-ourgos, or supreme artificer	274

Z.

Zoroaster, religion of	163, 194, 281, 335

www.ingramcontent.com/pod-product-compliance
Lightning Source LLC
Chambersburg PA
CBHW051745300426
44115CB00007B/692